GOODS FROM OVERSEAS

PRINTED FOR HIS MAJESTY'S STATIONERY OFFICE BY JORDISON & Cº Lᵀᴴ LONDON & MIDDLESBROUGH

EMPIRE'S

CHILDREN

TRACE YOUR FAMILY HISTORY ACROSS THE WORLD

ANTON GILL
selected books published since 1984

Martin Allen is Missing
How To Be Oxbridge
Croquet: The Complete Guide
Mad About the Boy
The Journey Back from Hell
Berlin to Bucharest
City of the Horizon
City of Dreams
City of the Dead
Several short stories (2001–2003)

EMPIRE'S
CHILDREN
TRACE YOUR FAMILY HISTORY ACROSS THE WORLD

ANTON GILL  Harper Press
An imprint of HarperCollins*Publishers*

Harper Press
An imprint of HarperCollinsPublishers
77-85 Fulham Palace Road
Hammersmith, London, W6 8JB

visit our authors' blog: www.fifthestate.co.uk

Published by Harper Press 2007
9 8 7 6 5 4 3 2 1

A catalogue record for this book
is available from the British Library

ISBN: 978-0-00-724714-1

Design by 'OMEDESIGN

Printed by L.E.G.O. SpA, Vicenza, Italy

FOR J. A.
(gratefully)

All empire is no more than power in trust

John Dryden

How is the empire?

King George V (attributed dying words)

*The wheels of fate will one day compel
the British to give up their empire...
What a waste of mud & filth will they
leave behind!*

Rabindranath Tagore

CONTENTS

ACKNOWLEDGEMENTS

Colette Flight, producer of the Channel 4/Wall to Wall television series which the book accompanies, who (despite her own busy schedule) has been unfailingly and generously helpful; Claire Hungate of Wall to Wall Media; and Jess Colmer and Caroline Miller, both assistant producers on the series. Arabella Pike, commissioning editor at HarperCollins, has been most sympathetic. My thanks as well to senior editor Kate Hyde at HarperCollins, and picture researcher Amanda Russell. My literary agent, Julian Alexander, has given me immeasurable, patient and timely help and support.

I thank my wife, Marji Campi, for essential help with the research, necessarily conducted under pressure. I thank Katie Mankin of Lucas Alexander Whitley and Alice Massey of HarperCollins. For the loan of books, for advice, and other support, I thank Sophia Akbar, Sharmini Ashton-Griffiths, Pamela and William Bennett, Major and Mrs Nigel Browne, Nicci Crowther, Bill Edmonds, Hilary and Stuart Ellis, Yves-Bernard Fogel, Nicola S. Gill, Alison Harris and Dr Harold Shukman. I thank Karl Leino, who can make a Mac computer sing and dance; Daniel Campi for additional com-puter advice; and Sir John Hammerton and Carlton Wallace, both unfailing sources of knowledge. Finally, my thanks to other friends and colleagues who looked things up for me and/or gave valuable insights.

My debt to the authors of the books listed in the Bibliography is profound. Anyone who finds this book interesting and wants to delve deeper could not be in better hands than theirs.

FOREWORD

This book accompanies the Channel 4 television series of the same name produced by Wall-to-Wall. It is designed to fill in the background of the stories (which are included here) told in the six television episodes, by describing briefly the rise and fall of the British Empire, but concentrating on its last days – those following the end of the Second World War – together with the impact of emigration to Britain from her former colonies, the effect of Britain on the immigrants and their effect on her, and the gradual and still incomplete journey towards integration and harmony. Recent events, including highly destructive and successful terrorism, and ill-advised and equally violent reactions to it, have interrupted the process. One can only hope that it will resume, but current damage will take a generation or two to repair.

Any opinions expressed in these pages which are not otherwise acknowledged are my own, and should not be associated with any of the individuals or organizations mentioned above, or elsewhere in the Acknowledgements.

British influence as a world power began to develop towards the end of the sixteenth century, grew to full flower in the nineteenth, and only began its long decline after the First World War, a decline which accelerated during the second half of the twentieth century.

During the entire period a number of things changed, among which place names and the British currency system are the most obviously striking. As names and references to the old British, non-decimal currency occur from time to time in the narrative which follows, it is good to be aware of them.

On 21 February 1971, the United Kingdom adopted a decimal system of currency similar to those already in use in most countries. Everyone born in the UK from the late 1960s onwards will be aware that 100 pence equals £1. It was not always thus. Before 1971, a system of pounds, shillings and pence existed. According to that system, which had been in use for centuries, there were 240 pennies (or pence) in a pound. Twelve pennies made up a shilling, and there were twenty of those in a pound. The pound was designated by the familiar £ symbol (denoting *libra*, the Latin for 'pound'), the shilling by '*s*.', and the penny by '*d*.' (the first letter of *denarius*, the Latin word for a small Roman silver coin). Sums of money were expressed thus: the modern £1.25p would have been £1. 5*s*. 0*d*., 25p would have been 5*s*. 0*d*. or 5/-.

Apart from the shilling and the penny there were several other coins, in use at various periods, each representing other subdivisions of the pound. Those that survived to 1971 were the half-crown, the florin (2*s.* or 10p), the sixpenny and threepenny bits, and the halfpenny.

There is one other measurement of money that the reader should be aware of: the guinea. The guinea ceased to exist as a coin long ago, and largely disappeared as a recognized unit of payment before the watershed of 1971. Before that it was used latterly as an expression of payment of professional fees. The BBC paid contributors in guineas, and the fees of medical specialists and lawyers were demanded in them. The guinea was worth £1.05p, or £1. 1*s.* 0*d.*

The origin of the guinea is interesting and has a direct connection with the early period of British dominion overseas. The coin was first struck in 1663, 'in the name and for the use of the Company of Royal Adventurers Trading to Africa'. It was intended for the Guinea trade and was originally made of gold from Guinea, the name given to a small portion of the west coast of Africa. The splendidly named company, headed by Charles II's brother James, Duke of York (later James II), dealt mainly in slaves. It had its ups and downs, but traded in slaves until 1731, when it switched to ivory and gold. It provided gold to the Royal Mint from 1668 to 1722. The slave trade continued to flourish until its abolition (by Britain at least) in 1807.

Place names and names of definition present a slightly more complicated problem. Names of definition change with assumptions of political correctness. Once, the term 'Black' was generally thought offensive, but 'Negro' was not, at least not to 'white' people. Now the reverse is true. Appalling as it seems now, people in the 1950s and earlier would quite innocently call a pet black Labrador 'Nigger' or a black cat 'Sooty' or 'Blackie'. Most of us have come a long way towards greater integration and understanding since then, but at some cost; and sensibilities must be treated with respect as a result.

Care has to be taken with other general definitions. It is okay to call 'Europeans' that as a catch-all, but we are well aware that Europe is made up of a number of very different nations, languages, religious sects and cultures. That has not always been true of Europeans' perception of other parts of the world. While the term 'Asians' appeared soon after the end of the Second World War as a useful umbrella-term for those peoples inhabiting what had been British India – that is to say, the Burmese, the modern Pakistanis, the modern Bangladeshis, the Sri Lankans and the Indians – nowadays the slightly more defining term South Asians appears to be preferred. The same sort of issue applies to the question of whether to use 'West Indian' or

'Afro-Caribbean' as a denomination of convenience when one cannot specify a particular island or island nation.

Such applications change with fashion and time. I have opted for those which, after consultation, seem most acceptable at the time of writing to those to whom they are applied. If any offence is caused by any reference in the pages which follow I apologize, for this is purely unintentional.

Two earlier usages which occur less frequently these days but will be found in older books, articles and so on are 'Anglo-Indian' and 'Eurasian'. The former can mean *either* a person born in India of mixed Anglo-South Asian parentage, *or* a native British white (Caucasian) person who had spent a considerable time in India, usually in government or military service, possibly born there, and who would have considered India, not Great Britain, his or her principal home. The term 'Eurasian' denotes only the former category, that is, a person born of Caucasian-South Asian parents. I have decided in this book to use Eurasian for a person of mixed race, and Anglo-Indian for the British Indian long-termers. But be aware that the latter expression will sometimes be found elsewhere denoting the former.

Place names can change with the political climate. Look, for example, at the progression over the last century or so from St Petersburg to Petrograd, to Leningrad, and now back to St Petersburg. If you look at an atlas published in 1937 and at an atlas published in 2007 you will see a large number of name and even frontier changes, in the Russian landmass, in what was British India, and in Africa. Only British India and Africa concern us here, and almost all the dramatic changes of name there had taken place by 1980, when the last British colony, Rhodesia (earlier, Southern Rhodesia), became Zimbabwe.

One or two countries have changed their names twice or more in the past half-century. For example, the Belgian Congo gained independence in 1960 and became the Republic of the Congo, a name it shared with a neighbouring state, the former French colony of Congo. In 1966 the former Belgian territory was renamed the Democratic Republic of the Congo. After a period of war and unrest one political leader, General Mobutu, became dominant, and under him the country became the Republic of Zaire in 1971. (The name 'Zaire' derives ultimately from *Nzere*, a local name for the River Congo.) But, as was the case in so many newly independent African states, repression and unrest continued, and Zaire's future was compromised in the mid-1990s by involvement in the war in neighbouring Rwanda. This led to the fall of Mobutu and the reversion under new leadership, in 1997, of Zaire to its earlier name of the Democratic Republic of the Congo.

Many other colonies – British and otherwise – in Africa changed their names on independence, often reverting to pre-colonial or ancestral names. Thus the first to attain autonomy, the Gold Coast, became Ghana. Tanganyika and Zanzibar merged as Tanzania, Nyasaland became Malawi, Northern Rhodesia became Zambia, Bechuanaland became Botswana, South-West Africa became Namibia (as late as 1990), and so on.

The situation in what had been known as British India (prior to the end of the Second World War) changed with the end of British rule there and the political partition of the subcontinent in 1947. The original divisions were India, East and West Pakistan, Burma and Ceylon, along with a couple of the former Independent States (separate countries within the Raj but more or less in thrall to it) which had refused to become subsumed within either the new Hindu or Pakistani divisions. One of these, Kashmir, is still being fought over today. Ceylon, independent of Britain since 1948, changed its name to Sri Lanka (meaning 'Venerable Lanka') following a socialist revolution in 1972. A year earlier, East Pakistan (itself formerly Bengal) broke away from West Pakistan (now Pakistan ('Land of the Pure') and became the independent state of Bangladesh ('Land of the Bangla Speakers'). Burma, which became fully independent of Great Britain in 1948, changed its name to Myanmar (its pre-colonial name) in 1989, and that of its capital from the westernized 'Rangoon' to 'Yangon'.

I have decided to follow my own judgement in what place names to use in the pages which follow. This means on the whole that for African and South Asian countries I will use their current names, with their former colonial names afterwards in brackets where appropriate. However, in some cases I have stuck to older usages as still being more familiar to most readers. Thus, for example, although I have preferred Beijing to Peking, I have used Madras rather than Chennai, Bombay rather than Mumbai, and Burma and Rangoon rather than Myanmar and Yangon. I have also used Mecca rather than Makkah, Cawnpore rather than Kanpur, Calcutta rather than Kolkata, and Mafeking rather than Makifeng. Where any elucidation or explanation is necessary, I have given it immediately in parentheses, but in the course of telling a complex story I apologize here and now for any inconsistencies.

Where it applies (England was a separate country from Scotland until 1707 and Scotland played only a tiny part in an independent colonization process before then) I have also decided to use 'Great Britain' or 'Britain' rather than 'the United Kingdom' because to me the former names reflect the period better than the latter, and tie in more euphoniously with what lies at the centre of this exploration of the British Empire.

PROLOGUE

But as the debate was nearing an end, I felt I had been too harsh with the man who would be my partner in a government of national unity. In summation, I said, 'The exchanges between Mr (F. W.) de Klerk and me should not obscure one important fact. I think we are a shining example to the entire world of people drawn from different racial groups who have a common loyalty, a common love, to their common country... In spite of criticism of Mr de Klerk,' I said, and then looked over at him, 'sir, you are one of those I rely upon. We are going to face the problem of this country together.' At which point I reached over to take his hand and said, 'I am proud to hold your hand for us to go forward.' Mr de Klerk seemed surprised, but pleased.

Nelson Mandela

At the end of January 2007 the Anglo-Dutch metals giant Corus, which had until a 1999 merger been British Steel, was bought by the Indian company, Tata Steel, of Jamshedpur. One hundred years earlier, when the British Empire was at its height, such a future concept would have been unthinkable. Even sixty years ago, when, in August 1947, India finally achieved its independence in a hurried and, some still argue, botched job by its last Viceroy, Lord Louis Mountbatten, the idea of an Indian concern taking over a British one would have been beyond the scope of most imaginations, Indian or British. The visionary novelist Salman Rushdie, whose seminal work, *Midnight's Children,* redefined the moment of independence for a new generation, could not have conceived of it when his ground-breaking work was published twenty-six years ago, when the author himself was a mere thirty-four years old.

The world has turned radically in a half-century, and in doing so it has submerged the greatest, largest and longest-lived empire that ever was, and seen the reduction of its mother country from a real world leader to one which on the one hand hangs on the coat-tails of the USA, and on the other refuses fully to integrate with its natural partners in Europe. We, the Children of Empire, still retain a memory that seems more concrete than ghostly of our powerful past, and it still influences our thinking.

But when I say 'we' in such a context I am immediately at fault, because there are Children of Empire who are not by descent British at all, except for the fact that the countries they or their parents or grandparents or even earlier forebears came from for generations – in some cases back to the seventeenth century – lived under the shadow and protection of the British Crown. As we settle into the twenty-first century, we must grow used to the idea that India will soon overtake China in terms of population size; and that both those countries will soon become the dominant industrial and economic powers of the world.

In the pages that follow we will hear some of their stories, but here at the beginning it is worth making one allusion to the first wave of Caribbean immigrants to British shores, in 1948, nearly sixty years ago, on the *Empire Windrush*. Small in number – there were fewer than 500 of them – the men and women of the *Windrush*, dressed in their best, who had come to seek a new life in a mother country they had always been taught to love, respect and revere, met a mixed reception. A nervous parliament prevaricated – though Prime Minister Clement Attlee stood firmly on the side of the angels – while the racist extreme right, headed by Oswald Mosley, who had previously supported Hitler's anti-Semitic policies, foamed at the mouth. A decade later, after suffering years of poor lodgings for high rents, and a gamut of racist prejudice from the locals, the immigrants had to suffer one more great indignity – the race riots of Nottingham and then Notting Hill in the summer of 1958. Here it will suffice merely to quote from Mike and Trevor Phillips's masterly account, largely through vox pop interviews, of early immigration to Britain, *Windrush – the Irresistible Rise of Multi-Racial Britain*, to give a flavour of those times:

> *Notting Dale differed considerably from Brixton or Paddington, and it might have been tailormade [sic] for the main event. Notting Dale had everything St Ann's Well Road [in Nottingham] had, and more, in much larger quantities. It had multi-occupied houses with families of different races on each floor. It had a large population of internal migrants, gypsies and Irish, many of them transient single men, packed into a honeycomb of rooms with communal kitchens, toilets and no bathrooms. It had depressed English families who had lived through the war years then watched the rush to the suburbs pass them by while they were trapped in low income jobs and rotten housing. It had a raft of dodgy pubs and poor street lighting. It had gang fighting, illegal drinking clubs, gambling and prostitution. It had a large proportion of frightened and resentful residents. A fortnight before the riots broke out there was a 'pitched battle' in Cambridge Gardens, off Ladbroke Grove, between rival gangs, and the residents of several streets got together to present a petition to the London County Council asking for something to be done about the rowdy parties, the mushroom clubs and the violence.*
>
> *Notting Dale also had a clutch of racist activists, operating at the street corners*

and in the pubs. Parties like Sir Oswald Mosley's Union Movement actually had very few members, but in the atmosphere of hostility and uncertainty which had begun to surround the migrants they provided the country with an idiom, a vocabulary and a programme of action which shaped the resentments of inarticulate and disgruntled people at various levels of society. In the week before the Notting Hill riots broke out a drunken fifteen-year-old approached a black man in a railway carriage at Liverpool Street station and was reported as shouting, 'Here's one of them – you black knave. We have complained to our government about you people. You come here, you take our women and do all sorts of things free of charge. They won't hang you so we will have to do it.'

Leaving aside the peculiarity of the boy's language after it had been filtered through various official reports, the style and content echoes precisely the rhetoric being peddled by such right-wing activists as Mosley, John Bean and Colin Jordan.

There follows an interview with Barbadian osteopath Rudy Braithwaite, who arrived in Britain in 1957:

I remember going to listen to some of the speeches that Mosley would make, you know. I was too young to really take on board what it meant when you talk about the Third Reich and all that sort of thing. And Britain is a white country and it's for white people, and that sort of thing. That was the gist of the discussion that he would have on this little soap box. And there were a lot of people, who are very respectable now, who used to be supporters of Mosley. I could put my finger on them. I know who they are.

Very massive crowds, big crowds used to come, you know. A lot of people would follow him. I mean, he used to have his meetings on one of the side streets off Westbourne Park Road. And there were people who would really come from everywhere and listen to Mosley, you know. And it was crazy. But that happened. He was a very convincing speaker. And he spoke without a breath, he didn't take much. He would speak and things would roll out of his mouth, so that he was very impressive. When I remember some of the things that were being said. It's very impressive. And he said, and perhaps that is true, he used to say, 'Many of the people who are in high places, who are politicians, would love to say what I am saying now.'

I remember those words. But they are too scared to say it because of the likelihood of jeopardising their wonderful, tidy positions. And, of course, that was borne out by Duncan Sandys [a right-wing Tory MP and minister with a chequered career], who talked about 'polka-dot grandchildren'. And Gerald Nabarro [a right-wing

*Tory MP and notorious roué of the 1950s and 1960s, mainly famous for his han-
dlebar moustache], who couldn't even drive on a main street without driving up the
wrong way. Yet he got away with it, his racism. He was very blatant about his
racist behaviour.*

The *Empire Windrush*, by the way, set off on her final voyage in February 1954,
sailing from Yokohama and Kure to the United Kingdom with 1,500 wounded UN
soldiers from the Korean War. The battered ship, long past her best, took ten weeks
to make Port Said, and she was later condemned.

Prejudice of a different kind hit Britain hard nearly fifty years after the Notting
Hill riots, and the form it took is indicative of how radically and dramatically our
culture has changed within a generation.

During the London rush hour on 7 July 2005 four bombs exploded, three on the
underground at 08.50, and another on a Number 30 bus in Tavistock Square, not far
from Euston Station, an hour later. Fifty-two innocent people were killed, and more
than 700 injured, some seriously disabled for life. The four suicide bombers were
young Muslim men, all of whom were British citizens and all of whom would have
had a perfect right to identity cards – the introduction of which as a means of coun-
tering terrorism is clearly invalid.

The London bombing (a similar attack was launched in the same city a fortnight
later, but miraculously failed) was the third in a series which started with the
destruction of the World Trade Center by Al Qaida in New York in 2001 (3,000
dead). The second was the bombing of the Madrid rail system on 11 March 2004
(191 dead, 1,700 wounded).

We can see how long a shadow an empire, even in its last stages, can cast.
England has been no stranger to bomb attacks in its recent past anyway, perpetrated by the IRA, and these outrages were also ultimately the result of decisions made
decades earlier and perpetuated in the name of the Empire, largely because irrecon-
cilable differences had been created.

It is true that following the bombings young Muslim men, or indeed anyone with
similar looks, ran the risk for a time of being regarded with fear and suspicion. But
there were no significant race riots such as those that had occurred four years earlier in Oldham and other major cities in northern England. There were race riots in
Birmingham in October 2005, but the confrontations then were not between whites
and blacks but between Afro-Caribbeans and South Asians, where the former local
population is predominantly Christian and the latter predominantly Muslim. The
riots, which took place over the weekend of 22/23 October, were triggered by

rumours that a black teenage girl had been raped by a gang of Muslim men.

Violent outbursts of this type have occurred from time to time ever since immigrants from the former British colonies began to arrive in noticeable numbers after the end of the Second World War. The first major race riots – not officially recognized as such – were those of Nottingham and Notting Hill in 1958. Though the Notting Hill Carnival came into being (in 1959, in St Pancras Town Hall) as a reply to the Notting Hill riots, tensions remained for many years after that. I can still remember the kind of looks I got when I was going out with a Guyanan girl in London in the mid-1960s.

We have – hopefully – come a long way since then. Most people, wherever they have come from, just want to get on with their lives, look after their families, have a more-or-less congenial job, and so on. That is self-evident. It is the few who muck things up for the many, and the many either have to put up with it or suffer. The people of Iraq, who as I write suffer outrages like the London bombs on a daily basis, are no different from anyone else in that respect. Prejudice against foreigners is endemic but it is essentially rare, and it is the child of propaganda. Many Muslims are in as great danger of tarring us white 'Christians' with the same sort of brush that we can be in danger of tarring them with. (And we should also be aware that as early as 1995 the French secret service had invented a nickname – 'Londonistan' – for our capital, as a result of their suspicion that it was a breeding ground for terrorists operating in Algeria; our reputation not helped by an initially, no doubt commendably liberal, but perhaps ultimately ill-advised indulgence towards such extremists as Abu Hamza al-Masri.)

The victims of the bombs in London, as they would have been in any concentrated multi-ethnic community, were random ones. Several members of what we still call ethnic minorities, including Muslims, inevitably died alongside 'native' Britons – something the bombers must have known. The hospital doctors and nurses who looked after the injured counted many non-ethnic Britons in their number. There was little racist reaction: we were united in common shock, outrage and grief. Ironically the most naked prejudice today – often stirred up by sections of the press – is against immigrants from the former Soviet bloc. But there is no stopping the tide, or the constant fluidity of demographics. The British Empire aside, an article appeared in the *Evening Standard* on 13 November 2006 pointing out that one-third of Londoners today were born outside Britain. This is a good thing. We should not forget that immigration has essentially enriched the country, not threatened or impoverished it. We had better get used to it, and the good news is that, slowly but surely, we are. This is only fair, since the British are a mongrel race anyway – and it is arguably that which has given them their edge in the past.

Britain is, generally speaking, a tolerant nation, though racism in many forms still exists. A thirty-five-year-old black London cabbie recently told me that when he was doing 'the Knowledge' his examiners – mainly ex-policemen – would tell him to drive to such destinations as Black Boy Lane (N15) and Blackall Street (EC2). However, there are some positive signs. About a year ago, I was pleased, if not 100 per cent convinced, by the optimism of a British-born Pakistani friend, who has had her share of racial abuse, who told me that she felt she was now living in a country whose institutions had become much more liberal in the last decade or so. She is about forty, and it seems to me, half a generation older, that a growing familiarity with other cultures is leading to a greater sense of ease. Many people have a South Asian doctor. Almost all city-dwellers have a South Asian corner shop or newsagent, or have eaten at one time or another in an Indian or Chinese restaurant. London probably has the greatest choice of cuisines of any city in the world, and Birmingham certainly has among the very best Indian restaurants. Many of our sporting heroes and heroines, whether they are athletes, cricketers or footballers, are of South East Asian, African or Afro-Caribbean origin. The Afro-Caribbean contribution to popular music since the late 1940s has been nothing short of revolutionary. Famously, chicken tikka masala (devised with the British palate in mind) has supplanted fish and chips (originally a French concoction) as the 'national dish'.

It is probably true to say that most people born since, say, the mid-1960s – people who are now middle-aged – have greater tolerance than their parents' generation, and *their* children will hopefully be more tolerant still – on both sides. After all, a large number of people of African, Afro-Caribbean and South Asian stock living in Britain today were born here, the children, grandchildren and great-grandchildren of Empire, and the flowers on the grave of that once mighty organization. And if it is depressing to reflect that the current leader of the British National Party was only born in 1959, it is also worth remembering that he was influenced in youth by his parents, and that the BNP has nothing like the clout of, for example, its Austrian or its French counterparts (the latter itself inexorably losing ground), and that Britain can at least be proud that it has never contained a political party of the extreme racist right which has had more than a derisory following, even in areas where 'blacks' now outnumber 'whites'. When the BNP leader was recently (in November 2006) acquitted (by an all-white jury) of charges of racial incitement, the official reaction of the government was an undertaking to re-examine 'race hate' laws.

There are still spheres of official life in Britain that are tainted by institutional racism, but in other public areas our record is good. In the sixties and seventies, sitcoms such as *Love Thy Neighbour* and *Till Death Us Do Part* dealt uncomfortably with the existence of racism. Although written from an ostensibly liberal point of view, and aspiring to show as ridiculous the characters who exhibited racism, all too often it was the non-European immigrant characters who were the butts of the jokes, and an uneasy sympathy sometimes bolstered the unpleasant protagonists. Such shows now seem to belong to a different planet. British television has nurtured a number of Asian and Afro-Caribbean sitcoms and series – from *Empire Road* by Michael Abbensetts and broadcast in the late 1970s to Meera Syal's *The Kumars at No. 42* and *Goodness Gracious Me*. That television is almost painfully aware of its responsibility is borne out by an article by Mark Sweney in the *Guardian* of 9 November 2006, detailing the results of an investigation carried out by the Open University and the University of Manchester for the British Film Institute (entitled 'Media Culture: The Social Organisation of Media Practices in Contemporary Britain'), which found that programmes such as *Coronation Street*, *A Touch of Frost* and *Midsomer Murders* have little appeal for members of the non-white ethnic minorities resident in Britain. It is a difficult gap to bridge, for portrayal of the predominantly white communities in the latter two programmes is still valid; oversensitivity to the sensibilities of ethnic minorities could be detrimental to harmony.

Britain has a good record too in the field of television journalism, at least in the area of news presentation, where, especially at the BBC and Channel 4, a large proportion of presenters in all fields belong to non-white ethnic minorities. This invites very favourable comparison with the situation in most other European countries. France, for example, has one black female newsreader on France 3, though ethnic minorities are better represented on the new twenty-four-hour news service. In politics and sport, Africans, Afro-Caribbeans and South Asians enjoy a high profile. This is not necessarily new. The first Asian MP, Dadabhai Naoroji, a Parsi, was Liberal Party MP for Finsbury Central for three years from 1892. Maharajah Kumar Sri Ranjitsinji Vibhaji made his cricketing debut for Sussex in 1895. Not that such men's achievements were anything but unusual for decades to come; nor were either politics or sport untainted by racism. In the year Naoroji lost his seat, Sir Mancherjee Bhownaggree won Bethnal Green for the Conservatives. Bhownaggree, a Parsi lawyer, was far from radical. He supported British rule in India and earned the nickname 'Bow-the-knee' from his Indian opponents. But the MP he replaced, a trade unionist called Charles Howell, was indignant that he had been 'kicked out by a black man, a stranger'. Seventy-three years later, the Conservative MP Enoch Powell distinguished himself by delivering perhaps the most racially inflammatory mainstream political speech of modern times.

In sport, as recently as 2004, the former player and manager Ron Atkinson, who twenty-six years earlier had distinguished himself by the pioneering introduction into his West Bromwich Albion team of three Afro-Caribbean players – Brendan Batson, Laurie Cunningham and Cyrille Regis – disgraced himself when commentating by describing the black French player Marcel Desailly as: 'He's what is known in some schools as a fucking lazy thick nigger.' For all that this may have been an isolated event, such a lapse in public can no longer be tolerated and Atkinson lost his jobs at ITV and on the *Guardian* instantly. The athlete Linford Christie has pointed out that when he won races, the press described him as a British athlete; when he lost them, he was either an immigrant or a Jamaican.

Christie came to Britain aged seven. For his services to athletics he was awarded, and accepted, the OBE. Meera Syal, born here, accepted the MBE in 1997. But the poet Benjamin Zephaniah, also born here, turned his down in 2003, defying convention by doing so publicly, and giving as his reason that it, and its association with the Empire, recalled to him 'thousands of years of brutality, it reminds me of how my foremothers were raped and my forefathers brutalised'. This sparked a discussion about whether the 'Empire' gongs should be dropped altogether, though this is unlikely to happen soon.

There is no doubt that elsewhere a dark ghost of Empire remains, exemplified recently by the trial, still ongoing as I write, of Thomas Cholmondeley, heir to the Delamere fortune. The Delameres are an aristocratic family who have farmed in Kenya since the 3rd Baron arrived there in 1903, and they own huge tracts of land, appropriated from the Masai, in the Rift Valley. Their name is associated with the Happy Valley set, which became notorious through the book and film of the same title *White Mischief*. They do not have a high tradition of tolerance with regard to native Kenyans.

In April 2005, game warden Samson Ole Sisina, aged forty-four, was killed by the then thity-seven-year-old Cholmondeley on the Delamere family's ranch near Lake Naivasha. Sisina was armed, and dressed in plain clothes, as part of an undercover investigation into the illegal trade in bush meat. Cholmondeley maintained that he shot the warden through the neck, but in self-defence, believing him to be a robber. Local whites immediately said it was the result of police failure to tackle a spate of car-jackings, burglaries and murders. Cholmondeley was acquitted, but in 2006 he was arraigned again on the charge of shooting another black Kenyan dead. This time, Cholmondeley claims that he mistook Robert Njoya for a poacher.

Matters remain tense. Assistant Minister of State Stephen Taurus told mourners at Njoya's funeral that 'it is time for these white settlers who are killing our sons to be kicked out of the country'.

Such events, tragic as they are, and whatever the truth behind them, are the very last twitchings of a dead age. More serious are the possible repercussions. There has been talk in Kenya of following Zimbabwe's lead in forcible repossession of farms owned by whites. Over all this falls the shadow of Empire.

In Britain, and much more positively, belonging as it were to a different age, perhaps the greatest recent flowering of 'immigrant' talent has been in the arts. Not only does Britain have established sculptors and painters of the calibre of Anish Kapoor (born in Bombay in 1954 but now living in England) and Chris Ofili (born in Manchester in 1968) as well as rising stars such as Raqib Shaw (born in 1974 in Calcutta, now living and working in London), but in the last decade or two she has been privileged to see a great wave of new novelists from the non-white ethnic minority community. Apart from established, eminent, even venerable writers such as R. K. Narayan, Anita Desai and Salman Rushdie and the Nobel prizewinners Sir V. S. Naipaul and Wole Soyinka, recent years have seen a flood of novels from the pens of such (predominantly female) writers as Chimamanda Ngozi Adichie, Monica Ali, Kiran Desai, Andrea Levi, Zadie Smith and Arundhati Roy. Not all of these, of course, live in Britain, but their work has exercised profound influence here and enriched her cultural heritage immeasurably, as well as having been influenced to a greater or lesser degree but always irresistibly by the old Empire.

And so the complicated, colourful story continues. But to understand the true roots of the Children of Empire, we must first look at the origins of that Empire itself, at the men and women who shaped it, and how it, in the course of three centuries, shaped them.

PART ONE

'RULE BRITANNIA'

JAMES THOMPSON

CHAPTER ONE

GOLD ᴀɴᴅ PLUNDER

Not only did it last far longer than any other in modern times, but at its height the British Empire was also the largest the world had ever seen.

⊠

THE EMPIRE REACHED ITS GREATEST EXTENT WHEN BRITAIN COMMANDED AROUND 500 MILLION PEOPLE.

The British Empire reached its greatest extent, ironically some time after its decline had set in, in the wake of the First World War, when Britain commanded nearly 40 million square kilometres of the earth's landmass and around 500 million people – about a quarter of the planet's terrain and about a quarter of the world's population at the time. Look at any world map published around the turn of the last century, and you will see a huge part of it marked in red, the colour of the Empire. Red stretches in a more-or-less unbroken swathe from the Yukon in the north-west to New Zealand in the south-east. When it is 6.00 a.m. in the extreme north-west of Canada, it is 2.00 p.m. in London and 3.00 a.m. the following day in Auckland. This great sweep of land, with its massive population, comprising scores of different nationalities and races and hundreds of different languages, was truly 'the empire on which the sun never sets'.

That Empire is gone, but its legacy is immense, and its effects are still felt in almost every corner of the world. Sir Richard Turnbull, among the last governors of Tanganyika and of Aden, once cynically told my mother that the Empire would leave behind only two traces of its existence, the game of football and the expression 'fuck off'. That is understating the case. To take one other frivolous example (and many would argue with my choice of that adjective immediately), the game of cricket, whose origins in England go back at least as far as the sixteenth century, is only played as a serious professional game in countries across the world which were once part of the Empire. In the case of the Caribbean island states, it is a game they have made their own and at which they famously trounced the mother country first as early as 1950. In more mundane areas, British approaches to civil and military administration, and law, have taken root and continued to develop in countries that were once ruled by Britain, their efficacy underpinned by the fact that, for all their faults, the British were able to run their Empire with relatively small numbers of soldiers and civil servants. Techniques of commerce and banking (adopted from the Dutch and the Italians) evolved in the seventeenth and eighteenth centuries have continued to influence international trade. And the greatest legacy of the Empire is the English language.

But what was all this built on? What was the lynchpin for the English (and later the British) to acquire and maintain their Empire? The answer is sea power. With the development of aeroplanes during and after the First World War and rocketry during the Second, the importance of the Royal Navy and its strategic ports across the world declined. Though ships and submarines as missile carriers would still make their contribution, the new craft could stay at sea for long periods. In the case of the submarines their whereabouts could be kept totally secret. They had no need of the old bases. The Empire was originally founded on maritime dominance. When this became a less important factor in world politics, and when other countries began to overtake us industrially, economically and in the development of new military technology, the Empire became far less easy to maintain.

One of the first monarchs to encourage overseas exploration was the Portuguese King Henry, called 'the Navigator', under whose sponsorship Portugal took and colonized the Azores as early as 1439. Having a west-facing coastline it was logical that the first line of travel should be westwards, and Henry's explorers were soon followed by others. The Portuguese were great seafarers, and their development of shipbuilding technology would be closely followed by the two other European seafaring nations.

Exploration in the name of enrichment and the extension of power was what motivated the early navigators. Spain was not slow to follow Portugal in setting forth across the Atlantic, commissioning the (probably) Genoese sailor Cristóbal Colón (Columbus). He made four voyages westwards between 1492 and 1504, making landfall in the Caribbean and on the coast of Central America.

The idea that the earth was a sphere, and not flat, was widely acknowledged, and had been for centuries. As early as the beginning of the Christian era the earth's spherical shape was accepted by most educated people in the West. The early astronomer Ptolemy based his maps on the idea of a curved globe and also developed the systems of longitude and latitude. Although arguments in favour of a flat earth still persisted, the modern idea that people in the Middle Ages generally believed in it is actually a nineteenth-century confection. A land route to the east had been well established since antiquity, and the Ancient Egyptians were already importing lapis lazuli – a hugely expensive luxury – from

C.Discovery · C.Columbia · C.Washington
Lockwood I. · C.Washington
Alfred Ernest · Hazen Ld
LINCOLN SEA
Grant Land · Britannia
L.Hazen · F.Conger · May
Lady Franklin · Hall Land
Grinnell · Washington Ld
Greely Fiord · Land · Peabody
Hayes Sound · Bay
Ellesmere Ld · Prudhoe Land
North · Inglefield Gulf
Lincoln · C.York

ARCTIC OCEAN · SPIT
Pr.Patrick · Parry Isles · King William Ld · GR
I.
N.Kellett
Melville · Nth Devon · Lancaster Sd
Sd · BAFFIN · GREENLAND
Banks I.d · BAY · Franz Josef · Jan Ma
Prince · Boothia · C.Bismarck
Wrangel · Albert · W.
Land · Barrow Pt · Land · Magnetic Pole · Disco I. · C.Brewster
Mackenzie · Egedes · Icela
Bay · Ld
ALASKA · DAVIS STRAIT · Reikiavik · Fare
Arctic Circle · C.Chudleigh · Shetlo
E.Cape · C.Pr.of Wales · Yukon · Great · C.Farewell · BRITISH
Behring Str. · (To U.States) · Bear L. · Quebec to Liverpool 3040 m. · ISLES
Cooks Inlet · Great · Labrador · Sub.Tel. · Glasg
Slave L. · HUDSON · Gulf St. · Newfoundland · Duh
Sitka I.V. · BAY · St.Johns · Louds E
Nelson · Str.of Belleisle · Gulf St.
Aleutian I.s · L.Athabasca · Nova Scotia · New York to Liverpool 3320 m. · Sub.Tel.
Vancouver I. · British · Winnipeg · Lawrence · Montreal · Southampton · C.Finistere
Victoria · Columbia · DOMINION OF CANADA · Quebec · Oporto
NORTH · Columbia R. · CANADA · NORTH · Lish
L.Superior · St. · Boston · C.Finistere
Missouri · NORTH AMERICA · Chicago · New York · Oporto
Salt Lake C. · Philadelphia · Azores · Madeira · C.Spart
San Francisco · UNITED STATES · Bernudas I. · Aspinwall to Southampton 5360 m. · Gib
Kanagawa to S.Francisco · California · Galveston · N.Orleans · Charleston · ATLANTIC OCEAN · Madeira · C.Spart
5470 m. · Tropic of Cancer · Sargasso Sea · Teneriffe
PACIFIC · G.of · C.S.Lucas · G.of MEXICO · Florida · Canary I.s
California · MEXICO · Havana · Bahama I. · Cape Verd · C.Blanc
Honolulu · Owhyhee (Hawaii) · Mexico · Vera · Cuba · C.Verd · Tin
Johnston I. · Sandwich I.s · Acapulco · Cruz · Hayti · WEST INDIES · St.Thomas
New Guatemala · Belize · Domingo · Windward · Barbados · C.Verd · Bathurst · Sierra Leon
OCEAN · CENTRAL AMERICA · Trujillo · CARIBBEAN SEA · Trinidad · Georgetown · Main Equatorial Current
Palmyra I. · COSTA · Panama · Amsterdam · Cayenne
Fanning I. · Christmas · RICA · Caracas · GUIANA
Equator · Equatorial Current · Galapagos I.s · Bogota · COLOMBIA · VENEZUELA · Amazon
Phoenix I.s · Malden I. · Humboldts · Quito · ECUADOR · C.S.Roque
Starbuck · Marquesas I.s · Guayaquil · UNITED STATES OF · Pernambuco · Ascension
Penrhyn · Caroline · Paita · PERU · BRAZIL · or Recife
Samoa I.s · Polynesia · Society I.s · Callao · Lima · Francisco · Bahia · SOUTH
Friendly I.s · Tahiti · Paumotu or · BOLIVIA · SOUTH AMERICA · Ouro Preto · St.Helena
Cooks I.s · (Otaheite) · Low Archipel.o · Sucre · Arica · Trinidad
Karatonga · Gambier I.s · Tropic of Capricorn · Rio de Janeiro
Pitcairn I. · S.Felix · Valparaiso · ATLANTIC OC
Easter I. · Calder · Coquimbo · Asuncion
CHILE · Prto · Porto · Alegre
Valparaiso · REPUBLIC · Monte Video · England 5390 m.
Juan Fernandez · Buenos · Rio de la Plata · Australia to · Tristan da Cunha
Aires · ream track
Valdivia · ARGENTINE
Chatham I.s · Patagonia
CHART O
Wellington I. · Str.of Magellan · SHOWIN
Tierra del · Falkland I.s
Fuego · Sth Georgia
Emerald I. · Cape Horn · Submarine Teleg
Arrows indicate the
Distances on the Stear
Sth Shetland I.s · Sth Orkney I.s
Graham Ld

180 A 160 B 140 C 120 D 100 I
a 80
b 70
c 60
d 40
e 20
f 20
o 0
g 20
h 40
i 60
k

PREVIOUS PAGE:
Chart of the World showing
British Empire at its
height, 1897.

Afghanistan. But the development and refinement of the ocean-going ship opened a world of new possibilities. Rumours of great wealth overseas, and of the legendary Christian kingdom of Prester John, fired the imaginations of kings and explorers alike. Soon after Colón's voyages, the Spanish realized that the lands he discovered did not belong to Asia as had been expected (his aim had been to find a westward route to the Spice Islands) but to an entirely new continent; and the reports he brought back of it were promising.

Although the Portuguese Vasco da Gama established a passage around the coast of Africa and the Cape of Good Hope to reach the south-eastern tip of India at the turn of the fifteenth and sixteenth centuries, the main thrust of exploration by sea concentrated on the faster westward route, the theory being that one would reach lands of great wealth 'somewhere off the west coast of Ireland'. The rivalry between Portugal and Spain needed some formal regulation, and Pope Innocent VIII presided over the negotiations which led to the signing of the Treaty of Tordesillas in 1494. It declared that all the undiscovered world to the west of a north–south meridian established about 1,550 kilometres west of the Cape Verde Islands should be the domain of Spain, and all of it to the east should be Portugal's. The line, about 39° 50' West, was not rigidly respected, and Spain did not oppose Portugal's westward expansion into Brazil, which is why Brazilians speak Portuguese and the rest of South America speaks Spanish, but a demarcation was established.

It was far from the last time Western European countries would loftily carve up the rest of the world by treaties and edicts with no reference either to the people who lived there, or, often, to each other. Possession was nine-tenths of the law, and native inhabitants, whom they quickly found relatively easy to crush, the more so since they had no gunpowder, were there to be exploited or evicted. The first explorer to show real sympathy for or interest in local peoples was William Dampier in the latter half of the seventeenth century. (He was quite a man: pirate turned explorer-zoologist-hydrographer, he identified, plotted and traced the trade winds and published a book on them which stayed in use until the 1930s. No wonder Samuel Pepys and John Evelyn invited him to dinner.) The first circumnavigation of the globe was accomplished between 1519 and 1522 by the ships of another Portuguese, Fernão de Magalhães (Magellan), though he himself died in the Philippines and so did not complete the voyage. A new route, though a perilous one, cutting through what is now called the Magellan Strait, in Tierra del Fuego just to the north of Cape Horn, was thus established, and a new ocean opened up, which Magalhães named *Mare Pacifico* – the Pacific Ocean – because of the apparent calmness of its surface. The impact of this discovery on human history (together with the stories Magalhães's surviving crew brought back when they finally returned home) was probably the greatest since that of fire or the wheel.

Meanwhile England, the other emergent maritime power of the time, had not been slow to pick up on the activities of Portugal and Spain. King Henry VII engaged another Genoese (some say he was Venetian), Giovanni (also known as Zuan) Caboto, to undertake a westward-bound voyage of discovery on his behalf, famously giving him:

> *full and free authoritie, leave, and power, to sayle to all partes, countreys... of the East, of the West, and of the North, under our banners and ensignes, with five ships... and as many mariners or men as they will have in saide ships, upon their own proper costes and charges, to seeke out, discover, and finde, whatsoever iles, countreys, regions or provinces of the heathen and infideles, whatsoever they bee, and in what part of the world soever they be, whiche before this time have beene unknowen to all Christians.*

John Cabot, as we call him, set off in 1497, after a false start the year before, and became perhaps the first European to set foot on Newfoundland since the semi-legendary Viking voyagers of about 500 years before (we only know for sure that Erik the Red reached Greenland, but he or his successors may have got further, and there is evidence to suggest it).

Henry had sent Cabot, hot on the heels of the Portuguese and the Spanish, in search of something more than a large northern offshore island – and Cabot himself had meant to make landfall further south. The myth of El Dorado did not become current until thirty years later or so, but people's imaginations had been fired by the possibilities of great wealth in the brand new continent that they suspected lay beyond the coastline they had hit. Cabot, it later turned out, had discovered wealth of another kind: the most fecund stocks of codfish in the world. In any case, he claimed Newfoundland for England. She had a foothold.

Henry VII was an extremely shrewd, financially alert monarch, and quick to realize that an investment in sea power would be a wise one. He accordingly started to build up his navy, a task which his son, Henry VIII, who succeeded him in 1509, took over with enthusiasm.

During the first half of the sixteenth century the Spanish developed

THE SPANISH REALIZED THAT THE LANDS COLÓN DISCOVERED BELONGED TO AN ENTIRELY NEW CONTINENT, AND REPORTS WERE PROMISING.

Queen Elizabeth I, c.1559, at the beginning of her reign, aged 27.

colonies in the Caribbean, conquered Mexico, and began to make inroads into the continent of South America. Spanish galleons soon began to bring back gold and other treasures from the New World, and King Carlos V became a rich man, aiming at world power. At the same time, Henry VIII instituted the English Reformation and withdrew from the Roman Catholic Church. Envious of Spanish success, and also worried by the threat of overweening Spanish power, the English now began to see themselves as the potential champions of a Protestant Europe.

This ambition was checked by Henry's ultra-Catholic daughter, Mary, whose reign saw England in danger of becoming a vassal of Spain, and it was not until Queen Elizabeth I came to the throne in 1558 that the Church of England finally became properly established.

During this time, however, England had been growing ever more confident as a naval power and in response, perhaps by one of those accidents of history, perhaps because so great an opportunity was there, came a flowering of brilliant English seafarers. Many of them – and the politicians who backed them – were also staunchly anti-Catholic and anti-Spain. Elizabeth had no desire to see Spain remain in the ascendant unchallenged, but she had inherited a weak exchequer. In order to fill her coffers and undermine Spanish power, she condoned, semi-officially, what amounted to a campaign of piracy. If Spain had stolen a march on England and colonized lands which were a source of gold, then England would take her gold from her when and where she could. The propagandist and chronicler for all this activity was Richard Hakluyt, whose *Voyages* remain essential reading for any serious student of this period. And pirates did not only take gold. Where they could, they relieved the Spanish of their charts, which were worth more, since they traced coastlines and showed harbours, which the English had no knowledge of.

It was not simple piracy, of course – only Spain was officially targeted – and the men who carried out the campaigns ranged from bold adventurers and explorers like Sir Francis Drake, through Sir Humphrey Gilbert and Sir John Hawkins, to the cultivated and sophisticated Sir Walter Ralegh, whose last disastrous venture to South America in search of Eldorado, for the unpleasant King James I, was to cost him his life, as a sop to the King of Spain. In the course of his adventures, Drake became one of the earliest circumnavigators of the globe (1577–80) and the first to complete the voyage as commander of his own expedition from start to finish. Hawkins contributed many technical improvements to warships, and is now credited with introducing both tobacco and the potato to England. On a less noble note, he was also the first English mariner to become involved in the nascent slave trade. Ralegh founded the first British colony in North America on Roanoke Island, just off the coast of what was then the putative colony of Virginia (named in honour of Elizabeth, who had granted Ralegh a charter to claim land in the New World in her name). It was not a success at first, but it established what would become a permanent British settlement in the Americas. However, for all their efforts, the English never did find gold of their own in the Americas. Even the

⊠ **ENGLAND HAD BEEN GROWING EVER MORE CONFIDENT AS A NAVAL POWER AND THERE CAME A FLOWERING OF BRILLIANT ENGLISH SEAFARERS.**

l to r, Sir Thomas Cavendish, Sir Francis Drake and Sir John Hawkins - pirates, slavers, traders, explorers and master mariners who laid the foundations of the British Empire.

Sir Walter Ralegh, courtier, poet, chemist and explorer.

potato did not become popular for two centuries, though tobacco did. It was the first money-making product to come to the Old World.

Spain found herself plagued by English ships in the Pacific, in the Atlantic and in the Caribbean, and decided in the end to punish the unruly northerners once and for all. There were other political and religious matters which forced the issue. Elizabeth was a nimble diplomat, managing to string Spain along for years with the possibility of an alliance by marriage, and keeping Mary Queen of Scots, her cousin and Catholic rival, and a Frenchwoman in all but name, alive as long as she could. But the plots against Elizabeth which centred on Mary could not be ignored or foiled for ever, and Elizabeth finally, reluctantly, had her executed in 1587. A strong response from Spain was inevitable, but the ill-advised and unlucky venture of the Grand Armada against England came to grief spectacularly in 1588. It confirmed the superiority of English seamanship, and from 1588 on England began to establish itself as the leading maritime power of the world, a position Britain was to maintain for three centuries.

The Elizabethans sowed the seeds of colonization, and by the 1620s Virginia was beginning to boom on the back of successful tobacco exports, just as, in a more modest way, a colony established in Newfoundland thrived on the cod fishery business. But in 1620 a new kind of settler arrived in what is now Massachusetts.

Puritans, who sought a plainer form of worship than the Church of England, which still maintained many of the trappings of the Catholic faith, began to feel the weight of religious prejudice on account of their nonconformist attitudes. As a result a group of them sought refuge in Holland, where they enjoyed greater freedom, but not the full autonomy they desired. After a decade or so they returned to England and, having obtained a grant of land from the Virginia Company which ran the colony there, set sail for the New World on the tiny *Mayflower*, along with a number of other immigrants. The *Mayflower* was blown off course and made landfall far to the north of Virginia, and the Pilgrim Fathers, as they came to be known, founded a colony where they landed. They were the first Europeans to settle on that coast, and had a hard time of it at first, but they stuck it out and eventually prospered, establishing farms and gradually spreading inland. About fifteen years later, Catholic religious exiles would form a colony which they called Maryland, in honour of Charles I's queen, Henrietta Maria. The English were now firmly established on the east coast of North America.

Francis Drake arrives in the New World. An uneasy first impression. There was to be little rapport between invaders and invaded over the ensuing centuries.

Contact with the local inhabitants – the Native Americans – was limited and generally unfriendly. The Spanish had managed to destroy huge numbers of the local populations they encountered with guns and – less deliberately but more effectively – with imported European diseases against which the locals had no natural resistance. Judged by European standards, and it would be a long time before anyone took an anthropological interest in the peoples of the colonized countries, the locals were 'brute beasts', who needed to be converted to Christianity and/or destroyed as an inconvenient thorn in the colonizers' side. Shakespeare's Caliban in *The Tempest* – itself in part a reflection on colonization – shows a sympathetic (for its time) take on the 'native'. And when emotional and personal contact was made, it was rare enough to enter into modern myth. The Native American princess Pocahontas, daughter of Powhatan, born about 1595, married an Englishman, John Rolfe, and returned to England with him and their son, Thomas, where she lived in Brentford. She was presented at Court, but later fell ill, and died at the beginning of her return voyage to Virginia in 1617. A few more exotic outsiders arrived here in the course of the century, prompting such literary responses as Aphra Behn's *Oroonoko*, and Defoe's Man Friday – who, however, kept his place.

England, still at loggerheads with Spain, had had an eye on the Caribbean islands since John Hawkins first took captured Africans there from Guinea and sold them to the Spanish as slaves to work the land (the native populations having largely been killed off). In 1627, Charles I granted a charter to settle the uninhabited island of Barbados and establish tobacco plantations there. They did not work, but tobacco was replaced with sugar cane and the sugar industry boomed. Then, in 1655, an army sent by Oliver Cromwell took Jamaica from Spain. Ravaged by dysentery and malaria, the first settlers held out on account of the money to be made, and the sugar plantations established there soon demanded an immense workforce, not least because life for the workers was hard and short. Initially, a system of indentured servants was introduced, generally poor people from the homeland who undertook to work for a fixed term – three to five years – on a very modest wage, in return for their passage out and their keep. These people endured extremely harsh conditions and were treated no better than serfs. Some went voluntarily to escape even grimmer or hopeless conditions at home; others were kidnapped – 'barbadosed'. Many Irishmen and women suffered this fate after Cromwell's crushing campaigns in their country, one of England's first and most abused colonies. Few lived long.

It was not a system that worked well, and it became harder and harder to fill places left vacant by the high mortality rate. Increasingly, Spanish and English planters in the Caribbean looked for a new source of labour, and in that search a new international trade was truly born.

The slave trade was so successful that it lasted from the seventeenth to the nineteenth century, formed the basis for the prosperity of such towns as Liverpool and Bristol, and made the fortunes of large numbers of individuals. Slavers were proud of their trade, saw nothing wrong in it, and one even had the figure of a slave incorporated in his coat of arms.

It was so profitable because the ships which plied it were never out of use. A ship would leave England for the coast of West Africa loaded with finished goods such as firearms, stoves, pans, kettles and nails, along with iron bars and brass ingots. These would be traded for slaves rounded up in the interior by local, often Arab, traders, but also provided by local chiefs from the prisoners taken in local wars. The slaves were densely packed into the holds of the ships in dismal conditions, but enough of them survived the crossing to make a profit for the traders, who, having sold their cargoes in such places as Barbados and Jamaica, but also trading with the Spanish since political enmity and reli-

TOP:
A child slave in Zanzibar, manacled to a block of wood to prevent escape.
ABOVE:
A group of freed slaves in Zanzibar, late nineteenth century.
OPPOSITE:
Oliver Cromwell, painted by Robert Walker, c. 1649, when the sitter, the new Lord Protector of England, was in his fiftieth year.

Taken on 1 November 1868, this photograph shows liberated slaves aboard HMS *Daphne*, after the Royal Navy had rescued them from Arab slave traders off the coast of Africa.

gious difference have never cut much ice with profit, then loaded their ships with refined sugar or tobacco to take back home. This was known as the triangular trade, and may be responsible for the fact that the British sailor employed to sail the ship had an even greater likelihood of death en route (usually from yellow fever, malaria or scurvy) than the slave. By 1700, it was estimated to be worth £2 million in contemporary terms – perhaps a hundred times that or more in modern money. Because the death rate was high, and because even when slaves bred the rate of infant mortality was high, demand for replacements was inexhaustible. Eric Williams, a former prime minister of Trinidad and Tobago and a historian of the Caribbean, gives an example from Barbados which is worth quoting: 'In 1764 there were 70,706 slaves in the island. Importations to 1783, with no figures available for the years 1779 and 1780, totalled 41,840. The total population, allowing for neither deaths nor births, should, therefore, have been 112,546 in 1783. Actually it was 62,258.' The slave population therefore was smaller by 8,448 people than it had been nineteen years earlier.

Chillingly, the slaves were referred to as 'product', in rather the same way as the Nazis later referred to the Jews. Rebellious slaves (and there were several rebellions) suffered vicious punishments, and those who stole sugar cane to eat themselves could, if caught, look forward to being flogged, to having their teeth pulled out, and to other cruel humiliations, as one Jamaican estate owner noted in his diary in May 1756, having caught two slaves 'eating canes': 'Had [one] well flogged and pickled, then made [the other] shit in his mouth.' Slaves who escaped headed for the hills where they formed their own communities, governed by a system of laws developed by themselves. The British, borrowing a word from the Spanish *cimarrones* (peak-dwellers), called them 'Maroons'. So successful and independent did these communities become that the British, despairing of destroying them, eventually concluded treaties with them, and, ironically, engaged them to hunt down other escaped slaves.

In the course of the eighteenth century, when the slave trade peaked, more than 1,650,000 people were uprooted, shipped and sold. The slave trade constituted one of the greatest migrations in recorded history. In England itself, and especially in London, there was a sizeable black population – Simon Schama tells us that there were between 5,000 and 7,000 in mid-eighteenth-century London alone. All of them were technically free, while resident in Britain, under the law, but many, despite the intervention of early activists

THE SLAVE TRADE CONSTITUTED ONE OF THE GREATEST MIGRATIONS IN RECORDED HISTORY.

William Wilber force (1759-1833), the Tory philanthropist best known for his work in abolishing the slave trade, shown here aged 68 in a splendid though unfinished portrait by Sir Thomas Lawrence.

**Head-Quarters, Montego-Bay,
St. James's, Jan. 2, 1832.**

TO

THE REBELLIOUS SLAVES.

NEGROES,

YOU have taken up arms against your Masters, and have burnt and plundered their Houses and Buildings. Some wicked persons have told you that the King has made you free, and that your Masters withhold your freedom from you. In the name of the King, I come amongst you, to tell you that you are misled. I bring with me numerous Forces to punish the guilty, and all who are found with the Rebels will be put to death, without Mercy. You cannot resist the King's Troops. Surrender yourselves, and beg that your crime may be pardoned. All who yield themselves up at any Military Post *immediately*, provided they are not principals and chiefs in the burnings that have been committed, will receive His Majesty's gracious pardon. All who hold out, will meet with certain death.

WILLOUGHBY COTTON,
Maj. General Command^g.

GOD SAVE THE KING.

A minatory notice directed at rebel slaves during one of the many Caribbean uprisings.

such as Granville Sharp on their behalf, were cruelly abused by their employers. Some, like Dr Johnson's servant, Francis Barber, enjoyed the benefits of education and became minor celebrities. Others, especially young men and boys, were often employed in aristocratic houses as pages – the modern equivalent of fashion accessories, dressed in exotic costumes believed suitable to their backgrounds. Yet others eked out a precarious living as musicians or waiters. There were a few soldiers and sailors. For women, the choice was stark: most only had recourse to either begging or prostitution.

By the end of the eighteenth century, an abolition movement gathered momentum in Britain. A medallion was struck by the pottery magnate Josiah Wedgwood in the 1790s showing a kneeling, chained slave, and bearing the legend 'Am I not a man and a brother?', which did much to popularize the cause; and its supporters succeeded in bringing about an end to the slave trade and then slavery itself by Acts of Parliament passed in 1807 and 1833. The institution itself did not die out instantly. It lingered long in India, and in the former British colonies in America it would survive for another thirty years at least. And abuse of colonized peoples and of former slaves continued even longer. In some places, it continues today. The descendants of slaves, of course, form the majority of the populations of the Caribbean states today.

England was not only expanding in the western hemisphere. Coffee – its name derives from the Arabic *qahwah* – spread to Europe from the Muslim world (its origins in antiquity are in Ethiopia), and towards the end of the seventeenth century it became an immensely chic, and expensive, drink in London, where coffee houses blossomed almost as fast as chains like Starbucks do today. Tea – even pricier – followed, imported from China. Chocolate, much drunk in the eighteenth century, quickly followed. These new and popular tastes for the exotic suggested new markets. The Dutch had established trading links with the Spice Islands of south-west Asia at the beginning of the seventeenth century, and colonized them under the aegis of the Dutch East India Company. Queen Elizabeth I granted a charter to the Royal East India Company in 1600, according it the usual high-handed carte blanche, irrespective of any other nation. Rivalry between the Dutch and the English concerns simmered throughout the 1600s, leading to a string of Anglo-Dutch wars towards the end of the century, but resolved by the accession of William of Orange to the British throne in 1689. The French East India Company established a base at Pondicherry (now Puducherry) in 1673, creating further rivalry as the trading possibilities opened up in India began to promise rich rewards.

⊠
ABUSE OF COLONIZED PEOPLES AND OF FORMER SLAVES CONTINUED EVEN LONGER. IN SOME PLACES, IT CONTINUES TODAY.

The English established trading stations in Surat, in what was to become Madras (now Chennai) and in what was to become Calcutta. In 1661 Charles II of England received Bombay (now Mumbai) as part of the dowry due on his marriage to the Portuguese Catherine of Braganza. The Portuguese had colonized the Goan coastal strip over one hundred years earlier. 'Bombay' derives from the Portuguese *bom baia* – 'good bay'. Much of the rest of India at the time was under the control of the fading Mughal empire (one of the last great emperors, Shah Jahan, created the Taj Mahal as a tomb for his wife in the middle of the seventeenth century), but the subcontinent was also divided into petty kingdoms whose warlike rivalries worked to the advantage of the European interlopers.

Trade dominated here initially, not colonization, and far from encountering unsophisticated tribes who could easily be dominated, the local peoples here were organized and powerful. Initially, the Europeans stuck to their coastal

Two views of the British garrison and fort at Bombay (Mumbai) in 1703, when the East India Company was in its golden age.

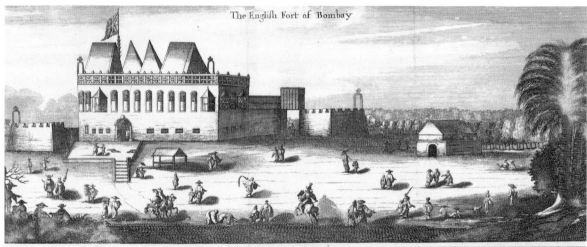

The English Fort of Bombay

The English Fort of Bombay towards y.ᵉ water side.

trading stations and bickered among themselves. The sea voyage east had to be made via the Cape of Good Hope (where Britain also established coastal bases) and was considerably longer (six months) than that to the Americas (about eight weeks), so East India Company officials enjoyed a great degree of latitude and independence, often making private fortunes on their own account.

The process by which India gradually fell under exclusively British control is long and complex, but, briefly, the Dutch were outmanoeuvred because they had a less versatile range of goods to trade with. The French, whose main centre was at Pondicherry, just south of Madras, ultimately foundered when the ambitious governor of the Compagnie des Indes, the Marquis Dupleix, fell foul of one of the first great heroes of the British Empire, Robert Clive. Clive, a severely flawed and pugnacious character who was to commit suicide (succeeding at the third attempt) at the age of forty-nine in 1774, was nevertheless a brilliant soldier and an able and astute administrator and negotiator. When the equally truculent Dupleix, with the aid of Indian allies, took Madras (then called Fort St George) in 1746, Clive recaptured it, and went on to take Pondicherry from the French, effectively neutralizing their influence. Not long after this campaign (1751–3), Clive, after a brief interval in England, returned to India to crush another enemy.

In 1756 the Nawab of Bengal, Siraj Ud Daulah, became disaffected with the East India Company's interference in the internal affairs of his country, and sensed (correctly) a threat to his independence. In June 1756, he ordered an immediate stop to improvements in the fortifications of Fort William in Calcutta. The Company ignored him. Thereupon the Nawab laid siege to the fort and took it after a bloody battle. His troops imprisoned about 120 British and Indian survivors – men, women and children – in a barrack which measured only about 4.5 by 5.5 metres, and left them there without food or water overnight. The air to breathe was limited among such a large number, the heat was atrocious, and when the prisoners were released the next morning it was found that only twenty-three were still alive. This was the famous Black Hole of Calcutta.

Apart from the need to nip this rebellion in the bud, for the British were indeed planning to use Bengal as a base for greater expansion in India, the affront demanded vengeance. Clive acted swiftly, moving north from Madras, and took Calcutta with relative ease on 2 January 1757. Siraj continued his fight, but the British forces had superior discipline and weaponry, and he was defeated finally at the Battle of Plassey towards the end of June. Titular control

TOP:
Rebel leaders. Many independent Indian rulers resented British influence and rebelled against it. Siraj-Ud-Daula, the Nawab of bengal, began an unsuccessful uprising in 1957 in Calcutta, and is remembered as the man responsible for the notorious Black Hole.
ABOVE:
Haider Ali of Mysore (1728-1782) allied himself with the French and was one of Britain's most tenacious opponents.

Haider Ali's son, Tipu
Sultan, continued his
father's campaigns against
the British and died
fighting them.

of Bengal passed to Siraj's former commander-in-chief, who was already in
Clive's pocket. The hegemony of the East India Company was assured, and,
incidentally, once Bengal was surely in its grasp, the Company took over the
lucrative opium trade, formerly the preserve of the Dutch, and exported the
drug to China.

Siraj was not the only Indian ruler to try to assert his independence against the
British. Tipu Sultan, the Tiger of Mysore (1750–99), was the eldest son of
Haider Ali. He succeeded his father as ruler of Mysore in 1782. Tipu was a cultivated man, a poet and a linguist, as well as an able soldier. He is one of the
heroes of Indian independence. An early opponent of the British, and quick to
see the danger of giving them too much rope, he fought alongside his father, then
an ally of the French, and defeated the British in the Mysore War of 1780–4. He

continued to resist the British for the rest of his reign, and died bravely, defending his capital, Seringapatam, when Mysore's resistance came to an end.

The most famous relic of his reign is his Tiger-Organ, a life-sized model of a Bengal tiger mauling a prostrate British redcoat. The organ is fitted with a number of pipes, and when operated, the tiger roared and growled and the soldier cried and groaned. After Tipu's fall, it was seized and sent for display to the East India Company Museum in London, where it created a great stir. Keats even alluded to it (rather foolishly) in his 'Cap and Bells'. It can now be seen at the Victoria and Albert Museum in South Kensington, but it is no longer played.

During its ascendancy, from the time of Clive's victories in the mid-eighteenth century to its demise in the wake of the Indian Mutiny of 1857, the British East India Company, or 'John Company' as it was nicknamed, through a policy of shrewd trade-offs with local rulers, and of playing them off against each other; through the placement of British 'advisers' in the various courts of the rajahs and maharajahs, and the development of a highly efficient private army, ran the subcontinent for the British with a minimum of fuss and a great deal of profit.

Another aspect is of interest. It was not until the nineteenth century that fraternizing with the local people began to be discouraged as a general rule. In the eighteenth and early nineteenth centuries, miscegenation was actively encouraged, and many a prominent 'British' officer was born as a result. James Skinner (1778–1841), the founder of 'Skinner's Horse' cavalry regiment, had an English father, but a Rajput mother.

BELOW:
Assimilation and mixed marriages were encouraged in the early days of British India. Colonel James Skinner, pictured here, founded a famous regiment of cavalry. His father was English and his mother Rajputani.
BELOW LEFT:
Tipu had this 'tiger-organ' built as a symbol of his dislike for the British. Almost life-size, the tiger mauls a British redcoat.

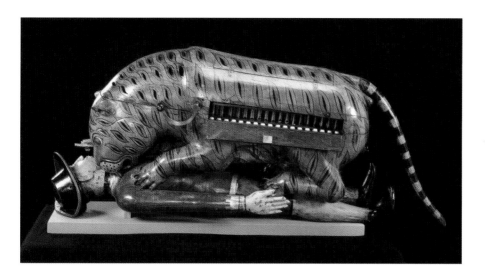

CHRIS BISSON

TRINIDAD

Chris Bisson is a familiar face on British television. He is probably best known for playing shopkeeper Vikram Desai for three years, when *Coronation Street* introduced its first South Asian family. He has also starred as Saleem Khan, the son of a Pakistani fish-and-chip shop owner in the 1999 film *East is East*, and as Kash, owner of the local mini-mart in the Channel 4 hit series *Shameless*.

Despite playing so many Asian roles, a lot of them as a shopkeeper or shopkeeper's son, Chris doesn't see himself as Asian. His paternal family's roots are in India but over the last century the family's history has been so changed by the British Empire that they have lost all connection with the subcontinent. Chris's grandfather and father were born in Trinidad and he has grown up feeling British West Indian, not Indian. It's a family history that made him question what it really means to be British in the twenty-first century.

Chris was born in Manchester in 1975. His mother, Sheila, who is white, grew up in a small family in Wythenshawe, a suburb of Manchester. Her relationship with Chris's father, Mickey, was the first she had had with someone who was not white. Mickey's lively household, with his nine brothers and sisters in Moss Side, was a culture shock. Sheila's parents found their daughter's relationship difficult initially but things changed when their grandson, Christopher, was born.

Chris wanted to find out how the British Empire has shaped his family's history. His father, Mickey, arrived in Britain in 1965. Chris went to talk to his father about his memories of that time. Mickey recalls how cold it felt in Britain in August. He also remembers the affluent lifestyle that the family left behind and showed Chris photographs of the large house they had owned in Trinidad. Mickey wondered why his father left that life and the successful businesses he had built up. It was clear that Chris needed to go to Trinidad to find out more. He had never been to the island before.

Although Chris's father was born in Trinidad he is ethnically Indian, like 40 per cent of the island's population. Chris knew that the key to unlocking the family story was his great-grandfather, whom he knew simply as 'Bap'. No one in the family had any idea of Bap's full name and no pictures existed of him. All they knew was that he came to Trinidad from India. When Chris arrived in Trinidad, his first stop was to visit his second cousin, Rajiv, whom he had never met before. Bap was Rajiv's grandfather so he is a generation closer than Chris. Rajiv was able to provide Chris with two vital pieces of information.

Sheila and Mickey sitting on a bench, 1974. At a cricket match in Manchester.

CHRIS BISSON

TRINIDAD

Sheila, Chris and Mickey. Christmas 1977 at Sheila's parents' house in Wythenshawe.

The first was that Bap's full name was Bishnia Singh and the second was that he came from Jaipur in Rajasthan. This was unusual for a labourer – firstly to come from Jaipur and secondly because he was a warrior cast.

Chris suspected that, like most of Trinidad's original Indian population, Bishnia came to the island as an indentured labourer. In the early nineteenth century Trinidad's economy thrived on its sugar, cotton and cocoa plantations, which were worked by African slaves. When slavery was abolished in the 1830s the British, who had ruled the island since 1797, needed a new source of cheap, plentiful labour. They began importing Indian peasants under the indentured labour scheme to replace the freed slaves, but refused people of a higher cast, which is why Bishnia's situation is unusual.

In order to confirm his suspicion, Chris enlisted the help of Shamshu Deen, an historian and genealogist. To his astonishment, Shamshu traced Bishnia to a book in the Trinidadian National Archives containing a register of Indian immigrants to Trinidad between 1901 and 1906. Among the 10,000 names in the book, Shamshu found Bishnia's. Bishnia's 'number' was recorded as

IT IS ESTIMATED THAT 2.5 MILLION INDIAN PEASANTS LEFT THEIR VILLAGES AND WERE SHIPPED AROUND THE EMPIRE TO WORK AS CHEAP LABOUR.

121,347, revealing that he was among the last of the indentured labourers to come to the island. In total, 147,592 labourers made the journey between the start of the scheme in Trinidad in 1845 and its abolition in 1917. But Shamshu had uncovered even more information for Chris. Each immigrant was issued with an Emigration Pass, signed by the 'Protector of Emigrants' in India. Bishnia's pass recorded that he was 5' 4", had a 'scar on left shin' and was only seventeen years old when he emigrated. He arrived in Trinidad in January 1905, after a three-month voyage with 620 others, on a purpose-built ship called the *Rhine*. Chris was amazed by the level of detail contained in the document, which included the village (Kownarwas) that Bishnia came from. The pass held another surprise and showed just how much his great-grandfather gave up when he went to Trinidad: it records the name of Bishnia's wife, whom he left behind in India.

Chris's next stop was Nelson Island, off the coast of Trinidad. Nelson Island was the disembarkation point and quarantine station for the new indentured labourers, who were kept there for ten days. Chris visited the barracks, originally built by slaves in 1802, which were created to house the Indians, like Chris's grandfather. The barracks were the first solid structure to be erected on Trinidad or Tobago. He found it an eerie and unsettling place, now inhabited by vultures and adorned with graffiti saying 'Fock da British'. Once they had been certified at the barracks as fit and well, the labourers would be sent from Nelson Island to work on one of Trinidad's 300 plantations.

In total, it is estimated that 2.5 million Indian peasants left their villages and were shipped around the Empire under the scheme to work as cheap labour in places they had never even heard of, including Mauritius, British Guiana and East Africa as well as Trinidad. Half a million of these so-called 'coolies' were brought to work on the sugar, coffee and cocoa plantations of the Caribbean. Although these labourers were not slaves and had signed contracts of employment, many were illiterate and could not read these contracts. It was not uncommon for people to be tricked into becoming labourers. Chris met ninety-six-year-old Nazir Mohammed who was brought to Trinidad as a baby by his mother, an indentured labourer. She was tricked by Indian recruiters who told her they were taking her to find her missing husband but instead took her and her baby to the labour depot. Nazir then grew up on a Trinidad plantation as a child labourer. He described conditions on the estate where he spent twelve years as being akin to slavery. The workers were forced to work and were whipped by the foreman.

TOP:
Emigration pass
of Bishnia.
ABOVE:
Mickey and Chris.
1976 in Wythenshawe.

Chris then travelled to the Bien Venue Estate where his great-grandfather had laboured in the early twentieth century. Bishnia spent five years there, unable to miss a day's work and forbidden from leaving the estate. Professor Kusha Haraksingh showed Chris round the plantation. He painted a picture of life on the estate but also explained the wider historical context. In the seventeenth and eighteenth centuries India had had a booming cotton and textile industry but the British had plans to make Manchester the textiles capital of the Empire. By imposing increasingly heavier tariffs on Indian imported cotton goods they made it impossible by the nineteenth century for India to compete with untaxed British goods. The poverty this gave rise to may well have forced Bishnia into becoming an indentured labourer. As Chris concluded, his fellow Mancunians managed to displace his great-grandfather. History had come full circle.

ABOVE:
Chris's uncle, Jameel, as a boy.
RIGHT:
Photo of Chris's grandfather, Harry. Apparently taken in the early 1960s in Trinidad.

Having discovered how his great-grandfather came to Trinidad as an impoverished labourer, Chris was curious to know how, in just one generation, his grandfather, Harry, achieved the wealth and success he has heard so much about. He decided to enlist the help of his eldest uncle, Jameel. He arranged to meet him at the family's old house in Stone Street in Port of Spain. Chris was amazed by how grand the house is and even more surprised to find out there are servants' quarters at the back.

Harry had always been ambitious. He had joined the British Customs Service but in 1959 decided to leave and see if he could make a living out of his favourite pastime: gambling. Jameel took Chris to one of the racetracks where Harry made his money and raced some of his own horses, some imported from England and Ireland. Jameel recalled that while Harry made sure his horses enjoyed air-conditioning on hot days, the family had no such luxury! Despite the grand house, two betting shops and owning his own race horses Harry had ambitions to move to Britain. Jameel revealed that Harry was motivated by two reasons: his children's education and a desire to be at the heart of the racing empire in Britain. Chris's ancestors were all Hindu and Harry's brother Lal in particular was a devout Hindu. Chris pondered that with the same fervour Lal embraced his religion, Harry had embraced capitalism.

Chris wanted to find out more about Harry. The impression he was getting was of a very determined and strong-willed patriarch who decided his family's future. He went to see his eldest aunts, Farida and Shaira, and great-aunt Dulcie, who remember Harry well. They agreed that Harry was an intelligent, disciplined and authoritarian figure. Failure to do homework properly earn 'licks with the belt'. Harry's iron grip extended beyond his children's education. His aunt Farida told Chris how she had married a Calypsonian singer called The Mighty Robin. But Chris was shocked when Farida revealed that Harry refused to meet Farida's fiancé. He didn't want one of his children marrying someone who was black. His aunts pointed out that there had always been racial tension between the Blacks and the Indians in Trinidad which still exists today. It made Chris wonder if there was more to Harry's plans to emigrate to Britain as Harry moved the family in 1965, three years after independence when a predominantly black government took over from the British.

In order to place this in context Chris went to see Professor Brinsley Samaroo from the University of the West Indies. Professor Samaroo explained to Chris that the island's ethnic tensions originated from the time when the British replaced the freed African slaves with Indian indentured labourers. It

Farida and Robin.

was another example of the British policy, which they practised throughout the Empire, of Divide et Impera, or Divide and Rule. These ancient antagonisms came to a head at independence and a considerable number of Indo-Trinidadians left at that time.

At the end of his journey Chris can see how his family's history has been shaped by the British Empire, causing his great-grandfather to leave India and his grandfather to leave Trinidad. But he still has one more question. How did the family end up in Manchester and what sort of welcome did they receive in Britain?

Back in Preston Chris went to see his aunt Patsy. She was the eldest of Harry's daughters to emigrate and was thirteen when she arrived in Britain. She had been excited about moving but was bitterly disappointed by the reality. Patsy faced enormous prejudice and found herself friendless. Chris's grandfather also found Britain unforgiving. He had hoped to open a betting shop in London but, before he could achieve his ambition, almost certainly hindered by the obvious racism there, had gambled all his money away. After three years in London the family had to rely on the Catholic Church, who

CHRIS
BISSON
TRINIDAD

Chris's Holy Communion.

helped immigrants find cheaper housing in other parts of England. The family made its final move, to Moss Side.

With his dreams of opening a betting shop gone, Harry put all his energy into his next great love, cricket. In 1972, with kit paid for from his winnings on the horses, Harry founded the Moss Side cricket team, the first black side in the area. The team was made up of blacks, Indians, and one white man. Chris's dad, Mickey, who played on the team, gathered together the former members for the first time in twenty years. The players reminisced about their games as well as the racism they encountered from both umpires and other players, and life in 1970s Britain. Leroy Hanley recalled how he and his friends were denied entry to clubs because of their Afros, which were claimed to be a fire hazard.

For Chris the journey into his family's past was illuminating. He now felt that he knew where he came from, something he never really understood before. As he concluded, 'whether my dad and my family were welcome here or not, I'm distinctly British and this is my country…If people still have racist attitudes, whether they like it or not, the Empire has affected this country in such a way that I am British and this is my home, and that's not going to change. It is now the responsibility of my generation to run the Empire!

CHAPTER TWO

TRIUMPH ᴀɴᴅ DISASTER

Political and trade rivalry between Britain and the two great Catholic powers, Spain and France, continued to simmer one way or another throughout the seventeenth and eighteenth centuries, boiling over into war now and then, with sniping as a constant factor.

Over the passage of time, Spain's power gradually waned, while France, especially during the long reign of Louis XIV, consolidated its position, a position it would maintain until the vainglorious Napoleon Bonaparte did it permanent damage. France took a knock, however, in the middle of the eighteenth century.

The conflict which concerns us here is the Seven Years' War of 1756–63. Winston Churchill called it the first *world* war, for it involved for the first time all the major world powers of the day, as well as spreading beyond the confines of Europe.

France had been building up its own empire, which extended to territories in the Caribbean and, later, in Africa. In the Caribbean, the most important possession was Saint-Domingue (now Haiti) occupied in 1697 on the western half of the Spanish island of Hispaniola. Saint-Domingue later became the richest sugar colony in the Caribbean. In America, France's colonial empire began in 1605, with the foundation of Port Royal in the colony of Acadia in what is now Nova Scotia. In 1608, Samuel de Champlain founded Quebec, which became the capital of a vast, thinly populated fur-trading colony – the start of what is now Canada. Unlike the British in the Americas, the French entered into alliances with the indigenous tribes, and through these had some control over much of the north-eastern part of the continent, but areas of actual French settlement were limited to the St Lawrence River area. Only late in the seventeenth century did France give its American colonies the proper means to develop in a way comparable to those of the British, but she was always more interested in power in Europe, and invested less time, money and effort in them than Britain did. France was not, however, unprotective of them, and the Seven Years' War, which grew out of a preceding conflict in Europe, brought overall rivalries to a head.

The causes of the Seven Years' War are complex, but in a nutshell it was

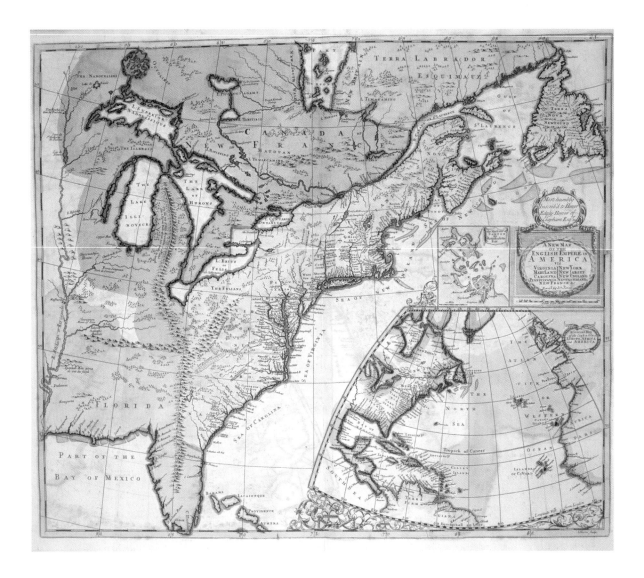

A 1721 map by John Senex of Eastern North America and Canada, entitled 'A New Map of the English Empire in America', and showing the thirteen colonies.

sparked by tension between Prussia and Austria over Silesia, which had come into Prussian possession. The Austrians formed an alliance with France and Russia, while Britain sided with Prussia to protect its own Hanoverian interests in Silesia. They were a powerful combination, since Prussia had the strongest army in the world, and Britain the strongest navy. Apart from the European dispute, Britain and France were already at daggers drawn over their colonial territories in North America, and in particular over the as-yet-unclaimed rich farmlands bordering the Ohio River.

In time, Sweden and Spain were drawn into the conflict on the side of the French alliance, and Portugal and Hanover on the side of the British. We need not concern ourselves with the European theatre of war (Britain and Prussia

Early settlers in New York, about 1650, seen bringing goods ashore and building a house. Apparently insouciant Native Americans sit under a tree in the foreground and observe them.

won overall), but the confrontation in America led to the collapse of French territorial ambitions there.

The decisive battle is a famous one in British history. In 1759, the British Army under Major General James Wolfe laid siege to Quebec for three months. In the event of the city not falling, Wolfe proposed 'to set the town on fire with shells, to destroy the harvest, houses and cattle, both above and below, to send off as many Canadians as possible to Europe and to leave famine and desolation behind me; but we must teach these scoundrels to make war in a more gentleman like manner'. Wolfe's asperity was rooted in his shock at the murder of prisoners and civilians by the local tribes allied to the French, for whose behaviour he held the French commander, the Marquis de Montcalm, responsible.

After pounding the city remorselessly but unsuccessfully, Wolfe then decided on a risky landing by river (among the mariners negotiating the difficult passage was a young man called James Cook, who had been busy mapping the mouth of the St Lawrence) at the foot of some cliffs to the west of Quebec – the Heights of Abraham. His army, dragging two small cannon with them, climbed up at dawn on 13 September 1759, surprising the French, who were unprepared for an attack from that quarter, believing the cliffs to be impregnable. Battle was joined on the Plains of Abraham, and the French were defeated, but both Wolfe (aged thirty-two) and Montcalm (aged forty-seven) were fatally injured. With the fall of Quebec, French rule in North America came to an end, for the victory paved the way for a successful attack on Montreal the following year. The French were left with two possessions: Louisiana, and the island group of St Pierre and Miquelon, off the eastern coast of Newfoundland – important bases for fisheries. Elsewhere, especially in the Caribbean, they got off relatively lightly, though this did nothing to mollify their resentment.

The Treaty of Paris, drawn up in 1763, saw Britain gain territories worldwide from France and Spain, though she did not keep as much as she had gained by force of arms, which led to some criticism of the government at home, which, however, felt its leniency to be in the interests of the balance of world power. The French slaving posts on the Senegal coast went to the British. The British also took Grenada, St Vincent and Tobago, as well as Havana. Britain gained Canada and tracts of land west of the Mississippi River, as well as Florida. However, these gains belied the fact that Britain was nearing the end of what historians often refer to as 'the first British Empire', by which is principally meant the thirteen North American colonies, which would gain their independence as the fledgling USA a little more than ten years later.

Just over a decade after the Treaty of Paris was signed, the Quebec Act of 1774 restored some aspects of French jurisprudence to Canada and allowed Catholics to worship freely, at the same time permitting French Canadians to participate in government, as well as annexing the area east of the Mississippi and north of the Ohio rivers (roughly, modern Michigan, Ohio, Illinois and Indiana). This bit of legislation was timely, since it secured the loyalty to Britain of the Canadian colonists. Along the coast, to the south and east, things in the American colonies were beginning to stir.

By the middle of the eighteenth century Britain's territories had spread along the east coast of North America, and were divided into thirteen colonies, from Maine in the north, through Pennsylvania and Virginia, to the Carolinas in the south. They were profitable but expensive to run. However, land speculation was booming, and interest in expansion westwards fired the imaginations both of the colonists, large numbers of whom were born Americans by now (Washington and Jefferson were born in Virginia, Franklin in Massachusetts), and developers at home. At the same time, immigration to the New World had rocketed: between 1760 and 1775, 125,000 English, Irish and Scots left home to seek a new life, escaping poor working conditions and a falling-off of employment in Britain.

However, all these prosperous new lands and this emergent new (and generally staunchly Protestant) people – who still saw themselves as British first and foremost – were governed from Westminster and had to accept whatever London told them to do. But they were beginning to think for themselves. As early as the 1750s, Anglo-French skirmishing had stimulated the British colonies to convene an assembly of representatives at Albany to agree the formation of a common front against the Catholic French and their Native American allies. Now, with the French threat removed, it was pressure from the mother country that induced them to assemble again.

The pressure came in the form of a Stamp Act, introduced in 1765, designed to impose a tax on all documents, including newspapers and even playing cards, throughout the Empire. The Congress convened in reaction to it placed an embargo on British goods. The demonstrations and riots which attended the introduction of the Act took London by surprise, but George III, together with his advisers, refused to bend with the wind, taking the view that the American colonies were junior members who had no right to question their authority.

BRITAIN WAS NEARING THE END OF WHAT HISTORIANS OFTEN REFER TO AS 'THE FIRST BRITISH EMPIRE'.

Though there was plenty of support in Britain for the Americans' point of view, the approaching rift was probably inevitable. The Americans, while still seeing themselves as British, were growing away from the mother country. There was no aristocracy in the colonies; men lived and worked together in a more egalitarian society, which was simpler and less sophisticated than that of England, certainly, but had its own integrity and pride, and its intellectuals were feeling their way towards a quasi-socialist *modus vivendi*. Chary of the French they may have been, but they were quite willing to absorb what such writers as Rousseau and Voltaire had to say. A sense of independence was in the air, for sure, and there was enough unity for the Americans successfully to apply pressure on Westminster to repeal the unpopular Act in the following year, 1766.

The repeal of the Act, however, did nothing to lessen tension, as the British promptly passed another law which emphasized London's right to make unchallengeable legislation for Britain's colonies. The Americans simply ignored it, and continued to refuse to pay taxes they deemed unfair. New taxes imposed on tea and imported finished goods were withdrawn after two years because no one paid them. Clearly military force could not be used – these were, after all, our own people – but something had to be done to break the deadlock. By 1770 there was still a stalemate. By ill-fortune, Britain had an increasingly intractable king and a series of vapid prime ministers at the time. In the American colonies, the British government's executives found themselves powerless to enforce any of the measures demanded of them by London. The foolish decision was made to use limited but selective force after all. It was also decided to apply it in Boston, the largest and wealthiest city in the American colonies, and an intellectual hub. It was like lighting a match next to gunpowder.

The tipping point was passed in the wintry March of 1770, and it was triggered by what on the face of it was a petty incident. A young wigmaker's apprentice, backed up by some cronies, brusquely told a British officer that he was late paying his barber's bill. The officer had actually paid it earlier the same day, but ignored the boy, who became more vociferous. When he would not go away, a British sentry hit him over the head with his rifle butt. This quickly led to a confrontation between a couple of redcoats and a small group of Bostonians who by now had gathered and threw snowballs and street filth at the British. The soldiers panicked and called reinforcements, who duly arrived, but meanwhile the crowd had grown, its mood turned uglier, and the people started to throw sticks and stones and lumps of ice. Then one of the

A SMALL GROUP OF BOSTONIANS WHO BY NOW HAD GATHERED AND THREW SNOWBALLS AND STREET FILTH AT THE BRITISH.

King George III, aged 62 in 1800, when this painting was made by Sir William Beechey.

The Boston Tea Party: 16 December 1773. In fact the protest took place at night and barely anyone witnessed it. Possibly not even a political act at all, it became a central plank in American independence propaganda.

soldiers was struck to the ground by one of the missiles. His gun went off as he fell, and in the confusion his comrades opened fire at the mob. Five men were killed and six more injured.

The British were not the brutal thugs depicted in the sillier Hollywood retellings of the War of Independence – arrogant officers with Eton accents leading troglodytic foot soldiers with bad Cockney accents. There was far less distinction between Britons and Americans than there is now, and one of the redcoats involved in what became known as the Boston Massacre fired his gun into the air rather than at what he and many like him regarded as fellow citizens. But the damage was done, and what was quickly to become the independence movement had its first martyrs. The next three years saw the burning of a revenue cutter at Rhode Island and, in 1773, the Boston Tea Party, when a group of Americans disguised as Indians tipped the cargo of tea – worth £10,000 – from an East India Company ship into the harbour in protest at new levies designed to protect the Company's monopoly.

However, the Stamp Act had not imposed huge duties, nor did the Tea Act, to which the Boston Tea Party had been a reaction. Tea, in fact, had become very cheap, and it has been suggested that the men who dumped it over the side of the East Indiaman were not aggrieved citizens but smugglers who objected to what amounted to a rebate on its cost, since the new tax imposed on the Americans was less than what the English paid.

These incidents were triggers, symptoms of a deeper unrest; and the Quebec Act, though it neutralized Canada, caused a furore in the American colonies. Recognition of Catholicism, associated as it was with the excesses of the Spanish colonizers to the south and the French alliances with native tribes whose cruelty in war bore no relation to European humanism (at least in theory), sparked panic, and there was outrage at the annexation of the lands south of the Great Lakes which, the Americans had assumed, would soon be theirs to settle. A new Congress was called, in Philadelphia, in September 1774 to decide on a course of action.

America was rich: Britain depended on it not only for luxuries like tobacco but also for timber for masts for the ships of the Royal Navy. Thus one logical line to take was to impose a trade boycott on Britain and its other colonies. Britain could not retaliate in the same way because although she exported a variety of finished goods to the Thirteen Colonies nothing she could offer was indispensable to them. But the cautious deliberations of Congress were quickly overtaken by men who wanted to take a much more radical course of action. British colonial governors were stranded, British executives were simply ignored and had not sufficient military backup to enforce their demands, and during 1775 actual power began to slip increasingly into the hands of what were alarmingly looking more and more like rebels. On neither side was there unity. Many Americans wished to remain within the British Empire, and many Britons supported independence. Either way, whether or not anticipated with dismay by many on both sides of the Atlantic, war seemed, and indeed was, inevitable.

Britain was still recovering financially from the Seven Years' War and did not relish the cost of sending a large army so far overseas and then supplying it. The Americans in general were more bullish, but the rebels faced at worst an experienced and well-honed military and naval power with more than the potential to crush them and make sure they never rose again. The Americans only had groups of militias to oppose them, though Congress moved in the summer of 1775 to establish a standing army, and engaged George Washington, forty-three years old and a veteran of battles with the French during the Seven Years' War, to organize and lead it. Black Americans fought on both sides. Those who managed to escape slavery and sided with the British were promised their freedom in return; a promise which in the event the British were unable to fulfil.

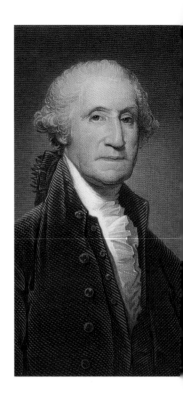

George Washington, 1732-1799, the first President of the United States.

The spoils of war?
A map of the fledgling
USA, from 1783.

Skirmishes and pitched battles took place during 1775, especially around Boston, and late in the year the Americans tried unsuccessfully to invade Canada. They remained confident in their cause, however, and as early as 1776 made their Declaration of Independence at Philadelphia.

The war continued unresolved until 1778, when the French, who were still smarting from the loss of Canada, signed a treaty with the colonial forces, by now fielding near-professional armies under Washington, and also adept at guerrilla techniques unfamiliar to their British counterparts. Spain joined the revolutionary alliance a year later, but held back from open support of American independence, having its own South American colonies to consider. The Dutch also joined in 1780, sharing with Spain and France a desire to see Britain curbed as a world power. The cooperation of these countries weakened Britain's dominance at sea, and with many at home opposed to this wasteful and expensive conflict with a people who were perceived as country-men fighting in a just cause, who should be allies and trading partners, not enemies, British resolve faltered.

In early September 1781 the French defeated the British in a naval battle at Chesapeake, cutting off supplies to Lord Cornwallis's land forces. Seizing the opportunity, Washington moved his army from New York and besieged Cornwallis at Yorktown. Cornwallis, the vanquisher of Tipu Sultan, but never a supporter of the taxes imposed by Westminster on the Americans, surrendered in October.

The war went on, but effectively it was over. Political support for the war crashed after the defeat, Lord North, the Prime Minister, resigned, and in April Parliament voted to cease hostilities. Although the articles of peace were not formally signed until the Treaty of Paris of 1783, the war was over. The British left the few Indian allies they had in the lurch, signing over their lands, between the Appalachians and the Mississippi, to the newly formed United States of America; and settled down to an amenable trade relationship with their new ally, soon finding that having the North Americans as partners was far more profitable than having to fund them as colonists.

The British were not the only ones to treat badly those for whom they had implicitly taken responsibility. This chapter should not close without telling the story of Toussaint Louverture.

In the wake of the French Revolution, in 1792, the new National Assembly declared that all blacks and mulattos in France and its colonies should have the same political rights as the whites. This did not please the rich sugar-planters of places like Saint-Domingue, who had already decided that the island would be better off if it left France and joined Britain. This proposal pleased Britain, but there had to be some very delicate and secret diplomatic negotiation to make sure she got what she wanted. The French revolutionaries were touchy and belligerent, and had to be handled with care. But the British were pleased to be able to pay back the French in a small way for the aid they had given to the Americans a few years earlier, and glad of the extra sugar revenue, so they garrisoned Saint-Domingue. The troops were soon succumbing to tropical disease and fearful boredom.

Nobody considered that the slaves of the island might play a role themselves, and when in 1794 the French government declared that all slaves should be free, they rose against the British under Louverture, a freeman and former coachman who was already a revolutionary leader, and kicked them out. By 1798, at the age of fifty-two, Louverture was effective ruler of the island, though he remained passionately attached to France and to the ideals of its revolution. However, times were changing in the mother country. Late in 1799, modern Europe's first major dictator, Napoleon Bonaparte, effectively took over the country which he was, through the next fifteen years, to sacrifice on the altar of his own ambition.

In Saint-Domingue, Louverture drafted a constitution that made him governor general for life with near absolute powers. There was no provision for a French official, because Louverture thought himself Frenchman enough. Bonaparte appeared to accept Louverture's professions of loyalty, and confirmed his appointment, but in fact he wanted to make Saint-Domingue a profitable colony, and to reinstate slavery to do so.

Bonaparte was conveniently forgetting that, had it not been for Louverture, Saint-Domingue would no longer have belonged to France in the first place.

The French dictator then sent a task force under his brother-in-law, Charles Leclerc, to regain control of the island. Leclerc landed in January and immediately moved against Louverture. The battle raged for several months, but some of Louverture's brigades defected, as did former allies on the island, and defeat loomed. On 7 May 1802, Louverture signed a treaty with the French, on condition that there would be no return to slavery, and retired to his farm, but three weeks later, on the pretext that he was plotting an uprising, Leclerc seized Louverture, put him on board a warship, and sent him to France. On the deck of the ship the Governor General declared: 'In overthrowing me, you have cut down in St-Domingue only the trunk of the tree of liberty. It will spring up again by the roots, for they are numerous and deep.'

Louverture reached France two months later. In August, he was sent to a castle high up in the Alps, a cold and bleak place deliberately chosen for its qualities, where he was put on a starvation diet and subjected to lengthy interrogations. 'On 27 April 1803 he was found sitting by the fireplace, his hands resting on his knees, his head slightly bent, dead. According to one account, the rats had gnawed at his feet. He was thrown into a common grave.'

There is also a footnote to this chapter. With the loss of the Thirteen Colonies, Britain no longer had anywhere to transport its convicts and other undesirables, though immigration to the United States still boomed as the burgeoning new country needed peopling as it ploughed westwards, sweeping, as is the way of all colonizers, the local residents aside. Fortunately for Britain, in 1770 Captain James Cook, whom we met briefly at the side of Major

General Wolfe before the battle for Quebec, reached the south-eastern shores of Australia, deftly assisted in his navigation to those parts of the world by John Harrison's recently invented chronometer, an instrument which for the first time allowed mariners to fix the lines of longitude. He was not the first European to enter these waters, nor even the first Englishman, for the pirate-turned-explorer and naturalist William Dampier, the first man to circumnavigate the globe twice, had arrived on the north-west coast over seventy years earlier. But Dampier had hit infertile and forbidding shores, was regarded with mistrust by the Establishment, and anyway Britain was quite happy as it was with America in 1699.

But Botany Bay was fertile and inviting. A new extension to the Empire presented itself, just as another part was falling away. Cook was the hero of the hour.

An extremely idealistic view of the founding of Port Jackson at Botany Bay in New South Wales. Various examples of the Australian cornucopia are illustrated. The man at the centre in naval uniform and a cockaded hat is probably Arthur Phillip, the colony's first governor.

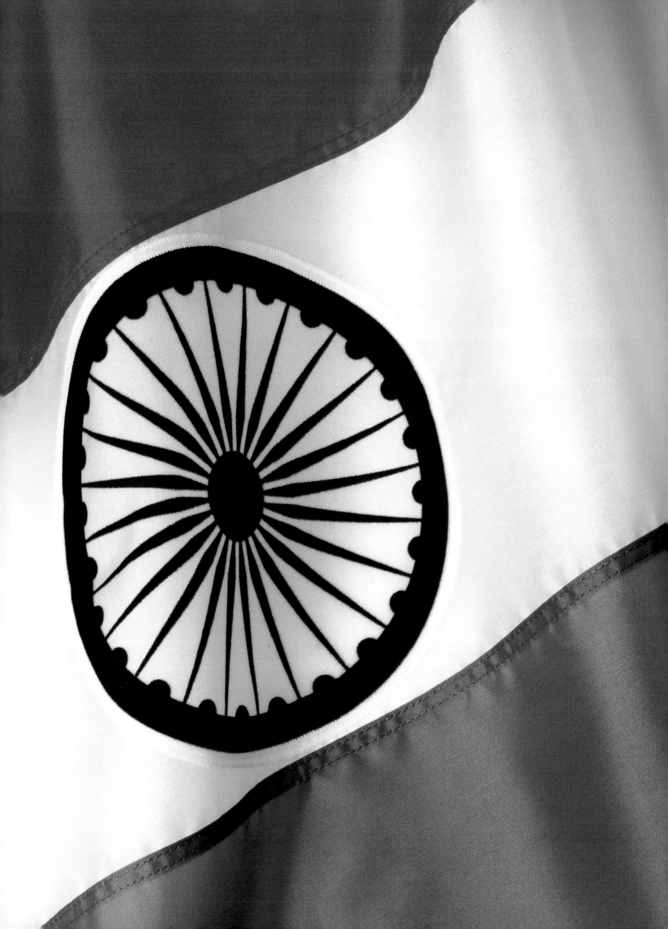

DIANA RIGG

INDIA

Dame Diana Rigg is one of Britain's best-loved actresses. She is perhaps best known for her iconic role as 'Mrs Peel' in the hit television spy series *The Avengers*.

She also starred as Tracy Di Vincenzo, the only woman James Bond ever married, in the 1969 film *On Her Majesty's Secret Service*. In a career that spans nearly fifty years, she has become a star of stage and screen, and has won both an Emmy and a Bafta for her performances. She is also a published author. One book, *No Turn Unstoned*, was inspired by a particularly unkind critic and is a compilation of the worst theatrical reviews. The other is a compilation of poetry on the English countryside entitled *So to the Land*. In addition to acting and writing, Diana is also Chancellor of Stirling University and is well known for her charity work. In 1988 she was awarded a CBE (Commander of the British Empire) and in 1994 she was made a Dame Commander. As part of her journey into the history of the British Empire, Diana reflected on the symbolism of these accolades. What exactly is she 'Dame' of?

Diana was born in India in 1938 but, before embarking on the programme, she knew very little about how she came to spend the early years of her childhood in India. She remembers leading a priviledged lifestyle, with several servants. She admits questioning her mother later on in life about the morality of this sort of lifestyle, but as her mother said, 'that's just the way things were then'. Diana started by visiting her brother Hugh to collect some photographs and letters that her mother wrote during the family's time there. Hugh remembers the food – goat's milk and lots of brain! But both Diana and her brother admit that theirs was a generation who didn't question their parents' actions and decisions. Diana needed to go back to a time before she was born, to find out why her father went to India in the first place.

Louis Rigg, Diana's father, was born in Doncaster in 1903. He followed in the footsteps of his father, who was also a railway engineer. Diana went to see historian John Scott Morgan at the National Railway Museum. Records show that Louis's father had spent £100 (nearly six months' wages in those days) on securing him a premium apprenticeship with the designer of the *Flying Scotsman*, Nigel Gresley. Such an impressive placement would normally have guaranteed him a job, but just as he was completing it in 1922 the government made the decision to rationalize the number of railway franchises from 122 to just four. Louis decided to look elsewhere for opportunities, to the British Empire. In 1925 he answered an advertisement in *The Times*, calling for railway engineers to work in India.

TOP:
Diana on her horse Araminta.
ABOVE:
Diana's father, Louis Rigg, in the 1920s.

India, like many of the colonies, appealed to the British working classes because it offered the sort of lifestyle that someone like Louis could never have enjoyed in Britain. But the change in environment and culture was vast, and many Britons found it difficult to adjust. Once in India, Diana's first destination was the city of Bikaner on the edge of the Thar Desert, Louis's first posting. Travelling on the railway that her father helped build, she can see symbols of the imperial legacy everywhere. Railways were built by the British all over the Empire, and were of vital importance to the infrastructure of the region. They are also one of the most important legacies of the Raj. Today 8,000 trains carry 12 million passengers daily over 75,000 kilometres of track.

As a young, unmarried man, James worked at 'the end of the line' where conditions were tough. The front of the track construction was far away from civilization. Temperatures rose as high as 50 ºC and the jungle harboured deadly wildlife. Diseases such as typhoid and cholera were also rife. Unusually, Louis did not work for a British employer, but for the Indian Maharajah (King) of Bikaner, Ganga Singh. Bikaner was one of the 500 princely states that was still ruled by its own king rather than directly by the British. In return for swearing allegiance to the crown the Maharajahs were allowed to continue raising taxes and governing all the internal affairs of their states. Ganga Singh was an extraordinary character. His feared camel corps fought in both world wars and, as ADC to King George V, he was present at the signing of the Treaty of Versailles. Far from the stereotypical decadent raja who spent his time kowtowing to the British, he was a benevolent despot who not only built railways and canals to bring water to his desert state but also made education free for all his subjects.

In Bikaner, Diana went to meet Shri Lal Nathamal Joshi, who worked with Louis on the railway. Many of the newly arrived 'sahibs' quickly developed a reputation for high-handed treatment of their staff but it seems Louis broke this mould. Diana learned that her father is fondly remembered as a man who, far from lording it over the locals, worked with them as equals. His contribution to the local area is remembered with gratitude and appreciation. When Louis left Bikaner in 1943, all the staff gathered together to bid him farewell and Joshi wrote a special poem in honour of the occasion.

By 1929, four years after moving to India, Louis decided it was time to get married. He was given six months' leave and returned home to Britain to seek his bride. He met twenty-one year-old Beryl Halliwell at the local Doncaster tennis club, and it was love at first sight. They were engaged almost immediately, but it took almost three years before Louis was able to persuade Beryl to make the six-week voyage to India. The couple were married in Bombay. Diana visited their first house, where she grew up, speculating how her mother would have tried to make it look as English as possible. She discovered from reading letters that her mother wrote home, that they were blissfully happy on their honeymoon.

BELOW LEFT:
Diana and her parents
leaving Bikaner, 30th
October 1943.
BELOW RIGHT:
Diana's mother, Beryl, and
her dog.

Life for a newly arrived bride in imperial India could be socially daunting. Beryl, the small-town girl from provincial England, had five servants to carry out every household task, and the comfortable bungalow the couple lived in was a far cry from Doncaster. Beryl faced other challenges, socializing with the most senior officials of the British Empire as well as Indian royalty. Diana visited one of the maharajah's private residences, where her parents would have been entertained, and was able to marvel at the opulence and luxury that they must have enjoyed. The Indian women were not so lucky. They were forbidden to socialize with men and were kept in 'purdah', only allowed to gaze down at the parties from balconies above.

The Rigg family were also regular guests at the Maharajah's lakeside hunting lodge at Gajner, about thirty miles west of Bikaner, another place that Diana visited. Louis's rank in the social order became apparent at such gatherings. One of Beryl's letters home provides a vivid description of one such hunt:

THE RIGG FAMILY WERE ALSO REGULAR GUESTS AT THE MAHARAJAH'S LAKESIDE HUNTING LODGE AT GAJNER, ABOUT THIRTY MILES WEST OF BIKANER.

ABOVE:
His Royal Highness Ganga Singh of Bikaner.
RIGHT:
Ganga Singh's Golden Jubilee celebrations, 1937.

Diana and her brother
Hugh and mother Beryl at
Kailana Lake 1944–5.

We didn't go into the butts with the men, I wanted to but H.H. [His Highness] said it was too hot for us, so we watched from the lakeside…An aide de camp or someone fired the first shot. That was to make the birds rise from the lake. It was extraordinary the way they all rose in a cloud when that shot was fired. Then H.H. fired the first one after the birds had risen, then all the men started. There were about 10 men shooting and they got 570 birds…H.H. himself got 170 birds but then he had 3 guns and 3 loaders so all he had to do was shoot…

Despite being a crack shot Louis, whose social status consigned him to a position at the end of the firing line, only bagged 3 birds that day.

When Diana was born in 1938, her brother Hugh was already four years old. Their mother kept a strict eye on them, making sure they did not stay in the sun too long and that they avoided local food. She was right to be cautious. Mortality among expats was high, and still higher in the local population. Even so, the imported tinned food from England was, Diana remembered, 'disgusting!'

In 1943 the Rigg family moved to the neighbouring state of Jodhpur. Louis Rigg accepted the post of Chief Mechanical Engineer – the highest posting he could ever hope for – to the Maharajah of Jodhpur. He was now in charge of some 3,000 staff and more than 100 locomotives. The equivalent position in Britain usually attracted a knighthood. The family's new home was commensurately grand, so large that today it is divided into four family flats. Maharajah Umaid Singh was another dynamic personality, a keen aviator who had opened the first airport in Rajasthan. He also had a 347-room palace built, still the largest private residence in the world.

Unfortunately, the good fortune did not last long. In 1944 Gandhi was released after being imprisoned for establishing the Quit India campaign in 1942. A year later the Second World War ended and pressure for independence was growing. Isolated bomb attacks began to occur, especially focused on disrupting the infrastructure, particularly the railways. Many expats believed that the time had come for them to leave. Louis Rigg took this view in August 1945 when he sent his family home on the SS *Mahonada*. After settling seven-year-old Diana and her brother Hugh at boarding school, Beryl returned to India until independence. Louis stayed on until 1948 to complete his contract. With his wife and children at home Louis spent much of his time at that great colonial institution: the Club. The Sardar in Jodhpur had a thirteen-hole golf course, small enough for members to get in a round between work and their sundowners.

When independence came in 1947 most of the Indian kings were persuaded to subsume their states within the greater new states of Muslim Pakistan or Hindu India. Louis returned, aged forty-five, to a post-war Britain still in the grip of rationing and suffering from severe unemployment. It was tough to adjust to life back home after over two decades away and even harder to find work despite his skills and experience. Louis did finally manage to get a job at a tanning factory in Leeds, but Diana remembers living in relative poverty.

Diana's final visit was to the girl's school that her parents scrimped and saved to send her to. She was not accepted at the local grammar after failing the entrance exams. Her education in India had left her very poorly equipped for English schooling but it was here that she discovered a passion for drama. The impact of the end of the Empire on her family is not lost on Diana, who knows how fortunate she has been to adapt and succeed in a newer, tougher world than that of her early childhood. Diana also learned that the British tyrannical reputation was not always accurate, as her father is testimony to. Although independence had to happen, many colonial subjects remember the British with fondness. After this journey, perhaps Diana can wear her DBE with a little more pride than she felt before.

DIANA RIGG

INDIA

ABOVE:
Home in Jodhpur,
August 1945.
LEFT:
Diana fishing with
her father Louis and her
brother Hugh,
Lake Kailana.

CHAPTER THREE

THE SECOND EMPIRE

The East India Company was already prosperous and powerful before Clive's victory at Plassey. Its bases at Calcutta, Bombay and Madras became thriving commercial centres, and its army was well on the way to becoming the most powerful in India.

Robert Clive, 1725-1774, by Nathaniel Dance. Clive, one of the heroes of early colonial India, who effectively secured the country for the British, was also a depressive who attempted suicide several times, and was not above shady financial dealings.

Its employees became rich; the governors general who succeeded each other at its head made vast and often partially illegal personal fortunes. At the same time it was developing an administrative system for the whole subcontinent which, with its centre at Calcutta, and with local rulers either cowed or collaborating, turned the whole country into a vast machine for generating wealth for Britain. Calcutta, the principal town of Bengal, which for a long period was the powerhouse of the Empire in India, was the capital of the British Raj until 1911, when the administration moved to the more centrally convenient Delhi, whence it removed again to New Delhi twenty years later. As a microcosm of the country the British managed, Calcutta is worth a quick glance. In 1911, its population was just over a million. Thirty years later, it had increased by 150 per cent. Separate nationalities, races and castes totalled 397, in a population speaking fifty-one different languages, twenty-eight of them belonging to India itself.

Opium, cultivated in Bengal and exported to China, was a huge earner. In return, silk was imported and re-exported home. Saltpetre for the manufacture of gunpowder was an important export, as was tea (though this suffered a slump about the time of the American Revolutionary War – and the North Americans never really returned to their tea-drinking habits). Cotton cloth, cheaply produced at home, was imported, to the ruin of local Indian cottage industries. Money-making was the name of the game, with scant regard for anything else.

However, running costs were high and the Company was a breeding ground for corruption, from the governors general to the lowliest private soldiers, which meant that while it was a profitable organization in the mid-eighteenth century, by the beginning of the nineteenth it was enormously in debt – to the tune of £40 million. By that time, too, wars and a slump in profits resulting

THE EAST INDIA COMPANY TURNED INDIA INTO A VAST MACHINE FOR GENERATING WEALTH FOR BRITAIN.

Two views, broadside and stern, of an East Indiaman, about 1685. The ship flies the flag of the East India Company. Big East Indiamen over 750 tons like this one would have mounted eighty guns, though of smaller bore than those of a man-of-war.

from events in Europe – a recession following the boom created by the Industrial Revolution, and the upheaval of both the American and French Revolutions – had drastically slowed things up. And although the Company had been successful in bringing more and more of India under its control, it became increasingly unable to govern the vast expanse of its territories. At the same time, in the early 1770s, a famine struck Bengal and wiped out 10 million people. Military and administrative costs mounted beyond control in British-administered regions in Bengal because of the ensuing drop in labour productivity. Three-quarters of its income was spent on its army, which, by 1815 consisting of 150,000 men, was essential to the enforcement of its function. The officers were British – Englishmen and Scotsmen. A high proportion of the NCOs and other ranks were Irish, and a large number of the soldiers were recruited from among the Indians themselves. The Company originally recruited these men from Hindus in Bengal, Bihar and Uttar Pradesh.

Many British colonisers in India were quick to appreciate native culture, to learn the languages, and even to adopt local customs and dress. This picture is believed to show Sir David Ochterlony, 1728-1825, born in Boston, Mass., though of Scottish descent. Ochterlony joined the British Indian Army as a cadet and rose to become one of its greatest generals. Here he is seen at home in Delhi, about 1820, wearing Indian clothes, smoking a hookah, and being entertained by a *nautch* dancer.

Known collectively as sepoys (from the Persian *sipahi*: soldier) they distinguished themselves by their selflessness and their bravery, qualities which were to make them in time not only the backbone but the true muscle of the army.

The home government began to wonder if the Company was not careering out of control, and Britain had no desire to lose India; but it had its hands and much of the fleet tied up dealing with Bonaparte, who had his own visions of empire. (Britain used colonial troops in its wars against the French dictator – in Sir David Wilkie's painting, *Chelsea Pensioners Reading the Gazette of the Battle of Waterloo*, now in Apsley House, you can see an African soldier rejoicing with his comrades.) However, towards the end of the eighteenth century, a new breed of governor general was brought in, and under Cornwallis and Wellesley much was done to clean up the Company's act – much to the discomfiture of several of its directors, unsurprisingly.

Increasing government interference in its workings, and increasing interest by the government in absorbing its profits, led to changes in the Company which had a significant impact on Indian society.

While medicine made great strides from the late eighteenth century, the impact of this was not widely felt at home, let alone in the colonies, until much later; but it is interesting to note that, apart from sexually transmitted diseases, there is not as much evidence of local populations in India being decimated by illnesses imported from Europe as was the case in the Americas, the

Caribbean, and even the East Indies. But equally in India the local populations, unless they rebelled against the colonizers, were not killed or swept aside in the same ruthless way. Europeans fought with each other for control of the subcontinent as much as with the natives, and by the time British rule was established through the East India Company, a spirit of tolerance and cooperation was found to be much more congenial to the making of money than any more violent course. Indians were co-opted into the junior ranks of the administration.

Not until some decades into the nineteenth century were white women in evidence in any numbers, and, far from home, the colonizers fraternized freely with local women. There were many mixed marriages, and a high proportion of white men found the company and the looks of Indian women more congenial than those of their compatriots. A relaxed view of homosexuality added to the sense of sexual freedom that prevailed. However, relationships between Indian men and colonial women were never condoned. By a strong double standard that existed throughout the Empire, white women were always regarded as shrinking violets in danger of being debauched by local men. (In fact, they did not shrink much, and affairs with Indian men – of the right caste – were not altogether unusual.)

Sex apart, the British in India, as long as the East India Company had free rein, were tolerant of local mores; not to have been so would have been bad for business and good relations, and the heavy hand of Victorian Christian morality, coupled with the desire to export it, was still some time in the future. Many of the British long-termers in India, up until the 1820s at least, found much to admire in Indian culture and ethics, so the toleration of local customs was not merely a response to material expediency. The Governor of Madras, Thomas Munro, writing in 1813, had this to say: 'If civilisation is ever to become an article of faith [between Britain and India], I am convinced that [Britain] will gain by the import cargo'; and he added: 'I have no faith in the modern doctrine of the improvement of the Hindus, or of any other people. When I read, as I sometimes do, of a measure by which a large province had been suddenly improved, or a race of semi-barbarians civilised almost to Quakerdom, I throw away the book.'

As far as proselytizing was concerned, East India Company chaplains were forbidden to attempt it with the Indians, and missionaries were severely discouraged. As one highly placed East India Company official wrote, diplomatically but firmly, to another in 1808:

MANY OF THE BRITISH LONG-TERMERS FOUND MUCH TO ADMIRE IN INDIAN CULTURE AND ETHICS.

We are very far from being averse to the introduction of Christianity into India... but nothing could be more unwise than any imprudent or injudicious attempt to induce it by means which should irritate and alarm their religious prejudices... Our paramount power imposes upon us the necessity to protect the native inhabitants in the free and undisturbed possession of their religious opinions.

Many Britons in India studied the cultures of their hosts and learned to speak and write the languages fluently. But this almost happy state of affairs was not to last. When the Company's charter came up for renewal in 1813, the Evangelicals – who had been, to their credit, involved in the abolition of slavery and the slave trade, and who were in the popular political ascendant at home – were able to put an end to the Company's power to veto missionary activity. Their motives were pure: they felt that Britain, privileged to have the vast riches of India fall into her lap, should not just enjoy the profits thereof, but also show some spiritual responsibility by bringing to the 'pagans' the light of Christianity. There was, of course, little or no attempt by the newcomers to reflect on the possible validity of the Indians' own religious beliefs.

Of course, the missions throughout the world brought some good with them: no one would criticize the hospitals and schools they established; and some missionaries learned the local languages and cultures of their postings. But the bottom line was always: convert. There are practices in any religion and in any culture which others regard as barbaric or taboo, often forgetting the violence in their own. In India, the British, for all their original policy of laissez-faire, were moved in the 1830s to do something about three native customs which they regarded as brutal and uncivilized.

The first was the killing of unwanted female children, who in high-caste families could be expensive to marry off, and in poorer families, where sons at least could work the land and earn their keep, were a drain on their slender incomes. Then as now, the population of India was huge, and attitudes to death were unsentimental. The British had been aware of the practice since the late eighteenth century at least, but the combined forces of Christian evangelism and a general modernizing and liberal impulse now induced them to act. Female infanticide was targeted, found to be widespread in the northern and western provinces, and strenuous and generally successful efforts were made to suppress it during the course of the middle years of the nineteenth century.

The same went for the practice of *sahamarana*, called by the British *sati* (or

suttee), whereby the widow of a deceased man was obliged to be burnt alive on the funeral pyre of her husband. Quite often the poor woman was drugged before she was made to face her cruel, but traditional and religiously condoned, fate. Vivid stories ran around fast. One told of a woman who twice managed to escape the flames, only to be caught and hurled back. At a third attempt, by now hideously burnt, she got as far as a nearby river, where her pursuers drowned her. In another case, the victim was rescued by one Job Charnock (once reputed to be the founder of Calcutta), who subsequently married her. By any modern standards (and lest we judge too harshly we should reflect on what was done during the Reformation and Counter Reformation in the name of Christianity) the practice was repugnant, and the liberal Governor General William Bentinck succeeded in suppressing it soon after he came to office in 1829. This was not achieved without resistance: many Hindus of the day regarded *sati* – the word actually refers to the woman herself and has the rough meaning of 'sanctified one' – as an expression of

The manicured British enclave in Calcutta, showing the fashionable influence of classical architecture, in a view by Henry Salt, 1809.

marital loyalty and of piety. In practical terms, it was akin to female infanticide: no one would have the burden of supporting a widow if she was dead.

It fell to an administrator under Bentinck's governorship, William Sleeman, to stamp out the third practice: *thagi* (or *thuggee* – from which we get our word 'thug' – one of many words in common use derived from Hindi and other Indian languages). This was not a religious custom; *thagi* is a generic term which refers to a large criminal organization which specialized in highway robbery, which always involved the deaths, often by strangulation, of its victims. The crimes were committed according to strict rules and certain rites were associated with them. Thugs prided themselves on leaving no trace of their activity behind: the victims were buried and everything they had which the thugs did not take was destroyed.

Since thugs preyed on fellow Indians and outsiders alike, Sleeman's remorseless and unrelenting campaign to break the vast organization, a campaign which took him years, earned him the gratitude of natives and colonizers alike and did much to enhance the prestige of the British in India.

But respect for the British, if not earned, could always be ensured by the

1879: British and Indian troops of the Queen's Own Corps of Guides observe the Khyber Pass from Sarkhai Hill while on reconnaissance duty during the Second Afghan War.

army. The British Army in India was, by the middle of the nineteenth century, a finely tuned fighting machine with a string of victories to its credit. Only in Afghanistan had it met with setbacks. Afghanistan was never fully taken over by Britain, though three wars were fought there. The first, from 1838 to 1842, left the British with a very bloody nose. The second dragged on from 1841 to 1881, when the British finally withdrew. The last, as late as 1919, in which the British ruthlessly used aerial bombardment, ended in victory for them, though the peace terms led to Afghan independence. In each case the crux of the matter was territorial rivalry between Britain and Russia, and British fear of Russian encroachment on its turf. Tsar Nicholas II once half-joked that all he needed to do to wipe the smile off the face of the British lion was to concentrate forces along his borders south-east of the Aral Sea and Lake Balkhash. Afghanistan's strategic importance was always clear. It, and the always volatile North-West Frontier Province, provided the arena for the Great Game – immortalized in Kipling's novel *Kim* – a cat-and-mouse contest between agents of the Russian and the British secret services.

In 1979, the then Soviet Union invaded Afghanistan, and it has been the scene of quasi-colonial conflict ever since. The same year saw the seizure of power in Iran by the Ayatollah Khomeini in the name of the Islamic Revolution.

In the nineteenth century, at approximately the same time as the Second Afghan War, the British Army and Navy in India were called upon to protect British trading interests in China. Owing to the difficulty of providing silver to the Chinese in exchange for such luxury items as tea and silk, the British had early turned to opium as a product easily cultivated in India and much in demand in China. The Qing government, alarmed by both the drop in silver income and the ill effects of opium on its people (in much the same way as gin had had on the English in the eighteenth century), decided to suppress the trade on health grounds. This did not suit the British Exchequer at all, and Westminster showed muscle by means of a favourite method of Victorian colonial enforcement – gunboat diplomacy. Between 1839 and 1842, British warships secured the mouths of both the Pearl and the Yangtze rivers, and British forces occupied Shanghai. Thousands of Chinese lost their lives, and the Qing dynasty did not have the means to oppose the British, who imposed their interests while not actually taking over the country. However, they left behind them a lasting mistrust and resentment of the West in general. The British gained Hong Kong, which became a Crown Colony in 1843.

A second Opium War broke out in 1856, sparked by the arrest by the

Chinese militiamen, armed with clubs and carrying wicker shields, photographed during the Second Opium War.

Chinese authorities of a Hong Kong-registered ship, the *Arrow*, which they suspected of smuggling. Once again the Chinese were attacked, this time by an Anglo-French alliance, and again came off badly, finding themselves forced to open more of their ports to foreign trade. When the Chinese then tried to veto the opening of embassies in Beijing, in 1860 the occupying forces marched on, and took, the capital. The Emperor fled, new treaties were signed, and the British gained Kowloon. When the American admiral Matthew Perry forced his attentions on the closed country of Japan in the mid-1850s, he pointed out to the Japanese that if they did not open their ports they might face the same fate as China. They took the hint, and by the early 1860s Japanese art, design and style were all the rage in Western Europe. The Aesthetic Movement was firmly rooted in *Japonisme*, which took Europe by storm in the wake of the London International Exhibition of 1862, at which the arts and crafts of Japan were the main attraction. In 1875, the thirty-two-year-old Arthur Lasenby Liberty set up his arts-and-crafts-inspired shop in

Regent Street, specializing in selling *japonerie*.

From its earliest colonization, the British realized that they had in India an empire within an empire, and until its independence in 1947 India remained incontestably the 'jewel in the crown'. It came, therefore, as a nasty shock when, in 1857, a large proportion of the Indian element in the army there rebelled.

By then, a high proportion – approaching 80 per cent – of the rank and file of the Indians who served, unlike their British and Irish counterparts, hadn't joined as a last resort, or because they could find no other employment, but because most of them came from martial peoples who saw soldiering as a true profession, to be taken seriously and conducted honourably.

To the Hindu soldiers, their patron deity was Kali, an ancient goddess who defeated the army of the demon king Raktavija by slaughtering them and drinking all their blood; but in her frenzied victory dance she made the earth tremble. When her husband, one of the avatars of Siva, tried to intercede with her to stop, she slaughtered him too, before coming out of her ecstasy and realizing what she had done. She is symbolic of wild, aggressive force, which, once unleashed, is hard to rein in again. She was the also the goddess of the thugs. It is prudent not to arouse her anger.

Sikhs and Muslims had by now joined the ranks, along with the Hindu tribes mentioned earlier. The three religions coexisted under the British in a cooperative, if not always harmonious way. Collectively, it was inadvisable to take them

British officers, seated in the foreground, of a North-West frontier brigade, c. 1880. Sepoys stand to attention behind them.

for granted, or ignore their customs and beliefs. In this the British erred.

They might have been warned. There had been a rebellion before, in 1806, over changes to the uniform which disregarded religious taboos. The one that was coming would be more serious.

A number of grievances had been building up among the native soldiers. Firstly, British officers tended to treat the sepoys with scant respect. Secondly, no native soldier had the remotest hope of a commission. Thirdly, Lord Dalhousie had arrived in India aged thirty-five as its youngest governor general. He had requested and been granted plenipotentiary powers; and while this energetic young Scot did much good in his nine-year tenure, his high-handed behaviour also humiliated and offended many Indians.

On the plus side, he planned and inaugurated India's peerless railway system, laid 6,000 kilometres of telegraph, built 3,000 kilometres of road, improved irrigation, cracked down even harder than his predecessors on *sati*, *thagi* and female infanticide, and opened the way, in a limited fashion, for Indians to enter the Civil Service and administration of the country. Other policies weighed against these. Chief of them was the Doctrine of Lapse, a policy of annexation by which any princely state or territory under the direct influence of the East India Company would automatically be taken over if its ruler was either 'manifestly incompetent or died without a direct heir'. This policy replaced the long-established right of an Indian sovereign without a direct heir to choose his own successor. Without consultation, the British decided if local rajahs and maharajahs were incompetent or not. Annexation by this means was humiliating, crushed local traditions and infrastructures, and left local administrations and armies unemployed. You can just see what kind of a man Dalhousie was. Unsurprisingly, as early as 1848 he was dealing with a Sikh uprising, and was soon fighting in what is now Burma as well. None of this stopped Dalhousie from annexing (with Westminster's tacit support – after all, if he could bring it off, the more of India brought under direct British control, the better) Satara in 1848, Jaitpur and Sambalpur in 1849, Nagpur and Jhansi in 1854, and Oudh (Awadh) in 1856.

Dalhousie, a small, frail, indomitable man, left India in 1856, having wrought the country to Britain's will with such firmness that, while some at home hailed him as a hero, others correctly feared that his bluntness and complete lack of tact had laid the foundations for revolution. Dalhousie himself looked forward to continuing triumph in his public career, but his always fragile health was shattered by overwork and the Indian climate. Misdirected by

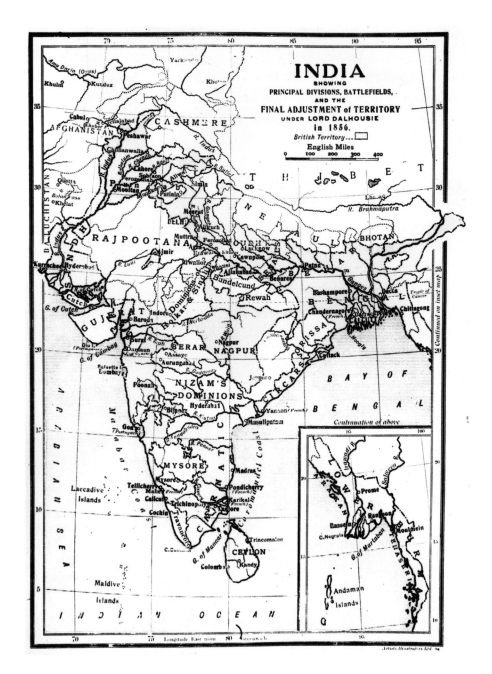

India after 1856, showing how the country was divided up following the interventions and annexations conducted by the over-zealous Governor-General, Lord Dalhousie.

his doctors, he lingered on as a semi-invalid for four years, finally dying at his family seat in 1860. Lacking a male heir, his line died with him.

Indians had been used to working alongside the British interlopers, conscious of the improvements they brought, and still feeling independent enough to squabble among themselves – something which, as we have seen, operated to the advantage of the colonizers. Now the beginnings of a sense of unity against the outsiders began very slowly to stir in the Indian consciousness.

Political discontent and a sense of being treated unfairly informed the thinking of the sepoys by the 1850s, though they were far from having any kind of coherent organization – luckily for the British. Ironically, the event that triggered the uprising was very similar to one of the elements in the rebellion of 1806. Then, it had been a question of whether or not a new cockade should be made of cow- or pigskin. Now, it was a question of whether the cartridges for the new Enfield rifles which had been introduced were greased with cow- or pig-tallow, or a mixture of both. It seems barely conceivable that the British could be so crass as to expect that the huge majority of their army, composed of Hindus and Muslims, would accept cartridges greased with the fat of two animals of such importance to them. The cow was sacred to the Hindu, the pig was taboo to the Muslim. But such seems to have been the case. On top of everything else, it was more than enough. Belatedly, the British, realizing their

British soldiers storm Delhi during the Indian Mutiny of 1857.

mistake, tried to make amends. The new cartridges, it was decreed, would be used only by European troops. Locals would receive a new issue, lubricated with beeswax or vegetable oil. But the order came too late.

The mutiny was far from unanimous among the Indian troops, but it carried great weight and spread rapidly. If it had been properly organized and focused, history might have taken a very different course. The first spark came at Barrackpore, when a young soldier of 34 Native Infantry fired without warning at his British sergeant major. When the adjutant rode up, the Indian shot his horse from under him and then slashed at him with a sword. This summoned the commanding officer who arrived with the garrison guard, upon which the young sepoy tried to shoot himself, but he failed in the attempt, was patched up, and hanged soon afterwards. The regiment was disbanded, the intent being to disgrace it, but, in fact, giving the mutiny its first *cause célèbre*.

When eighty-five troopers of the Bengal Light Cavalry stationed in Meerut (Mirath) refused to use the cartridges, they were promptly arrested, manacled and jailed for ten years; but this was akin to throwing a match to petrol. Their comrades' blood was up, and they resolved to free them. Without warning, late in the afternoon of the following day, sepoys rampaged through the town, killing people indiscriminately, burning and looting as they went. There was no stopping them, and the European forces were too weak to do so anyway. Then the mutineers fled to nearby Delhi, where lived in semi-retirement and on British sufferance the titular Mughal ruler, and sovereign of Indian Muslims, Bahadur Shah Zafar, around whose reluctant person they now rallied. He himself was powerless, and had no interest in rebellion, but he was in no position to repudiate his adoption as figurehead either. Later he would pay for his inadvertent role by being sent into exile to Rangoon, where he ended his days in a kind of bleak twilight. At the end of the mutiny, his three sons had been taken aside by a British officer, William Hodson, who summarily and personally shot them dead, and had their bodies thrown on a dungheap.

With or without him, the mutiny (called by many Indians today the 'First War of Independence') gathered speed, and spread among other places to Agra, Allahabad, Benares and Cawnpore (now Kanpur). By the time the rebels reached the garrison at Cawnpore, they had lost any awe of the British they once had. The British colony there was under the notional protection of Nana Sahib. Nana Sahib to the British was merely a local maharajah, but to the Hindu population he was the last of the great Mahratta dynasty, and to them what Bahadur was to the Muslims.

At the beginning of June 1857, sepoys under General Sir Hugh Wheeler had rebelled and besieged the Europeans in a vulnerable entrenchment offering little shade or other protection. The siege lasted eighteen days, during which time the British survived on what they had managed to bring with them – tinned herring, split peas and flour, and occasionally horsemeat from one of their dead animals – while suffering a constant bombardment in temperatures of more than 40ºC. They had little water, though, bizarrely, more than enough alcohol, including champagne.

On 25 June, Nana Sahib, apparently acting as a sympathetic intermediary, suggested surrender, with the promise of a safe passage out, expressly only for those 'who are in no way connected with the acts of Lord Dalhousie'. Wheeler accepted what seemed an honourable solution – he was responsible not only for his men but for the numerous women and children of the colony too, and besides, he really had no choice. His charges were dying like flies of heatstroke and disease, and some had gone mad. But when the British boarded the riverboats Nana Sahib had provided, no sooner were they in midstream than their Indian pilots dived overboard, and mutineers lying in ambush opened fire. Only four soldiers escaped, the rudder of their boat shot away, and finally, naked and starving, reached safety.

The surviving women and children – perhaps 100 of them – were taken to the *Bibighar* (the house of noblewomen), built for his mistress by an English officer long before. Just over a fortnight after the massacre on the river, a group of Indian men entered the building and killed every one of them. Their bodies were cut up and thrown down a deep well, almost filling its 15-metre shaft.

Cawnpore was something of a turning point for the mutiny. The British by now had had time to regroup and summon loyal forces from elsewhere, and the tide was turning against the mutineers. Furthermore, when news of the atrocity came out, duly embroidered with lurid embellishments involving appalling rape, torture and sexual, mental and physical humiliation, the British desire for vengeance knew no bounds. Nana Sahib, whose precise role in the business will probably never be known for certain, disappeared. It is significant that Cawnpore is situated in Oudh, a state which had been annexed by Dalhousie the previous year. There can be little doubt that Dalhousie's strong line, or intemperate action, depending on your point of view, and the ensuing Mutiny, were inextricably linked: some of the blood is on his hands.

The ruins of the British Residency at Lucknow after the relief of the siege there. The ruins were preserved as a monument to those who perished.

When General Sir Henry Havelock recaptured Cawnpore, the British took a terrible revenge. The sepoy prisoners were taken to the *Bibighar* and made to lick the bloodstains from the walls and floor. They were then executed by being tied across the mouths of cannon, and blown to pieces, this being a Mughal punishment for traitors. With the raising of the siege of Lucknow, 75 kilometres north-east across the Ganges, the end of the mutiny was signalled. The veteran British Resident of the town, Henry Lawrence, had foreseen the sepoy uprising there and managed to fortify, arm and provision the Residency there in advance of it. Taking his small force of 300 men, together with a few hundred loyal sepoys and all the European civilians of the town, he retired within it on 2 July 1857. Two days later he was dead, from a shell-wound, and his epitaph reads: 'Here Lies Henry Lawrence, Who Tried To Do His Duty'.

His foresight saved his compatriots and those loyal to him from almost certain death, for the siege dragged on for three months and even then the relief force found itself besieged in turn with the original defenders. It was not until November that Sir Colin Campbell was able to get the beleaguered garrison

After the Indian Mutiny, the Crown took over control of India from the East India Company. In this 1858 illustration from *Punch*, Queen Victoria graciously accepts the penitent submission of India, personified by the Rani of Jhansi, one of the leading rebels, who was killed fighting the British, aged 23. She remains a heroine in India.

and its civilian population out, and even then he was unable to take Lucknow definitively until the following March.

The Mutiny was extinguished by the summer of 1858. Later the same year, in a proclamation of 1 November, the East India Company was formally wound up and control of the colony and the Indian government was formally transferred to the Crown. In the same proclamation, mindful of Dalhousie's excesses, Queen Victoria renounced 'all further extension of our present territorial possessions', and undertook to 'respect the rights, dignity and honour of the native princes as our own'. The promise of amnesty contained in this message was carried out so diligently by Dalhousie's successor, the first Viceroy of India, Lord Canning, that he earned the nickname 'Clemency' Canning, which at first was derisive, but came to be honorific.

A period of active and benign development began. In 1860 a Penal Code drawn up by Lord Macaulay in 1837 was introduced, and in 1861 the Indian Councils Act awarded seats to Indians on the Governor General's executive council; this was the first step in the closer association of Indians with the government of their own country. In the meantime roads, railways and irrigation systems were greatly expanded. Canning was succeeded by Lord Elgin in 1862, and in 1864, following his demise, Sir John Lawrence, brother of Henry Lawrence of Lucknow, took office for five years. More social reform followed, despite setbacks in the form of a disastrous famine in Orissa in 1866 and the murder of Lord Mayo (Viceroy, 1869–72) by a demented Pathan convict in protest at what he regarded as an unjust sentence for another – vendetta related – killing. India was further wooed by the visit of the Prince of Wales (later Edward VII) in 1875, and its special Empire status was consolidated by the creation of Queen Victoria as Empress of India, an imperial title held by her successors until it was relinquished at independence in 1947.

The middle years of the nineteenth century saw Britain growing ever more confident as its dominance as a world power peaked. It expressed its prowess in such displays as the Great Exhibition of 1851, which took place in Joseph Paxton's astounding Crystal Palace, and made enough money for Prince Albert to build the museums which now abut Exhibition Road in South Kensington.

At Queen Victoria's Diamond Jubilee celebrations the crowds gathered to cheer the sepoy cavalry who rode in the processions. The Queen herself took a matriarchal interest in the greatest possession of her Empire, and though she never visited it, she surrounded herself with Indian artefacts. After the demise of

John Brown, her favourite body servant was Abdul Karim, better known as the *Munshi* (the Teacher), one of the earliest immigrants from India, though he exploited his position shamelessly and at Victoria's death found himself sent packing by her son. But immigration from the colonies was already under way. 1889 saw the appearance of Britain's first mosque, near Woking. In 1857 the Strangers' Home for Asiatics, Africans, South Sea Islanders and Others was founded on West India Dock Road, London. Lascars had been in evidence in the East End, the Liverpool docklands and other British ports for many years already. In 1830, Rammohan Roy had arrived as ambassador of the Mughal emperor Akbar Shah II, taken up residence in Bedford Square, and campaigned hard against the practice of *sati*. Duleep Singh, a Punjabi prince dispossessed by Dalhousie, arrived in the wake of one of his family's great treasures, the Koh-i-noor diamond, which he had surrendered to Victoria and which became *the* jewel in *her* crown. The African-American actor Ira Aldridge, born in 1807, took to the London stage in the 1820s, 'whited-up' to play Lear, Macbeth and Shylock, but also gave his Oroonoko in a stage version of Aphra Behn's eponymous, ever-popular novel. Mary Seacole came from Jamaica in the face of great resistance to nurse the wounded of the Crimean War. When it was over, the Brigade of Guards gave a concert and a dinner in her honour.

⊠
THE MIDDLE YEARS OF THE NINETEENTH CENTURY SAW BRITAIN GROWING EVER MORE CONFIDENT AS ITS DOMINANCE AS A WORLD POWER PEAKED.

The magical town of Simla, one of the greatest towns in the world, photographed by Alice Schalek in the mid-1950s.

Queen Victoria's successor and son, Edward VII, who came to the throne in late middle age in 1901, cared little for the Empire, preferring infinitely the delights of Paris and Deauville; and it has to be said that, for all the pomp and circumstance, few of his subjects did either, especially once Victoria's reign was over. The Edwardian era was in any case an autumnal one, and some could already see wintry clouds on the horizon. Rudyard Kipling wrote his poem 'Recessional' for Queen Victoria's Jubilee in 1897, but the text carries the intimation that his countrymen should not get too haughty, and remember the fate of all empires. This is a striking sentiment from the man who was and remains *the* poet, if not *the* artist, of Empire, and, at his worst, one of the worst! This poem, however, moved T. S. Eliot to remark that Kipling was the greatest of all writers of hymns.

God of our fathers, known of old,
Lord of our far-flung battle line,
Beneath whose awful hand we hold
Dominion over palm and pine,
Lord God of Hosts, be with us yet,
Lest we forget – lest we forget!

If, drunk with sight of power, we loose
Wild tongues that have not Thee in awe,
Such boasting as the Gentiles use,
Or lesser breeds without the law;
Lord God of Hosts, be with us yet,
Lest we forget – lest we forget!

The tumult and the shouting dies;
The captains and the kings depart:
Still stands Thine ancient sacrifice,
An humble and a contrite heart.
Lord God of Hosts, be with us yet,
Lest we forget – lest we forget!

For heathen heart that puts her trust
In reeking tube and iron shard,
All valiant dust that builds on dust,
And guarding, calls not Thee to guard;
For frantic boast and foolish word,
Thy mercy on Thy people, Lord!

Far-called, our navies melt away;
On dune and headland sinks the fire:
Lo, all our pomp of yesterday
Is one with Nineveh and Tyre!
Judge of the Nations, spare us yet,
Lest we forget – lest we forget!

If King Edward was not keen on his empire, there were still men who were. His Viceroy in India from 1899 to 1905 was George Curzon, an aristocrat of ancient lineage and overweening ambition. The viceregency was to him the fulfilment of one of his boyhood ambitions (the other was to become prime minister), and he loved the job. He was the last truly baroque figure in the Empire's history, and he did all he could to keep India firmly in the nineteenth century. The apogee of his career was organizing the Durbar for King Edward held in Delhi in 1903, a hugely theatrical event without the King-Emperor (Edward did not attend) but with his representative resplendent (one cannot imagine Curzon really wanting to be upstaged by his master); and with a parade of panoplied elephants bearing rajahs and maharajahs in all their bejewelled and turbaned magnificence. A last moment of hubris, perhaps, for Kipling was right: the Empire was already dying.

In the meantime, however, and particularly in the closing decades of the nineteenth century and the first few years of the twentieth, colonial life among the British in India continued insouciantly. There had been unfortunate moments, such as when the reforming and liberal viceroy, Lord Ripon, in the early 1880s had tried to reform India's legal system and permit Indian judges to try not only natives but Europeans, but he was faced down and his legislation was watered down. (The colonists crowed at this victory, but it was no accident that the Indian National Congress was formed soon after, in 1885, with the help of Ripon's successor, Lord Dufferin, and a Scottish civil servant, A. O. Hume.)

Ripon had made the strategic mistake of leaving Calcutta for the Empire's hill station, Simla, during the hot summer months, allowing his enemies a clear field to plot against him.

From Simla and Calcutta the Viceroy held sway over imperial territories stretching from Egypt to Hong Kong. But Simla (now Shimla), high in the foothills of the Himalayas, and the summer retreat for all who could afford the time or had the privilege, was also a playground. There were, of course, all the usual sports and games that delight the British, as well as pig-sticking and polo (more democratically available there than here). There were other diversions, too. As Maud Diver warned in *The Englishwoman in India*, two of the worst temptations that could befall a grass widow in the hills (whose husband, civil servant or businessman, was condemned to labour through the summer down on the plains) were presented by officers on leave and amateur theatricals. In other words, small town English society was authentically reproduced. In Simla, the Gaiety Theatre is still there, as is Christ Church. It is ages since I last

'My name is George Nathaniel Curzon,/I am a most superior person...' Curzon was Viceroy at the beginning of the twentieth century. Despite his political ambitions, it was the most important post he was ever to occupy.

visited, but I remember its mock-Tudor and Victorian Gothic, its churchyard and its immaculate lawns, being as reassuringly English as any leafy London suburb, except that it was all perched in the cloudy, tree-covered hills of Himachal Pradesh. Apart from the heart-stoppingly beautiful surroundings, the lumbering sacred cows daubed in ochre and yellow, and the bold, thieving monkeys, you could almost think yourself in Richmond or Pinner.

British architecture has left its stamp, now perhaps fading a little, on India. You will find it from Colombo to Rangoon. It served both as a reminder of home to the nostalgically minded, and as a political statement of power and possession. Calcutta, the first city to receive the stamp of English taste, reflects the cool elegance of the neoclassical style which was fashionable in the eighteenth and early nineteenth centuries. Bombay's large public buildings are in the later, ornate, Victorian-Gothic manner. Hill stations from Simla to Assam to Nuwara Eliyah reflect the Victorian ideal of the English country town, and even today you stay in guesthouses with names like St Agatha's and Mon Repos.

Last but not least came New Delhi, whose principal architects were Edwin Lutyens and, to a lesser extent, Herbert Baker. George V laid the foundation stone of New Delhi in 1911, during his visit on the occasion of the grand Durbar held for him to mark his coronation a few months earlier in London. The vast programme of large public buildings was completed in 1929, and the city was inaugurated two years after that. It was the last grand gesture. Sixteen years and another world war later saw the British quit India for good.

In India, Britain had a long time to develop its control, and apart from struggles with a handful of other foreign powers early on in that process, and the later border tensions with Russia, there was little or no competition.

But Africa presented a different set of problems. The northern countries and territories had long enjoyed a relationship with Europe, but by the 1870s, when colonization in sub-Saharan Africa first began, Britain was not the only power interested in seizing territory. There had been coastal outposts for centuries, along parts of the west coast on account of the slave trade, and in the extreme south because of the shipping lane round the Cape of Good Hope to India (the Suez Canal was not opened until 1869). Missionaries had been at work there since the beginning of the nineteenth century at least, and in the 1790s the young Scottish explorer Mungo Park traced part of the course of the River Niger. In 1792 Sierra Leone – initially known as the Land of Freedom – was established as an autonomous kingdom for a number of the liberated black slaves who had fought for Britain in the American War of Independence. Not all the 600 who signed up wanted to go, the whole project was fraught with disagreement and difficulty, and in the event only about 250 left England, in the company of about sixty poor white women from the East End of London – some of them married to members of the semi-reluctant expedition – who took their small children with them. The final complement was just over 400 people. The voyage was a disaster, many died en route, and Sierra Leone was not the land of promise that had been anticipated by the well-meaning and philanthropic English organizers. The emigrants were ill-equipped, the weather was foul, farming was next to impossible. Finally, in 1808, the British took over, making the country a Crown Colony, which it remained for about the next 150 years.

In the 1850s the explorers Richard Burton and John Hanning Speke opened up large areas of East Africa, in what is now roughly Kenya and Tanzania, and discovered Lake Victoria (named by Speke, who convinced himself (erroneously) that in it he had found the source of the Nile).

The most familiar adventurer was the missionary-turned-explorer David Livingstone, who traced the route of the Zambesi River in the (vain) hope of establishing that it would turn out to be a navigable waterway from the coast to the interior. But the British were not alone. Among other nations, Belgium, France, Germany, Italy and Portugal had explorers in the field, and a conflict of interests was inevitable. Competition between the European powers was sharpened by an economic depression which dominated the last two decades

The famous missionary-turned-explorer, David Livingstone, 1813–1873.

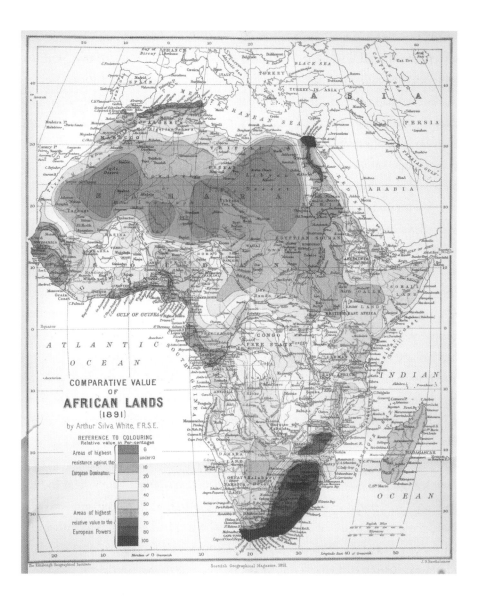

A political-economic map of Africa, 1891, showing the areas of greatest resistance to European interlopers, and those areas of highest relative value to the colonisers.

of the nineteenth century, coupled with a need for raw materials demanded by growing technological advances. The interior of Africa, which no one had taken much interest in hitherto, turned out to be a valuable source of rubber, copper and tin.

It did not take long for these European powers to carve up the continent between them. This led to the imposition by Europe of more-or-less arbitrary frontiers which ignored traditional tribal and ethnic divisions, the impact of which is still apparent today – as the recent tragic wars, for example in Rwanda-Burundi, indicate. To set some measure on this, the German Chancellor, Otto von Bismarck, convened a conference in Berlin in the winter of 1884–5, essentially to determine who controlled what, and which rivers and waterways should be deemed common to all for the purposes of transport. In the end, the whole of Africa, apart from Abyssinia (Ethiopia), Liberia (set up under the auspices and with the support of the United States for 'free men of colour' in 1822 and later badly crowded by Britain and France, without, however, losing its independence), the Transvaal and the Orange Free State, was divided up between Britain, the five powers mentioned above, and Spain, which was no longer a major player but which clung to settlements on the north-west and north coasts.

In the main, the arrangement worked for the colonizers. There was plenty to go round, wars were expensive, and although there were confrontations and tensions, Africa, as far as the occupying powers were concerned, in the main remained peaceful for the rest of the nineteenth century. Occupied territories not only in Africa but elsewhere in the world were traded between them like counters in a game. For example, Britain effectively swapped Zanzibar for Heligoland with Germany in 1890 (rather foolishly, as it turned out). Little attempt was made to understand the wishes or needs of local peoples, Africans being lumped together as being all alike, and the fact that the continent housed a vast and complicated agglomeration of peoples with their own racial differences, languages, cultures, traditions, enmities and rivalries was largely ignored. The Ashanti possessed a Golden Stool, the most revered object in their religion, deemed to have been delivered to them from heaven. Its destruction would mean the destruction of the nation. To desecrate it would wound the Ashanti to their very soul. The Ashanti had no desire to convert to Christianity, and in 1900 the Governor of the Gold Coast, Sir Frederick Hodgson (admittedly held even by his peers to be an oaf and a nincompoop) decided to teach them a lesson. He made his way with an armed guard to the Ashanti capital of Kumasi, and demanded that the Asantahene bring out the Golden Stool, 'and give it to me to sit upon'. The Ashanti saw him off – he was lucky to escape with his life – but true to form the British, who could not take this kind of behaviour lying down, retaliated in force. They could not find the Golden Stool, but they arrested the Asantahene and exiled him to the Seychelles for twenty-four years.

Local peoples who objected to the presence of the whites were easily subdued by overwhelmingly superior military technology, which was supported by new firearms of spectacularly destructive force – the Gatling gun, and then the infinitely more efficient Maxim gun, a belt-fed machine gun ultimately

THE CONTINENT HOUSED A VAST AND COMPLICATED AGGLOMERATION OF PEOPLES WITH THEIR OWN RACIAL DIFFERENCES, LANGUAGES, CULTURES, TRADITIONS, ENMITIES AND RIVALRIES.

produced in several versions and calibres and adopted by the British Army in 1888 only five years after its invention by the American Hiram Maxim. It was capable of firing 500 rounds per minute and the British, who retained superiority over their European rivals in Africa despite the competition, used it against native enemies with devastating effect. As Hilaire Belloc wrote drily in 1898, after the Battle of Omdurman:

Whatever happens, we have got
The Maxim Gun, and they have not.

The gun was first used effectively in Africa against the Matabele in 1893–4, establishing that the general African war strategy of mass charges by warriors wielding spears would no longer win the locals any battles. Local chiefs did resist bravely, however, and managed, if never actually to beat back the British, at least to dent them.

In the early 1860s, Emperor Tewodros II of Ethiopia (an ancient Christian land) sent a letter to Queen Victoria, a fellow-Christian monarch whom he regarded as being on equal terms with him, requesting aid in his struggle against Muslim incursion from the north. He received no immediate reply, and in retaliation imprisoned all the British residents he could find, along with a few Swiss, to teach the British manners. It should be added that Tewodros was not possessed of the most stable of natures, and the untimely death of his beloved wife had done nothing to improve a depressive personality. He was neither a fool, however, nor a savage, and Britain's King George III was certainly madder than he ever was. He was also leader of his own sovereign state.

After a delay of two years, a chilly letter of reply from Victoria was finally brought to him, but none of the requested aid came with it. Tewodros responded by imprisoning the British Mission which had delivered the reply. The result of this was a massive punitive invasion, using among others a huge number of sepoy troops brought in from India, under General Sir Robert Napier. Tewodros withdrew with his prisoners to his mountain fastness at Magdala, and the two sides met there, Napier's column having made an epic journey from the coast. Battle was joined on 10 April 1868 – which was, as it happened, Good Friday. The result was a foregone conclusion. Accepting defeat, the Emperor released his captives, but when Napier attempted to come to terms, Tewodros refused to become a prisoner, and barricaded himself with

⊠
IN AFRICA, AS IN INDIA, THE BRITISH CONSTRUCTED A HUGE RAILWAY NETWORK.

A market in Addis Ababa. This photograph was taken three decades after Emperor Tewodros II's death.

a few loyal troops inside his fortress. The British shelled it to pieces, and on 13 April – Easter Monday – the Emperor committed suicide rather than fall into their hands. Napier returned home to a hero's welcome and a peerage. Among his army somebody brought home a local cat or two. The breed – Abyssinians – became very popular.

The Indians in Napier's task force were not the first to arrive in Africa. Many had already settled there as workers in the service of the British. The British had managed to gain control of the best parts of Africa, held in an almost unbroken line (but not quite, Bismarck had been careful to see to that) from Cape Town to Cairo. It had been the dream of one of the greatest and most ruthless titans of imperial Africa, the entrepreneur-turned-politician Cecil Rhodes, to build a railway connecting the two towns. In this he failed, but, as in India, the British did construct a huge railway network. To do this, as in India, an Indian workforce was employed, particularly in East Africa. The British found it far easier to work with the Indians than the Africans, whom they regarded as intractable, untrustworthy and no better than savages, so they imported them in their thousands. Originally employed as indentured labourers, they remained after the work was done to develop their own small (and later, very large) businesses, and to serve in the humbler ranks of the administration. By 1920, when Britain took formal control of the country, there were 20,000 of them in Kenya alone, occupying the middle ground between the seigneurial whites (10,000) and the local population (3 million). These people's descendants were the Kenyan and Ugandan Asians we reluctantly took in after they had been hounded in their own countries in the late 1960s and early 1970s by native Africans jealous of the power and wealth they had acquired.

The British were often less harsh and more scrupulous in their treatment of local peoples in Africa than their European counterparts, but the scramble for Africa was a far speedier occupation than that of India, it utilized infinitely more sophisticated technology, transport was quicker and – thanks to the telegraph – communication faster. There was not time to take local people's sensibilities into account, as we have seen in the case of Tewodros. But the British also knew how to recognize courage and heroism in their opponents.

The Battle of Rorke's Drift is one of the most famous in the history of the British Empire. So nearly a disaster, and immortalized in the 1964 film *Zulu*, it involved the engagement of a beleaguered unit of British troops and the Zulu army of Cetewayo in January 1879. The invasion of Zululand had started ear-

THE RHODES COLOSSUS

STRIDING FROM CAPE TOWN TO CAIRO.

lier that same month, but towards the end of the month, a section of the British Army was attacked and routed by an overwhelming Zulu force at Isandhlwana. At the same time, the farmstead of Rorke's Drift was successfully defended by 150 men of the 2nd Battalion, 24th Warwickshire Regiment of Foot and their very efficient Martini-Henry rifles. They held their position for a terrifying day and night against 4,000 of Cetewayo's Zulus, who early in the morning of the second day, leaving a sea of dead behind them, withdrew. The incident passed into Victorian myth, a record eleven Victoria Crosses were awarded, and Cetewayo, defeated later at his capital by the irresistible power of the Gatling gun, but managing to escape, eventually visited London, in 1882, where he was feted, so greatly did the British admire the soldierly qualities of the Zulus. There was even a bit of music-hall doggerel written about him:

> *White young dandies, get away-o –*
> *You are now 'neath Beauty's ban;*
> *Clear the field for Cetewayo:*
> *He alone's the ladies' man.*

The colonization of Africa created other mythological moments, which Victorian propagandists were quick to seize on. There is no reliable eyewitness account of the death of General Charles George Gordon at Khartoum, but even today many of us can easily call to mind George William Joy's picture – painted in 1885, the year of Gordon's death – of the general standing at the top of some steps in his residence, defying the bloodthirsty hordes below, who aim spears at him. Others will remember a biopic made ninety years later and starring Charlton Heston, which perpetuated the myth, but the actor remarked, 'the middle of the twentieth century is not much of a time for heroes'.

Briefly, the situation was this. Since the opening of the Suez Canal, the British had shown a keener interest to involve themselves in Egyptian affairs – hitherto the domain of the French. Far to the south, a political opportunist called Mahomed Ahmed had proclaimed himself Mahdi (in Islam, this is the 'Guided One' – the redeemer who, alongside Jesus Christ, will one day come to change the world into a perfect Islamic society). His teaching carried nothing new: it recommended the virtues of prayer, leading a simple life, and a strict and unquestioning adherence to the tenets of the Prophet. But around that he built a popular resistance to Ottoman rule, and his brand of nationalism potentially threatened Egypt's stability. He declared a jihad against the Ottomans, and his army grew, and had many successes.

The Ottoman ruler of Egypt had appointed as Governor of the Sudan Charles George Gordon. Gordon's attitude to the Mahdi was an aggressive one, but the British administration had no interest in the Sudan and decided it was not worth fighting for. Westminster ordered Gordon down to Khartoum to evacuate civilians and withdraw the garrison. When he reached the city, all was well. The locals were still loyal, lines of communication downstream were open, but the Mahdists were not far away and soon he found himself all but cut off. He sent messengers north to request backup, but gained no support. He managed to get a number of foreigners out safely, however, and then set about building up the city's defences. At home, public support for him (the telegraph had revolutionized journalism) persuaded the government to send a relief column, but it encountered strong resistance and, receiving conflicting messages about the city's ability to hold out, it believed the more optimistic one and paused to refit.

Gordon, a career soldier from a soldiering family of inflexible Christian views, already had an established reputation for his service in the Crimea and China, not least for making some effort to understand the customs and languages of the people he came into contact with. In China he took part in an expedition in 1860, at the end of the Second Opium War, and later assisted the Chinese government in the suppression of the military Taiping rebellion against the Qing regime of 1863–4, where his great success gave rise to his nickname 'Chinese' Gordon. The emperor awarded him the rank of *titu*, the highest in the Chinese army. But now, finding himself let down by his superiors, years of strain turned an always stubborn man into a half-mad maverick who disobeyed orders in remaining at Khartoum at all. Gordon had lapsed into heavy drinking and conversations with a pet mouse as he finally lay

General Charles 'Chinese' Gordon, aged 51 in 1884, the year before his death, when this photograph was taken. The eyes already show signs of the madness which was to overtake him.

General Horatio Kitchener in his Egyptian Army uniform, photographed by Heyman in 1890, at the age of forty. A brutal warlord, his hobby was crocheting.

besieged at his residence by the Mahdi. The ending was not a happy one for Gordon: the city fell to the Mahdi and he was caught and executed – contrary to the Mahdi's orders – in January 1885. The British steamers arrived forty-eight hours later, retaking the city and beating back the Mahdists.

Gordon's character and work were fitly commemorated in the Gordon School for orphaned boys of the Empire, founded at Dover in 1885 by a Mr Blackman as a memorial to the young general. Winston Churchill wrote of him later: 'Of course there is no doubt that Gordon as a political figure was absolutely hopeless. He was so erratic, capricious, utterly unreliable, his mood changed so often, his temper was abominable, he was frequently drunk, and yet with all that he had a tremendous sense of honour and great abilities.'

The Mahdi held the Sudan, except for a couple of outposts defended by British Indian troops. He introduced sharia law and looked set to establish a fundamentalist state, but he died, possibly of typhus, a few months later. His state survived, however, withstanding an attempted invasion from Ethiopia. But his successors were to learn that the British had a long memory.

The expedition to the Sudan, which took place thirteen years after the fall of Khartoum, was not undertaken in a simple spirit of revenge. By now, France and Britain were joint shareholders in the Suez Canal, and while France still had the majority holding, the canal was protected by British arms. This was a reasonably amicable arrangement. The Nile was a different matter. While the British controlled its lower reaches, the French had tried to assert control over the upper reaches: but their plan had been ill construed and they had not the power to back their claim.

Kitchener and his men, wearing their Egyptian uniforms to avoid any diplomatic unpleasantness, were courteous to the wretched French major Jean-Baptiste Marchand who commanded a French force of 150 infantry who had set out from Brazzaville with orders to make the area around Fashoda a French protectorate. After an exhausting fourteen-month trek across central Africa, they arrived at the woebegone place on 10 July 1898. On 18 September, a powerful flotilla of British gunboats arrived at the isolated fort, led by Lord Kitchener. As the commander of the Anglo-Egyptian army that had just defeated the forces of the Mahdi at the Battle of Omdurman, Kitchener was reconquering the Sudan in the name of the Egyptian Khedive. Both sides were stiffly polite and each insisted on its right to Fashoda.

News of the meeting was relayed to Paris and London, where it stirred the imperial pride of both nations. Each side accused the other of aggressive expansionism. The crisis continued throughout September and October, and both nations rattled their sabres vigorously.

In naval terms, the situation was always in Britain's favour, a fact that the French had to acknowledge. The French army was far larger than the British army, but there was little it could do against Britain without effective naval support.

The French also reflected that they needed Britain onside in view of a feared future conflict with Germany, so they finally sought a peaceful resolution of the crisis. At the same time, people increasingly began to question the wisdom of war for the sake of such a remote part of Africa. In France, a political scandal, the Dreyfus Affair, distracted public opinion from events in the Sudan. The French government quietly ordered its soldiers to withdraw on 3 November, and the futile matter was closed. Kitchener went on to secure the Sudan for the Khedive of Egypt, and, effectively, for Britain, which also now enjoyed de facto control of the Suez Canal. After the Fashoda Incident there was no further question of France being a serious colonial rival in sub-Saharan Africa.

The Convention of Constantinople in 1888 had declared the canal a neutral zone under the protection of the British, their claim being that they had moved in to protect it during a civil war in Egypt in 1882. Nearly half a century later, under the Anglo-Egyptian Treaty of 1936, Britain still retained control of the canal. Only as late as 1951 did Egypt overturn the treaty and attempt to overturn British hegemony too. The Suez Crisis of 1956, as we will see later, was the last disastrous throw of the dice for Britain in her attempt to exert imperial authority in the old-fashioned manner.

There was, however, one European nation Britain would lock horns with. By the end of the nineteenth century, the Dutch had been in South Africa for over 200 years, occupying territory inland from the British-controlled coastal areas. These Afrikaners, or Boers (from the Dutch *boer*, farmer), established two provinces, the Orange Free State and the Transvaal, where they kept to themselves, farmed, observed very low-church rites, and turned their back on the outside world. They were a dour, tough folk, conservative and narrow-minded; but they knew how to protect what was theirs, they were familiar with European ways of thinking, and they had breech-loading rifles to defend themselves with.

The Orange Free State enjoyed a relatively cordial relationship with its British neighbours in the Cape Colony. The people of the Transvaal, who had pushed further north, across the Vaal River, to escape British influence, were

THE BOER WERE FAMILIAR WITH EUROPEAN WAYS OF THINKING, AND THEY HAD BREECH-LOADING RIFLES TO DEFEND THEMSELVES WITH.

The chaps of the Jameson Raid on board ship on their way to England and gaol following their disastrous venture. Their raid on Paul Kruger's Transvaal Republic was intended to trigger an uprising by the primarily British expatriate workers in the region, but failed to do so. No uprising took place, but it did much to bring about the Boer War. James Leander Starr Jameson is second from the left, in forage cap and bow-tie.

far less tractable. But their independence irritated the expansionist ambitions of Englishmen. In 1877 an experienced diplomat, and old Africa hand, Theophilus Shenstone, was sent to Pretoria, the tiny, modest capital of the Transvaal, in order to annex it. At the time the country was in a poor state economically, the President ailing and weak, and the people divided over Shenstone's proposition. Shenstone, backed by the British Army, carried the day and took the Transvaal under Victoria's wing. But when Britain and the Transvaal both got new leaders in 1880, and Britain showed every sign of tightening her grip, the Boers rebelled.

The First Boer War was a short one – it only lasted from December 1880 to March 1881. The Transvaalers, knowing they were badly outmatched, made the first move, mobilizing to corral and pin down the British in the seven garrisons they had, scattered through the country.

Over the years, the British Army had become accustomed to winning easy victories over opponents who had primitive weapons and whose methods of warfare lacked any subtlety. The Boers were different. They had no uniform as such, but fought in the drab colours of their everyday clothes, browns and greys which camouflaged them. The British still fought in red coats, which made them easy targets, and the Boers were expert marksmen. A notable ambush at Bronkhorst Spruit smashed a column of the elite Connaught Rangers only four days after the war had started, and, among other victories (the British had none), the Boers conclusively crushed the British at Majuba Hill at the end of the following February. There was no point in carrying on. Westminster opened peace negotiations soon afterwards, and acceded to the Transvaal's demand for independence, saving face by putting in a clause about 'the suzerainty of Her Majesty'.

Four years later, however, gold was discovered in the Transvaal. This led to another invasion, this time of prospectors from Britain and other nations besides. The newcomers rapidly outnumbered the Boers, who, glad of the money but resentful of their presence, refused them voting rights but taxed them heavily. The British resented this, and wanted to control the goldfields themselves. In the course of time, a powerful lobby formed, led by the self-made diamond millionaire, Cecil Rhodes, the Colonial Secretary, Joseph Chamberlain, and (later) the new Governor of Cape Colony, Alfred Milner. The Transvaalers allied themselves with the Orange Free State. In 1895, Rhodes funded an abortive military raid to seize power in Pretoria. It failed, but hackles were raised on both sides, and war broke out again in 1899.

In this second Boer War, the Afrikaners again took the initiative, invading British territory and besieging the towns of Mafeking, Ladysmith and Kimberley. Using guerrilla techniques and extremely mobile troops, the Boers enjoyed early success, but the British this time struck back effectively, relieving the sieges and advancing northwards, taking first Bloemfontein and then Pretoria. But the Boers refused to give up, and this led the British to resort to dirty tactics. Under Kitchener, Boer farmsteads were destroyed and their crops burnt. Their old folk, women and children were rounded up and placed in concentration camps, along with their black farm workers (who were put in segregated camps). About 30,000 Boers, mainly children, died in the camps, of disease and malnutrition; 14,000 of the 116,000 black internees also died – 80 per cent of them children. Kitchener was accused of genocide, but he did not flinch. The human rights activist Emily Hobhouse, whose visit to South Africa in 1901 sparked a series of debates at home, reported from a camp near

A formal photographic study of Cecil Rhodes in his forty-seventh year, at the height of his powers, and two years before his death.

The most shameful face of Empire (1). White children bathing, South Africa, 1956.

Bloemfontein, capital of the Orange Free State, that 'the atmosphere [there] was indescribable... the rations... became a starvation rate'. She witnessed Boer women and children herded into cattle wagons on a railway siding and the sight moved her to observe that she had now seen war 'in all its destructiveness, cruelty, stupidity and nakedness'.

Emily Hobhouse's report caused such outrage in London that measures were taken to improve the condition of the 'internees'. The war was brought to an end in May 1902, and the Boers were given £3 million in compensation and the promise of eventual self-rule again. However, eight years later the Union of South Africa brought both the Afrikaner states firmly under the sway of the British Empire. Thirty-eight years later still the policy of 'apartheid' – the Afrikaans/Dutch word for 'apartness' or 'separation' – was adopted as official policy by a National–Afrikaner Party coalition. It was responsible for some of the worst civil state-supported outrages of modern times.

Sharpeville, a black township about 65 kilometres south of Johannesburg, gained notoriety as a symbol of the infamy of the apartheid regime when, in March 1960, the police opened fire directly on an unarmed crowd of anti-apartheid demonstrators and killed sixty-nine of them, including women and children. The demonstration was held as a protest launched by the Pan-

African Congress against the pass laws, which required every non-white citizen to carry a passbook (ID papers not unlike those issued to the Jews by the Nazis). Ironically, the Israeli secret service, MOSSAD, worked as tutors to the white South African secret police, BOSS.

Soweto (an acronym for SOuth WEst TOwnship) was a segregated urbanization, south-west of Johannesburg which saw several outbreaks of anti-government unrest during the apartheid period. Soweto began life as a black shanty town in the 1930s and today it is the largest black city in South Africa. Its notoriety in popular political history dates from 1976, when, as a pendant to the disgraceful behaviour of the South African government and police at Sharpeville in 1960, it suffered an even more appalling massacre at the hands of the 'authorities'. In June 1976, a demonstration was held in protest against a new ruling that Afrikaans exclusively should be the language officially used in black schools. Police intervention led to the deaths of 176 innocent people, and injury to 1,000 others. International disgust at the incident led to grudging reforms, but unrest continued, notably in 1985, until justice was finally brought to the South African administration in 1994.

Such events led to South Africa's temporary expulsion from the Commonwealth – not abolished until the early 1990s, with the release of Nelson Mandela, who had served twenty-seven years in jail in the cause of his people's freedom.

Emily Hobhouse, whom Kitchener called 'that bloody woman', was not an isolated example of female integrity in the Empire. Among many brave missionaries, doctors and nurses who worked in the colonies and concentrated on nurture rather than subjugation, there were several outstanding women. Lest it should be thought that the Empire was exclusively a man's preserve, it is worth mentioning a few examples here.

Lady Anne Blunt was a granddaughter of Lord Byron. She spoke fluent Arabic, French, German, Italian and Spanish; she played the violin to a professional standard and she had studied art with Ruskin. Married not very happily to the poet and diplomat Wilfred Scawen Blunt, her *Journals and Correspondence 1878–1917* describe her life in North Africa and Egypt, and she wrote books about her travels in Arabia and the Near East. She became a famous breeder of Arab horses, popularizing them throughout the world. Always a maverick, she left England for the last time in October 1915 and spent the last years of her life at Sheikh Obeid, where she died aged eighty. Overshadowing her in importance is the tough and overbearing Annie Besant,

SOWETO, 1976: POLICE INTERVENTION LED TO THE DEATHS OF 176 INNOCENT PEOPLE, AND INJURY TO 1,000 OTHERS.

well known as a theosophist and as the champion of Krishnamurti, but whose real contribution to Empire (or rather, against it) lay in her support for Gandhi and Gangadhar Tilak. She arrived in India in 1893, already in early middle age, with the intention of learning more than she could at home about Hinduism. Twenty years later, when she was sixty-six, she produced her *Wake Up, India*, and proceeded to tour the country, lecturing on behalf of her All-India Home Rule League. Five years later she became President of the Indian National Congress. Amy Johnson pioneered air routes between countries, while the journalist Daisy Bates was an early champion of the rights of the aboriginal peoples of Australia. Mary Kingsley was a prodigious traveller and explorer, who did not start her career until she was thirty, and died in 1900 just short of her thirty-eighth birthday, yet studied the Fang cannibals of Angola, collected fauna and flora, navigated the Congo and the Ogowe rivers; and all this off her own bat, with no sponsors, but trading in palm oil and rubber to pay her way as she went. She criticized missionaries and managed to upset the doyen of the

The most shameful face of Empire (2). South African police beat women with truncheons during a protest at Durban in 1959.

EMPIRE'S CHILDREN

British in West Africa, Frederick Lugard. She was far from liberal, however, and took a hard-nosed capitalist line when it came to Africa's potential for trade. On the other hand, she argued that we should not interfere with the customs and religions of local peoples, and with great and prescient insight speculated about whether or not Africa might have been the cradle of *Homo sapiens*.

Also in this far from complete list is Gertrude Bell, born to a wealthy family in 1868. She took a degree in history at Oxford and after graduating travelled to Persia (now Iran) where her uncle was British Minister in Tehran, later writing a book about her experiences there. She then spent a decade travelling the world, mountaineering, studying archaeology, and picking up Arabic, French, German, Italian, Persian and Turkish. She played a major role in important archaeological digs in Turkey and the Middle East, wrote several books on travel and archaeology, and joined the Women's National Anti-Suffrage League as its honorary secretary. During the First World War she joined the Arab Bureau, and was instrumental, with T. E. Lawrence (though his fame unfairly overshadows hers), in the foundation of the Hashemite Kingdom. During the war, based in Basra, she was area spymaster and controlled, among other agents, the wayward father of Kim Philby. When Iraq fell under British control after the war, Bell was one of those instrumental in the creation of the modern state. In 1926, she founded the Baghdad Museum, many of whose treasures (it was a wonderful museum) as we know have now been looted and destroyed as a result of the anarchy and chaos following the recent invasion of that country by Britain and the USA. Somehow, gunboat diplomacy just does not seem to work any more.

It is a great pity that such a full life should have ended sadly. In 1926, Bell discovered that she had pleurisy. She recovered, but almost immediately learned of the death of her beloved brother, Hugo. She had never married, having lost the love of her life to the First World War, and now, still in Baghdad, aged fifty-eight, she began to feel lonely and old. She committed suicide on 12 July, and is buried in the British cemetery in Bab al'Sharji.

Apart from Lady Butler (born Elizabeth Thompson), who created large patriotic paintings adored by the Victorians no painter of note emerged to celebrate the Empire, and nor did any other major artist, apart from Kipling and Elgar. By contrast there was no lack of minor talents. Tennyson's successor as Poet Laureate, Alfred Austin, chosen because there really was not anyone else suitable (Swinburne was considered to be 'not quite the thing'), was really pretty awful. The novelist G. A. Henty poured out forty or so books, mainly

AMONG MANY BRAVE MISSIONARIES, DOCTORS AND NURSES WHO CONCENTRATED ON NURTURE RATHER THAN SUBJUGATION, THERE WERE SEVERAL OUTSTANDING WOMEN.

⊠

**"THE RIVER OF
DEATH HAS
BRIMMED HIS
BANKS,
AND ENGLAND'S
FAR, AND HONOUR
A NAME,"**

aimed at boys, using actual events as the basis for stirring tales of derring-do, generally pitching noble Britons against intemperate and rebellious foreigners. There is a certain elegiac nobility in some of the poetry of W. E. Henley and Henry Newbolt, but in general their work seems, to modern ears at least, stilted and faintly ridiculous. The only great poem we trot out on great national occasions, apart from Benson's 'Land of Hope and Glory' (and it is Elgar's music, not Benson's words, that carries the day), and Thomson's 'Rule, Britannia' (again we tend to remember Arne's music rather than the words), is 'Jerusalem'. This time we do remember the words – though Hubert Parry's music for it is also very familiar. But the poem – a truly great one – is by a mystical artist, Blake, and has nothing to do with Empire.

Perhaps despite all the aggression and bluster there is something fatalistically north European in our psyche. As George Orwell once pointed out, no war song sung by soldiers has ever been martial. People want to go home and be with their loved ones. We were quick to adopt 'Lili Marlene' from the Germans even when we were fighting them. There may be a lot of jingoism in Newbolt's 'Vitaï Lampada', a poem which he himself later repudiated; but its inspiration lay in the crushing defeat by the Mahdi's forces of a British column marching to relieve Khartoum:

> There's a breathless hush in the Close tonight,
> Ten to make and the match to win;
> A bumping pitch and a blinding light,
> An hour to play and the last man in.
> And it's not for the sake of a ribboned coat,
> Or the selfish hope of a season's fame,
> But his Captain's hand on his shoulder smote:
> 'Play up! play up! and play the game!'
>
> The sand of the desert is sodden red,
> Red with the wreck of a square that broke;
> The Gatling's jammed and the Colonel dead,
> And the regiment blind with dust and smoke.
> The river of death has brimmed his banks,
> And England's far, and Honour a name,
> But the voice of a schoolboy rallies the ranks:
> 'Play up! play up! and play the game!'

The most shameful face of Empire (3). This 1956 photograph doesn't need a caption.

This is the word that year by year,
While in her place the School is set,
Every one of her sons must hear,
And none that hears it dare forget.
This they all with a joyful mind
Bear through life like a torch in flame,
And falling fling to the host behind:
'Play up! play up! and play the game!'

Soon such sentiments would seem very old-fashioned indeed. The twentieth century would not be very old before the world would be shaken by a war of greater violence and destruction than any of its predecessors, a war which would signal the beginning of the end for the British Empire.

DAVID STEEL

KENYA

L

ord Steel is one of Scotland's most prominent political exports. During the 1970s and 1980s, his most politically active period, he became leader of the Liberal Party in 1976 and led it to merge with the Social Democratic Party in 1981 to become the Liberal Democrats.

But his career was not restricted to British politics. From 1966 to 1970 he was President of the Anti-Apartheid Movement in the UK. A firm supporter of Nelson Mandela, his campaigns led to his expulsion from Rhodesia in 1971. He was knighted in 1990, and in 1992 he was a monitor at South Africa's first democratic election, and continued to campaign for a multi-party democracy in Kenya and Malawi. Later on, he became the first Presiding Officer of the Scottish Parliament from 1999 to 2003 after which he retired to the House of Lords.

David Martin Scott Steel was born on 31 March 1938 in Kirkcaldy, Scotland to parents David and Sheila Steel (née Martin). David Steel Senior was a Church of Scotland minister. In 1949 when David was eleven, his parents made the decision to move David and his four siblings to Kenya, where Mr Steel had been appointed Minister of St Andrew's Church in Nairobi, and the Parish of East Africa with responsibility for the Scottish population throughout Kenya, Uganda and Tanganyika. As their ship left Tilbury to the sound of 'Rule Britannia', David remembers being very excited about going on such an adventure. When he arrived in Nairobi the sights, sounds and smells of Africa were overwhelming. He remembers going into a café and having his first banana split. 'I'd never even seen a banana!' he exclaimed.

David had always known that his father was a well-respected public figure in his Kenyan parish. As a child he often travelled with his father to the 22 sub-parishes where he preached, and aged fourteen watched his father open a new church, St Andrew's, which he had built in the centre of Nairobi. After his death in 2002, David discovered a briefcase full of documents relating to his father's time in Africa. David knew that his father made a controversial sermon which had been broadcast throughout Kenya but, from the papers he found, David realized that there was much more to the story than he had realized. He wanted to find out more about the political controversy in which his father had become embroiled.

Since it had been declared a colony in 1920, Kenya had been a land of opportunity for British settlers. Segregation was standard practice. White colonials led a life of luxury, while Africans were treated as second-class citi-

TOP:
David and his dog Duke, c. 1950.
ABOVE:
On board the ship that took David (at back) and his brother home from Africa.

ABOVE:
On board ship going back to Scotland, 1953. David at top, Michael second to bottom.

ABOVE RIGHT:
The SS. *Kenya Castle* docked in Cyprus.

RIGHT:
Their voyage took them through the Suez Canal.

zens. This was coupled with a local sense of injustice that white settlers had arrogated to themselves rich farmland formerly worked by the Kikuyu, the dominant tribe of Kenya. By 1949, when the Steel family arrived, agitation for political change was intensifying, although it would be over a decade before independence would be achieved.

A rebel movement, known as the Mau Mau (which you can read more about elsewhere in this book), was gathering strength. The British naturally regarded it as a terrorist faction and clamped down on it hard, but it was difficult to police. In the end, despite the publicity given in the white press to the atrocities committed by the Mau Mau, there were only thirty-two white casu-

Christmas at the
Kibuyu mission
hospital in Nairobi.

alties. Most of the thousands of Mau Mau victims were black, murdered because they were suspected of 'collaboration' with the British. However, when the Ruck family was murdered on their isolated farm in 1953, the press had a field day, and a tremor went through the entire white community.

David met ninety-five-year-old Arthur Woolsey Lewis who came from Britain in 1930 to capitalize on what he regarded as undeveloped land. A proud pioneer of the British Empire, like many expatriates of his generation, Arthur believes the British brought civilization to an uncivilized, tribal society. But the Mau Mau did not want to learn the lessons that the white man had come to teach them. Arthur's farm eventually fell victim to terrorism and was burnt to the ground. White colonials were living in fear, and in 1952 a state of Emergency was declared.

Baby in a pail.
Taken by David in 1952.

Thereafter the Reverend David Steel was obliged to make his tours of duty with a loaded revolver in his car (though the family never experienced the effects of terrorism at first hand). It was either that, or accept an armed escort, which Mr Steel was disinclined to do in case it suggested to locals that he was an agent of the colonial government. Most liberal white people acknowledged that the black African Kenyans had a reason to feel disenfranchised. 75,000 of them had fought in the service of the Empire during the Second World War and understandably they were angered when they returned home to find their land occupied by the British. Many Kenyans agreed with the Mau Mau's plight to regain their rights to the land, but very few sympathized with the

brutal acts of terrorism committed in the name of their campaign.

The Mau Mau intensified their campaign. Their methods became more brutal, and began to alienate many moderate supporters who were given a choice: swear an oath of allegiance to their cause, or die a traitor. David remembers the tension of the times, when local white farmers, their hosts at a dinner party, had pistols on their side plates; and when David himself formed part of a night patrol – 'a kind of Home Guard–Dad's Army-style defence force' – in which the men carried guns and boys like David armed themselves with heavy sticks.

David continued to travel deeper into the Kenyan Highlands, where he came face to face with a group of Mau Mau veterans. They now admit that the British brought many improvements in health and sanitation, but in return they took away their land and freedom, and that is what they were fighting for. He then visited the Very Reverend John Gatu, who knew his father during his time in Kenya. He is shocked to learn that Dr Gatu admits to taking the Mau Mau oath of allegiance. Gatu explained that before they stepped up their campaign of violence, he agreed with the basic principles behind the Mau Mau movement. But he only participated for a short time before turning to the Church. After the meeting David could only speculate on what his father would have thought had he known that a fellow Church leader had previously been a Mau Mau supporter.

By 1953 the situation in Kenya was worsening. The family returned to Scotland on leave when David was fifteen, and he and his brother Michael were left behind to continue their education when their parents returned to Kenya. David remembers being terribly sad to see them go. He would not see his father for another four years.

Meanwhile, events in Kenya were coming to a head, becoming progressively more violent and bloody. British forces were sent out to deal with the problem. Their methods were harsh and direct. Large numbers of the African population were herded into concentration camps and detained without trial, in an attempt to try and isolate the terrorists and their supporters. David went to visit James Foster, who still lives in Kenya and came to the country as a young policeman in 1954. David questioned him over the methodology of the British campaign to defeat the terrorists. James admits that looking back now, the British security forces did behave very badly, and he certainly felt uncomfortable about it at the time. He particularly remembers one occasion when the police chief inspector instructed his men to let an African go and then shot him in the back. When Foster reported the incident he was posted elsewhere. Foster also told David that he remembers hearing his father's monthly broadcasts on the radio, and that the Christian Church played a major part in bringing the Emergency to an end.

But what part did David's father play specifically? How did he come to deliver a sermon, which would embroil him in such political controversy? David visited the Kenyan National Archives in Nairobi to try and find more clues. He found an amazing array of letters written by his father to the Church in Scotland, expressing his concerns about the treatment delivered by the colonial authorities to the Africans in Kenya. He was clearly aware of the implications of expressing his opinions publicly.

I know I have the reputation at times of being hasty but if ever I was careful, I have been careful here. I have evidence of indictment including murder. I am aware of the very dangerous position in which the Church may be placed if we come to an open clash with the Government and have to make a public indictment, and I will avoid that clash if possible, so long as the Church can keep its integrity.

David also found a letter from his father to the governor detailing the brutality he had witnessed, and explaining that the British were in danger of losing local support if they continued to use these methods.

BELOW:
David, aged 15, and Michael, aged 13, just before the family returned to Kenya without them.
BELOW LEFT:
David, c. aged 16, near Edinburgh.

DAVID STEEL
KENYA

At the height of the Emergency, 80,000 Africans were detained without trial. Of those who were tried, over a 1,000 were hanged for their alleged crimes.

David went to see John Nottingham, who was a District Officer at the time. He revealed to David's surprise that his father was receiving information from the head of Kenya's Police CID, whose job it was to investigate these incidences of brutality. Duncan MacPherson was also a member of Mr Steel's congregation. It was this that finally made him feel compelled to act. On Sunday 9 January 1955 he used his monthly broadcast to speak out against colonial repression. It was entitled 'The Massacre of the Innocents'. David met Reverend Dr Wanjau, who remembered the sermon for very personal reasons. His mother and father were both detained in one of the British concentration camps. He believes it represented a very important turning point in the Emergency, and was instrumental in bringing it to an end.

The Reverend David Steel also knew of Africans associated with his church who were being detained in the camps. David returned to the archives and found a list of the people whom David's father lobbied to be set free. He went

DAVID RETURNED TO THE ARCHIVES AND FOUND A LIST OF THE PEOPLE WHOM HIS FATHER LOBBIED TO BE SET FREE.

1952, St Andrew's
Church Nairobi,
exterior and interior.

back to Dr Gatu, who told him that one of the people on the list, Habill Kimenge, was still alive and in Nairobi. After some searching, David managed to track down Habill, and in a very moving interview he told David that he remembered his father's tireless efforts to help people like him. In recognition of his father's work, Habill presented David with a gift: a wooden stool, which he had made. It was only then that David truly became aware of how many lives his father had touched during his time in Africa.

Reverend David Steel left Kenya for the last time in April 1957, six years before independence. He died in 2002 aged ninety-two. Half of his ashes were interred in Scotland, and half were flown out to Africa to be buried at the Kikuyu Mission Station. This was David's final destination. Here he visited the grave, to reflect on the contribution his father made to the Kenyan struggle for independence. With his emotions running high, he read an extract from the St Andrew's Journal, which documented his mother's and father's departure.

On leaving, the people crowded round Mr and Mrs Steel to wish them goodbye and expressed their sincere hope they would meet again. Many of us felt like the little girl who fixing a determined smile on her face said, 'but I'm crying inside'. And yet, bearing in mind the words of the moderator and of the minister's last sermon, our hearts are full of thanksgiving for all that had been accomplished under God during our 8 years together, and it was holding that comfort to us that we said our last farewell.

PART TWO

'ALMOST INEVITABLE CONSEQUENCES'

RUDYARD KIPLING

CHAPTER FOUR

WAR AND PEACE

By the 1880s Britain was already beginning to lose ground as an industrial power to both the USA and Germany. British imperial skills were still much admired, however, and it would be another three decades before Britain's standing as the leading world power would be seriously challenged.

In Japan, senior officials were obliged to read Sir John Seeley's bestseller, *The Expansion of England*, as a kind of guidebook on how to establish and manage an empire.

But at home, despite the best efforts of that arch-publicist King George V, who succeeded his father as King-Emperor in 1910 and was the first British monarch actually to visit India, interest in the far-flung colonies was waning among ordinary people. They tended to take its benefits for granted, and remained incurious about it as a whole, being more concerned with problems closer to home, especially in view of the slump which affected Britain in the closing two decades of the nineteenth century.

True, there were still isolated examples of old-fashioned British aggression. As late as 1903, George Curzon rubber-stamped a military expedition to Tibet, led by Sir Francis Younghusband, to ensure that that country would not let the Russians in. His force, to make it seem the more impressive, was to have, in addition to strong brigades of Sikhs and Gurkhas, a mountain battery of British soldiers, of whom 'not a single man was to be under six feet'. This was stipulated by that master of detail, Kitchener, then commander-in-chief, who also saw to it that Younghusband was equipped with two Maxim gun detachments. In all, there were 1,200 troops, whose kit was managed by 10,000 porters and carried by 20,000 beasts of burden, including yaks, camels and two experimental zebrules (an animal resulting from crossing a mule and a zebra, which was not a success). The expedition moved unimpeded into Tibet over the winter of 1903, but in March the following year it encountered the army sent to oppose it. The Tibetan army had erected a vast barricade in the river valley ahead, placed across the track, though with plenty of room either side to pass it by. Manning it was an army that, apart from a few ancient muskets, might not have evolved since the twelfth century.

On confrontation, Younghusband gave the Tibetans fifteen minutes to withdraw and let him pass. They did not. Battle commenced on 31 March. Pounded by artillery and rifle fire, and strafed by the Maxim guns, within two or three minutes 700 Tibetans lay dead; the rest, dazed and horrified by the unimaginable maelstrom that had hit them, wandered away, back up the valley. They did not even hurry. Tibet was brought to heel, and the forty-year-old Younghusband underwent a mystical experience which was to shape the rest of his life.

In the meantime, the large white-settler colonies of the Empire were all but seceding from it. This process had, in fact, begun many years before, and carried the seeds of what would ultimately be the transformation of Empire into Commonwealth. Canada, which had long tended to exercise an independent voice, took dominion status as early as 1867 – 'daughter I am in my mother's house, but mistress in my own', as Kipling disingenuously wrote – followed by

December 1921. A simpering Prince of Wales (centre; later he was briefly to become King Edward VIII) stands over his first tiger kill in India during his successful Empire tour.

Australia in 1901, New Zealand and Newfoundland (later to join Canada) in 1907, and (as we have seen) South Africa in 1910. The foreign relations of these dominions were still carried out through Westminster, however; and though Canada created its own Department of External Affairs in 1907, diplomatic relations of the dominions were channelled through British governors general and high commissioners.

Meanwhile, trouble was brewing very much closer to home, in the shape of Kaiser Wilhelm II of Germany. More than slightly mad and more than slightly megalomaniac, he had cast an envious eye on his near-neighbour's empire since his accession, wanting a similar one for himself. Wilhelm had a close family association with Britain – Queen Victoria (whose offspring fertilized dynasties throughout Europe) was his grandmother, and George V was a first cousin once removed, but his ambitions were for a German 'place in the sun'. He supported the Boers and intervened when and where he could to undermine British influence, but made no more than a nuisance of himself until, stealing a march on British complacency, he built up the most powerful army

George V and Queen Mary in full fig at the Delhi Durbar.

Mixing and mingling: a
banquet held for Ranjit
Nawanagar in Delhi, 1907.

in Europe (Germany had 124 divisions to Britain's ten, and each and every infantry division was equipped with Maxim guns); and a navy which came close to rivalling Britain's: the tonnage ratio was 1:2 in British favour in 1914, but it had been 1:7 in 1880, and the Germans used wireless, not semaphore. As early as 1907, the German-born British diplomat Sir Eyre Crowe had warned of Germany's ambitions, and stated that they might include colonial expansion and the breaking up and supplanting of the British Empire. Eight years later (when it was clear to their high command that Germany was not going to be able to sustain its efforts), Feldmarschall Colmar von der Goltz chillingly but also perceptively wrote: 'If we are defeated this time, perhaps we will have better luck next time. For me, the present war is most emphatically only the beginning of a long historical development, at whose end will stand the defeat of England's world position... [and] the revolution of the coloured races against the colonial imperialism of Europe.' And in the long run, whatever else Britain did, she probably could not have done much to avert that.

The old order was changing inexorably. It was not only the British Empire that was facing its end: colonization in general was breathing its last in the form at least that it had taken up to now. Britain's behaviour as an imperial power may not have been impeccable (she behaved appallingly in Ireland for 400 years, for example), but it did compare favourably with that of the

⊠

**THE KAISER WAS
NOT A MAN TO
BACK DOWN, AND
WHEN HE SAW AN
EXCUSE TO OPEN
HOSTILITIES, HE
DID SO.**

Belgians, French, Germans, Italians and – in the east – the Japanese. (It is astonishing that during the Second World War some elements of the Indian independence movement should have looked to Japan for succour. Had they not heard about the atrocities committed by the Japanese army on Chinese civilians during the 'Rape of Nanking' in 1937?)

In 1904 Britain reached an entente cordiale with her old enemy, the French, with the French acknowledging British dominance of Egypt in return for a free hand in Morocco. France was allied with Imperial Russia. Battle lines were already being traced. A number of neurotic and admonitory books appeared, fiction, non-fiction and futuristic, about the German threat, the best known of which to survive is probably Erskine Childers's espionage thriller, *The Riddle of the Sands* (1903). John Buchan's wartime novel, *Greenmantle* (1916), makes interesting reading, too, since Buchan's hero from his earlier novel, *The Thirty-Nine Steps*, Richard Hannay, has to chase down rumours of an uprising in the Muslim world, and travels hazardously through enemy territory to rendezvous with a contact in Constantinople. Once there, he and his allies have to counter the Germans' plans to use Islam to help them win the war. German plans to woo Islam were real enough, though Buchan, who worked for the British Secret Service, probably had no inkling of them as they were very strictly classified. What is interesting too is his vision of an aggressive Islamist movement almost a century before the fact.

A handful of historians have suggested that 'Kaiser Bill' never really wanted it to come to war with the English, whom the Germans have always considered close 'relations'. After all, until 1917, when he changed it to Windsor, George V's family name was Saxe-Coburg-Gotha, just as the First Sea Lord in 1914 was Ludwig Battenberg (later Louis Mountbatten, father of the eponymous Viceroy to India); but the Kaiser was not a man to back down, and when he saw an excuse to open hostilities (naturally in the interests of world peace), he did so. Luckily, under such men as Lord Battenberg/Mountbatten, the Royal Navy had belatedly modernized, switching (on Churchill's initiative) from coal to oil, and the army had learned valuable lessons from the Boers. There would be no more fighting in squares or wearing red tunics to war any more (in fact, the army had adopted khaki – the word is the Hindi for 'dust' – uniforms first as early as 1848, and worn them in Afghanistan in 1878–80 and South Africa in 1899-1902, after which they were generally adopted for the field).

Nor would there be any more easy victories. Wilhelm II, who had parted company with the most experienced and cosmopolitan of his advisers,

OPPOSITE:
George, Prince of Wales, photographed in 1905, aged 40. Five years later he would succeed his father as King George V, the last great entrepreneur of the British Empire.

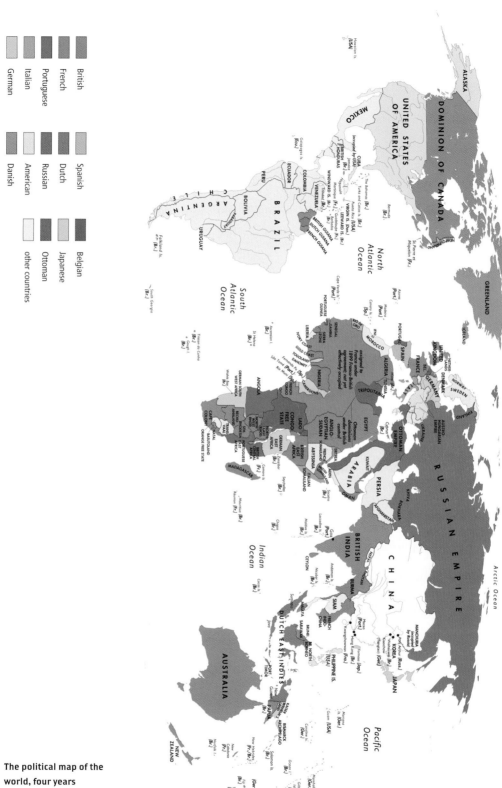

The political map of the world, four years preceding the onset of the bloody and long Great War.

Bismarck, in 1890, had also shown an early interest in buying the Maxim gun. Aerial bombardment and the use of poison gas would soon make even the machine gun a relatively conventional weapon. The 'Great War', when it came, would provide the arena for the development and advancement of other technologies which would enjoy an overall peacetime application as well. The telephone had been in existence, however primitive, since the 1880s and 1890s; and 1915 saw the introduction of wireless field telephones. Marconi got his patent for wireless telegraphy in 1897. The wireless itself developed alongside the telephone. Marconi sent the first transatlantic wireless transmission in 1901; the first voice broadcast was in 1914. Police cars in the USA had wireless transmitter-receivers fitted in the 1920s; and frequency modulation (FM) was introduced as early as 1935. The world was changing fast, and the Empire, based on sea power and slow communication – worldwide information quickly available was not in its interests – was having difficulty keeping up.

The Pax Britannica, which, with the exception of the Crimean War, had been maintained since 1815, allowed for the consolidation, maintenance and expansion of the Empire. All that was about to change, fast and for ever; but the seeds had been sown long before 1914.

The First World War was fought between the central European Powers – Germany, the Austro-Hungarian Empire, and their allies, and the Triple Entente – Britain and its Empire, France and Russia, and their allies, including the United States of America, which joined hostilities in 1917. The war was fought in Europe, Africa, the Middle East, and at sea, though there was only one truly major sea battle, led on the one hand by Admiral John Jellicoe, and on the other by Admiral Reinhard Scheer – that of Jutland, off Denmark, (the German name for the battle was the Skaggerachtsschlacht, named after the Skaggerak Strait between Norway and Denmark) in 1916, the outcome of which was inconclusive.

The causes of the war are complex. Early in the last century, commercial and territorial competition had together led to a rise in nationalist sentiment. King Edward VII did not care much about the British Empire, then a candle flame waxing before its wane. His nephew Wilhelm II of Germany was an ambitious expansionist who envied the Empire ruled over by his grandmother, Queen Victoria. Industrially, Germany was already taking the wind out of Britain's sails, but that was not enough for the Kaiser as he was styled; and nationalism created political tension to a significant degree between the single-nation states (of which Germany had recently become one thanks to Chancellor Bismarck who had been a great unifier in the closing years of the nineteenth century); at the same time the multi-national and rather old-fashioned states such as, most significantly in Europe, Austro-Hungary, found themselves threatened by nationalistically inspired schism. As tension mounted between the competing and jealous nations, principally of France, Britain and Germany, it led to an arms race, to trade barriers and tariff walls, and to increasingly aggressive jingoistic propaganda. The unrest between the principal nations of Europe which inevitably followed, coupled with nascent nationalist movements within the Austro-Hungarian Empire in particular, led ultimately to tension between that patron state and Serbia, a hotbed (in the view of conservatives) of nationalism. Matters came to a violent head on 28 June 1914, when, while on a visit to Sarajevo, then capital of Bosnia-Herzegovina, an Austro-Hungarian province at the time, the Archduke Franz-Ferdinand, aged forty, and his wife, were assassinated by a terrorist called Gavrilo Princip and his confederates, whose sponsors were the Serbian nationalist Black Hand Gang.

The Austro-Hungarian authorities naturally condemned the act, and Germany supported them, though aware that the action might arouse the ire of Russia, which tacitly supported Serbian nationalism, *inter alia*, in its bid to undermine Austro-Hungarian power in Central Europe. Soon, German military intelligence would be allying themselves secretly with Lenin, and it was only to be a few years before the ultra right-wing General Ludendorff, a later supporter of Hitler, would be arranging Lenin's secret train journey back to Russia.

Austro-Hungary presented Serbia with an ultimatum which required a response by 25 July 1914, forty-eight hours after its issue. Following Russian diplomatic advice, Serbia agreed to all the conditions save two, which conflicted with its own self-assertion as a sovereign state. Austro-Hungarian forces along the Serbian border were immediately mobilized on receipt of the response. Russia reacted by mobilizing on 29 July. When Berlin got the news two days later, it issued a demand that the Russians should stand down, and also required of France an undertaking of neutrality, despite the fact that France had an independent treaty of entente with Russia. For its part, Britain evoked an agreement regarding Belgian neutrality promulgated in 1839 to formalize its pro-Franco-Russian stance, and asked France and Germany to honour that agreement. Taking its cue, France agreed, but Germany demurred: the Kaiser may have been reluctant to cross swords with his cousin George V, King of England, but neither was he a man to back down if pressed.

On 1 August, Britain informed Germany that it could not countenance any threat to Belgian neutrality; but the day after German troops entered Luxembourg, and engaged in skirmishes with the French in the Germanic border area of Alsace-Lorraine (Elsaß-Lothringen). Germany would not stand down, and demanded the right of passage through Belgium to counter the French, with whom they were already de facto at war. The British prime minister, Herbert Asquith, ordered a mobilization on 2 August, and the following day Belgium denied any German right of passage over its soil. Thereupon Germany formally declared war on France and invaded Belgium. When a British demand for withdrawal received no formal reply, Britain declared war on Germany for the first time, beginning midnight on Tuesday 4 August 1914.

Britain faced the First World War bravely, and its colonies and dominions rallied round. Not unanimously, however. There were dissident voices and movements in Ireland, among the French-Canadians, among the Boers and in other parts of Africa, and in India. Some Muslim-Indians more than hesitated at the thought of fighting their fellow-Muslim Turks (Turkey and Germany were allies), the more so as the Turkish Caliph, who had declared a jihad against Britain, France and Russia, was spiritual leader of all Sunni Muslims. But the bulk of the Empire was quick to respond. Naturally, those countries still within the Empire found themselves automatically involved as subject nations to Britain, but that is not to say that they did not respond generously in any case. Germany and her allies had started a war with a nation that had 450 million people at her disposal. The response of the dominions, especially when you consider that they were sending their men to a battleground far from home which did not immediately threaten them, was also generous. 'Our duty is quite clear,' declared the Australian Prime Minister. 'To gird up our loins and remember that we are Britons.' Over 320,000 Australians would serve in the war. Many would lose their lives at Gallipoli (April–December 1915), when they were thrown against Turkish machine-gun emplacements in much the same way as the Mahdi's forces had thrown themselves against Kitchener's Maxim guns at Omdurman. The whole Gallipoli campaign lasted 259 days and cost over 200,000 lives.

Within ten days of its outbreak, 8,000 New Zealanders, including Maoris, had gone off to join the war. They would send 130,000 *in toto* – a tenth of the entire population of the two islands. They were joined by 31,000 Canadians (this figure would grow to 630,000). The majority of these people (many women went as nurses) were volunteers – there was initially no conscription overseas. The South Africans, who committed 125,000 people, neutralized the Germans

During a march-past of Indian troops (Sikhs here) in London during the First World War, a woman pins flowers on the chest of one of the soldiers (you can just see her arm protruding from the left).

Lt Ernest Brooks photographs Australian troops charging up the beach at Gallipoli to meet their fate in 1915.

in their colonies. Over 2 million black Africans served in the war, nearly all in supply and transport corps, in Africa and Europe, where they sustained losses of over 100,000 men. When the USA entered the war, black American troops entered it, too, though they were segregated from white American troops, and the USA actually refused to command them, handing them over to France, under whose officers the men of 93 Division fought valiantly.

Naturally it was not one smooth, friendly and efficient alliance, and naturally African, Afro-Caribbean and South Asian troops bridled when subjected to racist or patronizing treatment. As Niall Ferguson points out, European British officers (military regulations precluded coloured people from commissions) could treat their fellow countrymen (for that is what the colonized peoples were, in law) with contempt. The British West Indies Regiment was largely deployed as ammunition carriers, a very dangerous task, and it was hard for the men not to feel regarded as expendable. One Trinidadian sergeant noted in 1918 that: 'We are treated neither as Christians nor British citizens, but as West Indian "niggers", without anybody to be interested in or look after us. Instead of being drawn closer to Church and Empire we are driven away from it.' But bungling, arrogance and mismanagement were not uncommon among the British Army during the Great War, and, as Ferguson also points out, other colonial troops, black and white, as well as British, often had cause to complain of them.

There were other tensions: Australian troops were paid 5 shillings a day — five times as much as the British 'Tommies' (who referred to their Antipodean comrades as 'fucking five-bobbers'). And there had been misgivings about recruiting black soldiers for practical reasons. In 1915 the Colonial Office reminded the War Office that 'it must not be forgotten that a West African native trained to use of arms and filled with a new degree of self-confidence by successful encounters with forces armed and led by Europeans was not likely to be more amenable to discipline in peace time'. This was another reason why Africans were relegated to service corps, though many tens of thousands did, in fact, face the enemy in anger. Nevertheless, taboos and prejudices were being broken down willy-nilly: white men encountered black men of sophistication and education; black men encountered poor white men who did menial work for a living, and, in places like the Liverpool docks, they encountered women who were very far from the *memsahibs* and colonial wives of their previous experience.

Although already embarked on their own political journey towards independence, Indian leaders endorsed Britain in its time of need. 'We are, above all, British citizens of the Great British Empire,' declared Mohandas Karamchand Gandhi, who had served with the Indian Ambulance Corps during the Second Boer War. 'Fighting as the British are at present in a righteous cause for the good and glory of human dignity and civilisation... our duty is clear: to do our best to support the British, to fight with our life and property.' But he also said: 'They [his followers] would go to fight for the Empire, but they would so fight because they aspire to become partners in it.' More than one million Indians served in the war, seeing service in Europe and the Middle East, and providing, together with the Australians, the New Zealanders and the Canadians, the cream of the fighting men. India contributed as much manpower as the four white dominions put together, and as early as autumn 1914 one third of British forces in France were from India. These men, too, were volunteers, many of the races born to a military tradition, and to the credo *dulce et decorum est pro patria mori*: 'it is sweet and fitting to die for the motherland'. However strange the terrain and the weather of north-western Europe must have seemed, for them that motherland was Britannia.

At the end of the Great War, the number of casualties was over 37 million — over 15 million deaths and 22 million wounded. This included almost 9 million military deaths and about 6.6 million civilian deaths. Britain lost over 700,000 men; India, 64,000; Australia and New Zealand, 67,000; Canada, over 56,000.

No one had expected the war to last as long as it did. But when it ended, the British were by then expecting it to go on even longer. Germany was exhausted, but Germany's wilful and stupid ambition had sapped the rest of the world, especially its enemies in Europe and among them particularly the British. And they had achieved a part at least of von der Goltz's prophecy. The Empire would never be the same again, though soon it would become even bigger than it had been. But the break-up was close. The German war provided an important catalyst, but the break-up would have come anyway. The war had simply speeded up the rate of change.

After the end of the war in Europe, Poland at last emerged as an independent country again, after over a century. Yugoslavia and Czechoslovakia were entirely new creations, following the Treaty of Trianon in 1920 in the case of the former 'country'. Russia became the Soviet Union in 1917 and lost several client states, including Finland, Estonia, Lithuania and Latvia which became independent countries.

As for the Near East, the ailing Ottoman Empire was replaced by a secular state under Kemal Atatürk, Turkey; and many other new nations appeared on a radically different map of the world on which the Empire still held sway, but with its weaknesses already exposed by the burgeoning new powers in the world, not least that of the USSR which had replaced the former Russian Empire. Tsar Nicolas II, cousin of King George V and a virtual lookalike, was dead, assassinated with his family at Yekaterinburg in July 1918 (a month later the tsar was canonized by the Russian Orthodox Church in a political manoeuvre which didn't pay off).

As we see elsewhere in the story of the Empire's children, Iraq was created as a British Protectorate in 1922; and the ill-fated Palestine, which was to bring so much grief to the world in focusing Jewish/Islamic tensions for what is now ninety years, also fell to unfortunately inept British charge in 1917.

As far as the British Empire was concerned, the war gave birth to new expressions of nationalism. In Australia and New Zealand, the First World War, and especially the Gallipoli campaign, became known as the nations' baptisms of fire. The Great War was the first in which the recently established dominions had fought – unconditionally – on behalf of the mother country, and it is one of the first cases in which Australian troops fought as Australians, not just subjects of the British Crown. ANZAC Day commemorates the

Australian Army's and New Zealand Army Corps' sacrifice to what has been seen by many military historians since as a grotesque tactical blunder by General Staff and a severe blot on the British military escutcheon. (Peter Weir's film, *Gallipoli*, 1981, and the Turkish director Tolga Örneks's film of the same name (2005) both movingly capture the terrible waste of war.)

The toll was greater in Canada, though Canadians made sure that they were regarded as independent nationals, not, as some Britons in high political office, Churchill among them, were still inclined to regard them, subjects of the British Empire. Canadians refer to their country as a nation 'forged from fire'. However, participation in the Great War assured Canada's status as an independent nation as far as international regard was concerned thereafter. Canada entered the war as a dominion of the British Empire. By its end, Canada was a wholly independent nation. Canadian diplomats played a leading role in negotiating the treaty to end the war; and Canada signed the treaty in her own right, whereas other dominions were still represented by Britain.

The experiences of the war led in its wake to trauma for all the participating countries. The optimism of the 1900s was entirely gone, and those who fought in the war became what was known as 'the Lost Generation', as the

A bugler of 3 Battalion Nigeria Regiment sounds the House Farewell on board ship - sounded when officers and NCOs leave the country. Photographed by Lt. L. A. W. Powell in 1917.

American novelist Scott Fitzgerald gracefully and accurately defined it, because they never came round from their experiences.

For the next few years, much of Europe was in mourning. War memorials were placed in thousands of villages and towns. The homecoming troops suffered greatly in the wake of the peace; they had seen horrors beyond common experience and many were suffering from 'shell-shock', or as we might term it today, post-traumatic stress disorder.

The social trauma manifested itself in many different ways. Many were now appalled by nationalism and what it had caused, and began to work towards a community of nations. In this spirit the League of Nations was founded. Pacifism too became increasingly popular. But others felt that only strength and military power could be relied on for protection in such a divisive and uncertain world. The rise of Nazism and fascism led to a revival of the nationalist spirit that had sparked the Great War, and in a sense this reaction meant that the Second World War became an inevitable consequence of the First. Each generation lives under the shadow of the last, and by that token such mid-nineteenth-century throwbacks as Hitler could thrive – briefly but

Lt. Ernest Brooks photographs the British West Indies Regiment on the road to the Somme, 1916.

EMPIRE'S CHILDREN

fatally – in a world which had already moved on, and in which the centres of power had already shifted from Europe to Washington and Moscow.

Many people between the wars believed that 1918 had heralded the end of the world as they had known it, including the collapse of capitalism and imperialism. Communist and socialist movements around the world drew strength from this sentiment. These feelings in Europe were most pronounced in countries especially affected by the war; and in the USA, as far as European socialist thinking existed. It was later exported in terms of exiles by Hitler, who so managed things that Europe lost most of its greatest intellectual talent to the United States.

The tragedy and the waste of the Great War is summed up best by a poem by one of the less lauded war poets of his generation. John McCrae (a lieutenant colonel in the Canadian army) wrote 'In Flanders Fields' as a tribute to those who had died:

> *In Flanders fields the poppies blow*
> *Between the crosses, row on row,*
> *That mark our place; and in the sky*
> *The larks, still bravely singing, fly*
> *Scarce heard amid the guns below.*
> *We are the Dead. Short days ago*
> *We lived, felt dawn, saw sunset glow,*
> *Loved, and were loved, and now we lie*
> *In Flanders fields.*
> *Take up our quarrel with the foe:*
> *To you from failing hands we throw*
> *The torch; be yours to hold it high.*
> *If ye break faith with us who die*
> *We shall not sleep, though poppies grow*
> *In Flanders fields.*

Canada was not the only nation to have its nationalist instincts stirred by the Great War. The Great War had left the mother country, Britain, distracted and hard hit financially. The terrible influenza epidemic in 1919 would strike another blow, and the ensuing two decades would see increasing economic hardship and volatility serve as the run-up to another world war, after only twenty years of peace, far too short a time for any kind of recovery, morally or financially

'TO YOU FROM FAILING HANDS WE THROW / THE TORCH; BE YOURS TO HOLD IT HIGH.'

JENNY
ECLAIR

MALAYSIA

Jenny is one of Britain's most successful female comics. She began her career as a punk performance poet in the 1980s, and became famous for her outrageous, and occasionally obscene, stand-up. In an industry dominated by boisterous male comedians, it was an uphill struggle for a woman to get recognized.

But Jenny managed it, and was the first woman to win the coveted Perrier Award for Comedy at the Edinburgh Festival in 1995. Jenny now has her own Saturday morning radio show on LBC and is also a published novelist. But it is probably her hilarious contributions to the hit BBC show *Grumpy Old Women* (the live version of which she co-wrote and stars in) for which she is most famous nowadays.

Jenny Clare Hargreaves was born in 1960 in Kuala Lumpur, Malaysia. Up until embarking upon *Empire's Children*, Jenny had never known much about how she came to be born in such an exotic location, and admitted that it had never occurred to her to ask. Her father Derek Hargreaves is now eighty-two and in poor health. Jenny knew this might be her last chance to find out what her parents were doing in Malaysia forty-six years ago.

Growing up, Jenny says she was a typical forces child. Derek had joined the army after leaving school and travelled all over the world on tours of duty. Naturally, when he married Jenny's mother June, his family went with him. 'I think the showbiz world is littered with forces children,' she says. 'The itinerant lifestyle sets you apart from everyone else.' Jenny had never really considered her unusual place of birth and 'child of the Empire' status. At the beginning of her journey she said, 'When I think of Empire I think of India, *The Little Princess* and that's about it. I know almost nothing about the circumstances that led up to my being born in Malaysia, what my father was fighting for and indeed the culture and country of my birth.'

Jenny began by visiting her parents in Lytham St Annes, Lancashire. She asked Derek why he was in Malaysia (or Malaya as it was known then) in the first place. He explained that he carried out two tours of duty there, the first in 1952–3 and the second in 1959–62. He knew that he was being sent out there to fight a communist uprising called the Emergency, being led by the Chinese population in Malaya, but he could not tell Jenny much more about the political side of things. 'We didn't ask questions,' he said. 'It was simply a case of goodies versus baddies.' Finally Jenny showed Derek what she was most curious to ask him about. As a child, she stumbled across some disturbing photo-

Jenny as a baby on her mothers knee waiting for the Temerloh ferry, Malaya, 1960.

New born Jenny with her parents Derek and June and sister Sara, 1960.

graphs of dead soldiers, and one of a severed head. She had never asked her father about them before and was nervous about telling him that she had found them all those years ago. Derek told her that it was commonplace to take photographs of the dead communist soldiers, so that they could be identified for intelligence. Sometimes, when the body was too heavy to carry out of the jungle, the head would be severed, as it was easier to transport. Jenny was quite shocked to hear this, but relieved when Derek told her that he had never done any 'severing'. In fact he'd never even seen a live communist, let alone killed one.

Jenny embarked on her journey to Malaysia full of questions. Who were the communist terrorists and what did they want? Why were the British involved? And how could this business of decapitation be sanctioned? But first she wanted to get some background information on Malaya when it was part of the British Empire. She went to see Tristan and Joan Russell at the Selangor Club in Kuala Lumpur, an old colonial hang-out of her parents. Tristan is head of one of the oldest colonial families in Malaysia. Born there in 1932, he was educated abroad and then returned to Malaysia to work for the family business in 1954, right in the middle of the Emergency. He explains that after the British colonized Malaya in the eighteenth century as part of the trading activities of the British East India Company, it became Britain's most valuable colony, economically and strategically. Technically only two states of Malaya were under British rule, Malacca and Penang. Although Malay sultans governed the others, each of these had a British 'adviser' who was heavily influential. One of the most profitable exports from Malaya was rubber, which the British had introduced from Brazil in 1877. Many more Britons soon caught on, and set up hundreds of very lucrative plantations all over the country.

To find out more about how the Emergency started Jenny met up with Captain Michael Bleeck. Like her father, he was sent to Malaya in 1951 to fight for the British. They met in God's Little Acre, a cemetery that commemorates some of the solders who died in the conflict. Perhaps the most significant gravestone there is that of three British planters who were shot dead by communist terrorists (CTs) on 16 June 1948. Although tensions had been bubbling beforehand, it was at this moment that the British government decided to declare a state of Emergency and began sending in British troops to tackle the insurgency.

The communist insurgents were mainly made up of Chinese farmers and squatters living in poverty in remote locations in and around the jungle. During World War Two, the Chinese had fought alongside the British and Malayans to defeat the Japanese. But as soon as the war was over, a mainly Chinese communist faction took up arms and retreated into the jungle. Their aim was to rid Malaya of the British, and establish communist rule. The British, who would do anything to prevent the spread of communism, sent in troops to defend one of their most profitable colonies.

Captain Bleeck explained how difficult it was to locate the enemy in such hostile conditions. Jenny's father had told her about Dyak trackers from a tribe indigenous to Malaya, who were recruited by the British to help track the CTs. She was lucky enough to meet two trackers, Itam and Legan, who worked with the British during the Emergency. She read in her tourist guidebook that the Dyak were known for headhunting, and Jenny was curious to ask the trackers more about this practice, but when she did so they denied all knowledge. Later Jenny reflected that decapitation probably isn't something you would be very ready to admit to nowadays.

In 1951 the British High Commissioner Henry Gurney was ambushed and murdered by the CTs. This was a massive coup for the terrorists and triggered a wave of new British troops to be sent into Malaya. Jenny's father was one of

TOP:
Malay sign taken waiting for the ferry, Temerloh, 1960.
ABOVE:
Beach by the ferry, 1960.

**Jenny and her sister Sara,
Ampang Road, 1960.**

these. After a short time, Derek was promoted to intelligence officer. Sir Gerald Templer replaced Gurney as High Commissioner. He immediately turned what had been an unsuccessful shooting war into what he called 'a battle for hearts and minds'. At the centre of this battle was intelligence. Jenny went to see ex-head of Special Branch Dato (Sir) Seri Yuen Yuet Leng. He explained that through various methods they were able to build up a comprehensive list of the main perpetrators. Therefore it was essential to identify the bodies of dead CTs, and when a body could not be carried out of the jungle or a camera was not to hand, decapitation was the only option. Dato Yuen then showed Jenny, much to her shock, an article from a British newspaper, the *Daily Worker*. It exposes the practice of decapitation and shows a photograph of a British Royal Marine proudly holding aloft two severed heads. Dato Yuen admitted that on the odd occasion 'trophy' photographs like this were taken, but while a government inquiry into the matter condemned this particular incident the practice of headhunting for the purposes of identification was never officially terminated.

At this point Jenny confessed that she thought the film would be more of a travelogue than such a close examination of the Emergency. Despite the fact that the *Daily Worker* incident had nothing to do with Derek or his regiment, Jenny was concerned and visibly upset about how her parents might react to some of the more gruesome aspects of the film.

Steeling herself to carry on, Jenny wanted to understand just what would make the communists turn on the British like this. Mr Ban, a Chinese historian whose father was a well-known communist leader during the Emergency explains that they wanted to rid Malaya of British oppression, in order to have a fair chance of progressing economically. Again Jenny was told of some of the unsavoury behaviour of the British in Malaya. Mr Ban's father was shot by British troops. His body was then strapped to the back of a truck and paraded around the village as a warning to other communists.

Jenny felt defensive on behalf of the British troops who were carrying out their duty. Then she met K. L. Chye who worked with the British Coldstream Guards. He explained to her that the CTs were a ruthless and barbaric enemy, and that in his opinion the British were heroes who did what they had to do to win the war. He explained his involvement in what was to be the turning point of the Emergency. One of the lifelines for the CTs was terrorizing the local farmers squatting in the jungle into giving them food and supplies. In an

Jenny's sister Sara in front of a house in the Cameron Highlands, Malaysia, 1960.

Jenny's mother June in the Cameron Highlands, 1960.

✗

JENNY'S JOURNEY ENLIGHTENED HER TO A PART OF HER PARENTS' LIFE SHE WAS PREVIOUSLY UNAWARE OF AND TO THE CULTURE SHE WAS BORN INTO.

attempt to flush the CTs out, the British implemented the Briggs Plan. Every Chinese villager was rounded up and put into camps to prevent them from fraternizing with the CTs. The plan worked and the terrorists were forced out of the jungle. Conditions became so bad for them that many surrendered. Meanwhile, these camps developed into villages with running water, electricity, medical supplies and even democratically elected town councils, all things to which the Chinese villagers had never before had proper access.

Derek left Malaya in 1953 and eventually returned to England where he met and married June. By the mid-1950s the Emergency was all but over. In 1957 Malaya was granted its independence. Unlike many of the other former colonies, the British retained a heavy economic interest in Malaya, and some argue that it wasn't until much later than 1957 that Malaya truly won its freedom from colonial rule. Yet the most troublesome legacy of the British in Malaysia is an issue of ethnicity. Jenny met the former Prime Minister of Malaysia, Dr Mahathir

Jenny with her mother and sister, at her christening, 1961.

Mohammad, who explained to her that native Malays see themselves as 'sons of the soil', i.e. the rightful owners of the land. He believes that the racial tensions that exist in Malaysia today are a direct result of the British importation of foreign, particularly Chinese, labour during the ninetenth century.

In 1959 Derek was once again stationed in Malaya, to work on intelligence needed to rid the country of the last pockets of communist activity. Not long after this Jenny was born in Kinrara Military Hospital. The family remained in Malaya until 1962, when they left for Berlin. Jenny's final visit was to the house they lived in on Ampang Road, Kuala Lumpur. She was shocked and upset to find it in a very dilapidated state. Jenny's journey enlightened her to a part of her parents' life she was previously unaware of and to the culture she was born into. But reminders of Britain can be seen all over Malaysia, from driving on the left to the plug sockets, and the comfort she found from these things ultimately reaffirmed a sense of British identity that Jenny never knew she had.

CHAPTER FIVE

BEARING UP, BEARING DOWN

Apart from anything else, the imperial map of the world had changed radically.

To deal with it, the League of Nations was convened – an international body committed to world peace and arbitration when discord arose – the forebear of the United Nations, founded after the Second World War. Among the League's responsibilities was the administration of countries that were formerly colonies or dependencies of the defeated powers. These were passed under the control of Allied powers as mandates. The process is complex and variable, but in essence the mandates differed from protectorates or colonies in that those controlling them were ultimately answerable to the League. The country holding the mandate was not allowed to fortify or raise an army within the mandated territory, for example. But in practice these territories were subsumed within the rest of those controlled by the mandate holder.

There was no longer a Russian empire. The Tsar was gone. Instead, there was a new and unfamiliar kind of government and a new and unfamiliar kind of political doctrine in place where he had ruled his vast domain. But it was still a vast domain, and although it was not an immediate threat, still emerging from the egg, as it were, it was a country to watch. The Union of Soviet Socialist Republics, with its vast resources of oil and its enormous farmlands, would modernize quickly and establish Russia as a major player again in next to no time.

There was no longer a German empire either – that country forfeited its holdings in Africa after losing the war. German South-West Africa nominally became a British mandate, but it was taken over by South Africa (by a political sleight of hand) and remained under her control until it achieved independence as Namibia in 1990. German East Africa was split up. Belgium took what is now Rwanda-Burundi; Portugal got part of the south, which went to Mozambique, and the rest went to Britain – the mainland part of what is now Tanzania. Kamerun in the west became a League of Nations mandate territory and was split between the French (Cameroun) and the British

(Cameroons). Togoland was similarly divided between them. In the southern hemisphere, German New Guinea (Kaiser Wilhelmsland) also fell to Britain, though again, practical control went to Australia.

The defeat of Germany and her allies was also the death blow of the Ottoman Empire. Turkey was allowed to keep her existing frontiers but ceded territories in the Near and Middle East, including Palestine and Iraq, which both became mandates under Britain. The Caliphate was abolished, and Turkey became a secular republic under Kemal Atatürk.

In this way, the British Empire became bigger than ever before. But ironically, the huge cost of fighting the war meant that Britain could barely afford to run it any more. In 1918, victory had been achieved by a massive effort in modernizing the existing armed forces and developing an air force. Unfortunately, after the war there seemed neither money nor stomach for capitalizing on this. The tank, the submarine, the bomber and the fighter would, on the whole, have to wait twenty-odd years until another war called for another forcing of technological development.

Moreover, the war had created not only terrible human losses, but demanded

1st March 1919: Two men wearing and advocating the use of flu masks in Paris during the Spanish flu epidemic which followed World War I. The placard on the left reads 'The Boches are beaten but the flu isn't'.

massive financial sacrifice. In its wake, in 1918–19, a terrible influenza pandemic – the Spanish Flu or La Grippe – struck Europe, killing between 20 and 40 million people, and hitting younger adults hardest. Far more people died in it than had died in the war, and the hardest loss (for brutally practical reasons as well as sentimental ones) was the death of so many more young men. Britain was hard hit, and at the same time was having to cope with an increasingly intrusive and interfering USA (which never joined the League of Nations). In obedience to the USA Britain set aside her alliance with Japan; in obedience to the USA she agreed not to develop Hong Kong; in obedience to the USA she scrapped much of her battle-fleet.

The wartime US president, Woodrow Wilson, paid little attention to military affairs, but did provide the funds and food supplies that made Allied victory in 1918 possible, leaving Europe in general and Britain in particular significantly in the debt – financially, morally and ethically – of the USA, which had long since gained a material advantage through superior industry over the mother country. In the later stages of the war, President Wilson took personal control of negotiations with Germany, especially with the famous 'Fourteen Points' and the Armistice. He went to the Paris Peace Conference in 1919 to create the League of Nations and shape the Treaty of Versailles with a high-handedness and sense of independence that have attended America's status as world leader, though at the same time declining to belong to the League itself (just as the USA today studiously neglects to pay its UN dues). The US finally joined the Allies in 1917, by which time it was already clear that the war was nearing its end.

The Fourteen Points in Wilson's celebrated speech were based on the research of the INQUIRY, a team of 150 advisers led by Colonel Edward M. House, the president's foreign policy adviser, who had researched diligently the topics likely to arise in the anticipated peace conference. Wilson's speech embraced US principles of free trade, open agreements, democracy and self-determination; it was also the only full statement of war aims by any of the Allied combatants of the First World War. In his speech, Wilson also responded to Lenin's 'Decree on Peace' of October 1917, which proposed an immediate withdrawal of Russia from the war, calling for a just and democratic peace that was not compromised by territorial annexations, and led to the Treaty of Brest-Litovsk in March 1918. The exchange effectively established the USA and the newly formed USSR as the main powers in the world and saw the beginning of the squaring up that was to lead, despite temporary and always uneasy alliances between 'West' and 'East' to the Cold War. For Britain

OPPOSITE:
The signing of the Treaty of Versailles in 1919, which finally marked the end of the First World War. Original Artwork: Painting by Sir William Orpen.

as a world power, the writing was already on the wall.

The Fourteen Points projected by Woodrow Wilson were as follows (it will quickly be seen that, principled as they were, they also went a long way to castrate the economic and military power of the British Empire):

1. Open covenants of peace, openly arrived at, after which there shall be no private international understandings of any kind but diplomacy shall proceed always frankly and in the public view.

2. Absolute freedom of navigation upon the seas, outside territorial waters, alike in peace and in war, except as the seas may be closed in whole or in part by international action for the enforcement of international covenants.

3. The removal, so far as possible, of all economic barriers and the establishment of equality of trade conditions among all the nations consenting to the peace and associating themselves for its maintenance.

4. Adequate guarantees given and taken that national armaments will be reduced to the lowest point consistent with domestic safety. This also said that this safety would be kept in place for years to come.

5. A free, open-minded, and absolutely impartial adjustment of all colonial claims, based upon a strict observance of the principle that in determining all such questions of sovereignty the interests of the populations concerned must have equal weight with the equitable claims of the government whose title is to be determined.

6. The evacuation of all Russian territory and such a settlement of all questions affecting Russia as will secure the best and freest co-operation of the other nations of the world in obtaining for her an unhampered and unembarrassed opportunity for the independent determination of her own political development and national policy and assure her of a sincere welcome into the society of free nations under institutions of her own choosing; and, more than a welcome, assistance also of every kind that she may need and may herself desire. The treatment accorded Russia by her sister nations in the months to come will be the acid test of their good will, of their compre-

hension of her needs as distinguished from their own interests, and of their intelligent and unselfish sympathy.

7. Belgium, the whole world will agree, must be evacuated and restored, without any attempt to limit the sovereignty which she enjoys in common with all other free nations. No other single act will serve as this will serve to restore confidence among the nations in the laws which they have themselves set and determined for the government of their relations with one another. Without this healing act the whole structure and validity of international law is forever impaired.

8. All French territory should be freed and the invaded portions restored, and the wrong done to France by Prussia in 1871 in the matter of Alsace-Lorraine, which has unsettled the peace of the world for nearly fifty years, should be righted, in order that peace may once more be made secure in the interest of all.

9. A re-adjustment of the frontiers of Italy should be effected along clearly recognizable lines of nationality.

10. The people of Austria-Hungary, whose place among the nations we wish to see safeguarded and assured, should be accorded the freest opportunity to autonomous development.

11. Romania, Serbia, and Montenegro should be evacuated; occupied territories restored; Serbia accorded free and secure access to the sea; and the relations of the several Balkan states to one another determined by friendly counsel along historically established lines of allegiance and nationality; and international guarantees of the political and economic independence and territorial integrity of the several Balkan states should be entered into.

12. The Turkish portion of the present Ottoman Empire should be assured a secure sovereignty, but the other nationalities which are now under Turkish rule should be assured an undoubted security of life and an absolutely unmolested opportunity of autonomous development, and the Dardanelles should be permanently opened as a free passage to the ships and commerce of all nations under international guarantees.

THE ARMISTICE WENT A LONG WAY TO CASTRATE THE ECONOMIC AND MILITARY POWER OF THE BRITISH EMPIRE.

13. An independent Polish state should be erected which should include the territories inhabited by indisputably Polish populations, which should be assured a free and secure access to the sea, and whose political and economic independence and territorial integrity should be guaranteed by international covenant.

14. A general association of nations must be formed under specific covenants for the purpose of affording mutual guarantees of political independence and territorial integrity to great and small states alike.

The League's goals included the usual sops: the Cerberus of disarmament, preventing war through collective security, settling disputes between countries through negotiation diplomacy and improving global welfare. But the League lacked an armed force of its own and depended on the Great Powers to enforce its resolutions, keep to economic sanctions which the League ordered, or provide an army, when needed, for the League to use. However, they were often very reluctant to do so. Mussolini stated with acuity that 'the League is very well when sparrows shout, but no good at all when eagles fall out'.

After a number of notable successes and some early failures in the 1920s, the League ultimately proved incapable of preventing aggression by the Axis Powers in the 1930s. The onset of the Second World War suggested that the League had failed in its primary purpose – ironically to avoid any future world war. The United Nations replaced it after the end of that war with the same ultimate aim, in which it has so far succeeded, though effectively its teeth are no sharper than the League's were.

The Treaty of Versailles in 1919 formally ended the Great War, after six months of negotiations. Although there were many provisions in the final treaty, one of the more important and recognized provisions required Germany to accept full responsibility for causing the war and, under the terms of Articles 231–48, make reparations to certain countries that had formed the Allies. This it never fully did, and tensions remained throughout the two decades of uneasy peace, which were also an economic switchback for the whole world.

The post-war period saw the dominions drawing further away. Britain had signed the declaration of war on their behalf, but they signed the peace treaty at Versailles for themselves. Equally tired of war, and shocked by the grim harvest it had reaped, they did not respond immediately when, in 1922, Westminster took their aid for granted when British (and French) troops stationed at Çanakkale (Chanak) in south-western Turkey to guard the neutral zone of the Dardanelles found themselves threatened by Atatürk's nationalist forces.

The poor handling of the situation indirectly led to the downfall of Liberal Prime Minister David Lloyd George. The British Cabinet met on 15 September 1922 and decided that the British forces should maintain their positions. On the following day, in the absence of the Foreign Secretary, Lord Curzon, a number of Cabinet ministers issued a communiqué threatening Turkey with war on behalf of Britain *and its dominions*. Three days later, on his return, Curzon pointed out that such a move would upset the pro-Turkish Prime Minister of France, Raymond Poincaré. Curzon promptly left for Paris to smooth things over. Poincaré, however, had already ordered the withdrawal of the French detachment at Chanak. Curzon reached Paris on 20 September, and after a series of volatile meetings with Poincaré, reached an agreement to negotiate an armistice with the Turks.

The British public was alarmed by the Chanak episode and the possibility of going to war so soon after the dearly bought victory of the Great War; and public opinion had taken note through the press that Lloyd George had not consulted the dominion prime ministers anything like properly. When the Great War had broken out, Canada especially did not automatically consider itself involved. Now, the Canadian premier, William King, insisted that his parliament should debate whether or not to join the hostilities. By the time the issue had been discussed, the confrontation in Turkey was over. But King had made his point: his parliament would henceforward decide the role that Canada would play in external affairs, and it was not up to Britain to presume the automatic acquiescence of its former colonies.

Lloyd George's rashness was a major factor in the calling of a meeting on 19 October 1922, when Conservative MPs decided that they would leave the coalition and fight the next general election as a single, united party (this was the original 1922 Committee). The decision spelt the end for Lloyd George: the Conservative Party made up the vast majority of the 1918–22 post-war Coalition government. Lloyd George also lost the support of Curzon, who considered that the Prime Minister had simply gone behind his not uninfluential and very experienced back.

Following the Chanak incident, in 1926, and following the League of Nations meeting at Geneva in the same year, British statesman and former premier Arthur Balfour led a conference for the dominions in London to settle the question of status once and for all, which resulted in the Balfour Declaration of 1926.

THE BRITISH PUBLIC WAS ALARMED BY THE POSSIBILITY OF GOING TO WAR SO SOON AFTER THE DEARLY BOUGHT VICTORY OF THE GREAT WAR.

NURSE BRITANNIA : " Now, children, don't cut yourselves off. Remember the high cost of separate living."

Cartoon by London-based New Zealander David Low showing Britannia (prime minister Stanley Baldwin) trying to cope with a fractious and fragmenting white empire. 1926.

The Imperial Conference met in London immediately after the autumn General Assembly of the League of Nations. The Balfour Committee held 'long and intricate' discussions over fifteen meetings from October to November 1926. The Committee rejected the idea of a written constitution for the British Empire, preferring the British model of implicit rather than explicit constitutional guidelines and guarantees. Balfour opened the first meeting of the Committee by stating that the 1914–18 war had left the Empire 'unexplained and undefined', a situation complicated by the role of the Dominions 'in framing and signing the Treaty'.

In the report Balfour wrote that the Dominions' 'tendency towards equality of status was both right and inevitable' and that geographic and historic differences meant that this could not be achieved by a federation of nations within the Empire, but had to be sought 'by the way of autonomy'. Balfour declared that the British Empire depended

essentially, if not formally, on positive ideals. Free institutions are its lifeblood. Free co-operation is its instrument. Peace, security and progress are to be among its objects... And though every Dominion is now, and must always remain, the sole judge of the nature and extent of its co-operation, no common cause will, in our opinion, be thereby imperiled. Equality of status, so far as Britain and the Dominions are concerned, is thus the root principle governing our Inter-Imperial Relations.

Four years later, following a conference in London, a formal declaration was issued to the effect that Great Britain and her dominions should be considered 'autonomous countries within the British Empire, equal in status, in no way subordinate one to another... and freely associated as members of the British Commonwealth'. This declaration was ratified by the Statute of Westminster in 1931. The British monarch was still acknowledged to be the overall head of state, but the executive power of British governors general was reduced and the office was gradually replaced by that of high commissioner, the functions of which were effectively ambassadorial. The Empire was already shading into the rather more nebulous 'Commonwealth', but the 'black colonies' would have to wait a good while longer for their independence.

On top of this there was unrest in Egypt, another country over which Britain maintained unfair and barely legal control in her own strategic interests, and there were anti-white riots in the Caribbean. In Palestine and Iraq trouble was already brewing. The USSR was pouring out anti-colonial propaganda, and the Comintern offered support to any revolutionary independence movement which sought it. The growing importance of oil meant that the West looked anxiously at the problem of Russian encroachment in the Near and Middle East.

The British and the French had divided the Middle East between them after signing a secret treaty during the war. In Iraq, the British established a puppet ruler, Faisal, and managed the country through him until 1932, when Iraq gained independence again at Faisal's own request, though the British retained bases there, and took over again in 1941 in order to secure their oil supplies. The occupation ended in 1947, when the Hashemite dynasty was restored. Palestine was controlled by the British from the end of the war until the establishment of the independent state of Israel in 1948, after one of the bloodiest and most mismanaged handovers of all those which characterized the end of Empire. Much of the trouble arose from a short statement from the British Foreign Minister Arthur Balfour to the powerful Jewish banker Lord Rothschild in 1917. Known as the Balfour Declaration of 1917, what it proposed might well have seemed ideal on paper, but in practice, and in view of

THE GROWING IMPORTANCE OF OIL MEANT THAT THE WEST LOOKED ANXIOUSLY AT THE PROBLEM OF RUSSIAN ENCROACHMENT IN THE NEAR AND MIDDLE EAST.

the Jewish genocide that took place between 1941 and 1945, proved impossible to resolve. This is what it said:

Foreign Office
November 2nd, 1917

Dear Lord Rothschild,
I have much pleasure in conveying to you, on behalf of His Majesty's Government, the following declaration of sympathy with Jewish Zionist aspirations which has been submitted to, and approved by, the Cabinet.

'His Majesty's Government views with favour the establishment in Palestine of a national home for the Jewish people, and will use their best endeavours to facilitate the achievement of this object, it being clearly understood that nothing shall be done which may prejudice the civil and religious rights of existing non-Jewish communities in Palestine, or the rights and political status enjoyed by Jews in any other country.'

I should be grateful if you would bring this declaration to the knowledge of the Zionist Federation.

Yours sincerely
[signed Arthur James Balfour]

Britain was still trying to be grandiose, and possibly altruistic, but it had no real business to indulge in such meddling. There was Arab unrest at the relatively small Jewish presence in Palestine by the early 1920s, but nobody paid it much heed; and Jewish lobbies in the Diaspora were influential and persuasive. Ironically, though, the declaration served an immediate political purpose: that of pre-empting German efforts to woo the Zionists to their side. The Jewish position was not helped by the appearance in 1919 of *The Protocols of the Elders of Zion*, which purported to be a collection of documents proving the existence of a worldwide Jewish conspiracy for world domination but was, in fact, a concoction by anti-Semitic elements of the White Russian secret service. The *Protocols* was quickly shown up for what it was, but people believe what they want to believe, and in the wrong hands – Hitler's, for example – it proved a useful and effective tool.

Meanwhile, the situation in Palestine remained tense, with frequent clashes between Jews and Arabs. In 1933 there were about 400,000 Arabs in Palestine and 200,000 Jews. Islam, in contrast to Christianity, had always taken a tolerant attitude to Judaism, but the British ordered a commission of inquiry in the mid-1930s, which concluded that one day the two groups should be separated and accorded their own territories within Palestine. In 1948, that goal was achieved, though far from as amicably as the British had hoped and by then, against their better judgement.

In India, which Britain correctly still saw as the most important possession of their remaining formal Empire, she seemed to have a freer hand. But there was enormous fear of the Russians, reinforced by British secret service discoveries that during the Third Afghan War of 1919 the Afghanis had been seeking support from Russian planes and pilots. Two years later, Afghanis were training as pilots in Russia (as were the disarmed Germans, secretly).

Britain had always succeeded in India by a policy of divide and rule, which had been relatively easy when communications were slow and races, religions, sects and languages were so heterogeneous. But the British themselves had given India better communications, Western education (which was unifying) and a unifying language, or at least a lingua franca. By the late nineteenth century such developments were beginning have an effect with the emergence of an independence movement. In 1885 the Indian National Congress was formed in

For King and Country. Lt. General Sir Pratap Singh photographed by Ernest Brooks, with his son (to his left) and the Rajah of Ratlam, at Sir Douglas Haig's château at Montreuil, June 1916.

Mohandas Gandhi, photographed in 1946.

Bombay as a liberal debating society and ginger group for speeding up an increase in the numbers of Indians working for the country's civil service. Most of its members were moderate and Western influenced, and believed that the British would listen to rational argument. (Muslims – a significant minority in the population – were not well represented in the Congress, and in 1906 the Muslim League was founded to promote their interests within the community.)

There seemed little advantage to India in British rule. Britain had ten times as many doctors as India, pro rata, and only later instituted proper medical training schemes when it suited her own political purposes. Life expectancy was twenty-three years. Poverty was rife and showed no sign of going away. Many were asking: what had the Raj actually done for them in those areas?

The First World War provided a significant forward thrust to the nationalist movement, as thousands of Indian troops were drafted (without consultation) to fight in Europe and the Near East in a war that was not their own, though most did so sincerely believing in the democratic values for which they had taken up arms. At the end of the war, realizing that some gesture must be made to India in acknowledgement of its indispensable contribution, Westminster passed a Government of India Act (1919), which gave Indians more power in local – i.e., provincial – government than they had had. At the same time the Secretary of State for India, Edwin Montagu, stated that Britain aimed in the long term at the introduction of what he called 'responsible' Indian self-government. Crucially, though, there was a rider: it was to be self-government within the Empire. Neither Act nor statement satisfied the Indians, who, Muslims and Hindus alike, were by now fully committed to the idea of absolute independence from Britain and the Empire.

Hugely influential in the independence movement, from the time of his return to India from Africa in 1915 right up to his assassination (ironically at the hands of a Hindu extremist) in 1948, was Mohandas Gandhi, best known by his honorific, 'Mahatma' ('Great Soul').

A lawyer by training (he studied in London), Gandhi first cut his teeth on the political stage in South Africa, where, practising as a barrister, he led the Indian community there in its struggle against racial discrimination. Always an astute politician and publicist, he developed a canny persona as a simple, unworldly man, which was emphasized by his later adoption of the simplest peasant dress and his very public asceticism. He was able, between the wars especially, to act as a unifying force to the enormously diverse peoples of the subcontinent The image he cultivated carried the advantage of appealing to the country's vast rural population also, thus expanding the cause of nationalism beyond the ranks of urban intellectuals and creating a mass movement which he skilfully manipulated. He was a master publicist and an astute politician, and he made as much use of the newly emerging media as he could to further his cause.

When at the end of the First World War there seemed to be no move towards paving the way to independence, Gandhi and his followers embarked on a programme of *satyagraha* ('grasping the truth'), a form of non-violent protest which he had developed in his South African campaigns. *Satyagraha* was a systematic programme of non-cooperation with the authorities, of withdrawal of labour, and of boycotting foreign products, the campaign was designed to bring the administration and general functioning of the country to a halt. Arising from *satyagraha* came *hartal*, or strike action, which could mean

⊠
AN ASTUTE POLITICIAN AND PUBLICIST, GANDHI DEVELOPED A CANNY PERSONA AS A SIMPLE, UNWORLDLY MAN.

the closing of shops, courts, civic offices or schools for a short period as an expression of civil disobedience.

For a while it was successful, but to succeed it would have taken a very long time and even Gandhi could not inspire the collective will for long enough to achieve his ends by this means. Though the desire for independence did not falter, different ideas about how to get it sprang up, and some resorted to violence. The worried British overreacted and in 1919 introduced the Rowlatt Act, named after the Fettes-educated lawyer who drew it up. This series of discriminatory measures gave the British military and police pretty much a free hand to deal with whatever they might construe as rebellious behaviour, and authorized the imprisonment without trial of anyone suspected of terrorism. Politically, this intemperate reaction was a gift. *Satyagraha* neatly called into question the traditional British assumption that they ran India by common consent. Gandhi called for a nationwide *hartal* on 6 April to protest against the Rowlatt Act.

The *hartal* broke down in many places into a series of violent anti-British riots. Some of the most aggressive outbursts took place in the Punjab, where the governor was, most unfortunately, a tough and implacable old-school Empire administrator. He decided to unleash the dogs, in the person of the equally peppery Brigadier-General Reginald Dyer, CB, an irritable man in his mid-fifties whose nature was not helped by the constant pain of old war wounds. Dyer was given orders to establish martial law and restore the peace in Amritsar, the epicentre of the protests.

No doubt his boss intended to make an example of Amritsar, and Dyer certainly obliged. There was already great tension in the town. On 10 April a missionary called Marcella Sherwood was shoved off her bicycle in a side street and beaten up by louts, who ran away when other Indians came to her aid. This incident alone infuriated Dyer. When calls for a ban on public meetings were ignored, the Brigadier-General, with two armoured cars mounted with machine guns and a detachment of about 100 troops from Gurkha, Pathan and Baluchi detachments (who had no qualms about shooting plainsmen), moved on a large crowd which had gathered on 13 April in the Jallianwalah Bagh, and ordered his men to fire into it. The Jallianwalah Bagh was a large walled enclosure, accessible by five narrow gateways, one of which was covered by the armoured cars (Dyer apparently later regretted that he had not been able to use them as the gates were too narrow to admit them). When the soldiers opened fire, the crowd, which included large numbers of women and children, stampeded for the exits, where Dyer ordered his men to direct their fire. After ten minutes they ceased, leaving 379 dead and over 1,000 wounded. Afterwards, Dyer had suspected ringleaders publicly flogged – deliberately selecting members of the higher castes for maximum humiliation. Any Indian caught in the street where Miss Sherwood had been beaten up was forced to crawl along it on his hands and knees. No nod was made in recognition of her rescuers.

The massacre at Amritsar was a pivotal point in the Indian fight for independence. From now on they knew what they were up against, for the mask had slipped for ever. As a military and diplomatic faux pas it could not have been worse, for it galvanized the freedom movement in the Punjab, intensified anti-British sentiments, unified nationalists within Congress and the League even more intensely, and smoothed the way for Gandhi's non-cooperation movement. Gandhi called off the *hartal*, but capitalized indirectly on events. It also led to the rise of many revolutionaries. Among them was Lala Rajpat Rai, an author and politician who led the demonstrations in protest at the massacre. Rai was later, in 1928, to lead protests again the commission convened under Sir John Simon to investigate the political situation in India, but which Indian politicians boycotted as it did not have a single Indian member. Rai's protest was peaceful, but it was broken up with extreme brutality by the British police and Rai was beaten to death. The Marxist Bhagat Singh attempted to avenge Rai's death, but shot the wrong policeman. Later, in 1929, arrested for a non-lethal bomb attack on the assembly convened to pass the defence of India Act (drawn up to give more power to the police – it was defeated by one vote), he was sentenced to life imprisonment, but his earlier murder of the policeman was discovered and Singh was hanged for it in 1931, immediately achieving martyrdom status. Across the political divide, another aggressive nationalist affected by the massacre was Subhas Chandra Bose, later leader of the Axis-allied Indian National Army in the Second World War.

Intellectuals and artists were also appalled into protest. The internationally famous poet and Nobel laureate Rabindranath Tagore returned his knighthood to George V, who privately regretted Dyer's action and knew what permanent damage it had done to the British image in India, though the British reaction for some time remained to answer violence with violence.

On the British side, there was an inquiry and Dyer was removed, though he had many sympathizers in Britain and the conservative *Morning Post* set up a

THE BRITISH REACTION FOR SOME TIME REMAINED TO ANSWER VIOLENCE WITH VIOLENCE.

Future leaders of partitioned India:
ABOVE:
Mohamed Ali Jinnah – Pakistan – Muslim.
ABOVE RIGHT:
Jawaharlal Nehru – India – Hindu.
Both were English-trained lawyers.

fund for him which quickly yielded a huge £26,000. The great and the good of the time quickly lined up for and against (there had been a similar demonstration sixty years earlier, when Governor Edward Eyre of Jamaica bloodily put down a rebellion there; his British supporters included Tennyson and Dickens). Dyer, the 'Butcher of Amritsar', though he was condemned by Churchill, found support from Kipling.

Dyer, an Anglo-Indian to his bootstraps and, as a plain soldier, a brave and loyal officer, was haunted by his deed to the end of his days. After his retirement, he lived quietly in the English countryside, and when death approached in 1927, he said to his daughter-in-law: 'I don't want to get better... I only want to die... and know of my Maker whether I did right or wrong.'

In 1929, a decade after the Government of India Act, Congress demanded unconditional and immediate independence of the British. Gandhi rallied to the cause, and in defiance of the British government's tax on salt, and its prohibition of salt manufacture, he embarked on his famous salt march – 250 miles across India to the sea at Dandi, where he duly proceeded to extract salt for himself. This was the work of a publicist of genius. It attracted worldwide press attention and once again galvanized the Indian people, though the three-year campaign of civil disobedience which followed it once again splintered before it could achieve its ultimate aim of forcing the British to let go.

Gandhi remained a charismatic and influential figure throughout the rest of his life, turning his attention to social issues within the Indian and Muslim communities and subjecting himself to two long fasts – one of which, lasting three weeks, very nearly killed him – in protest at injustices in the legal system and at discrimination within the Hindu caste system against the 'untouchables'. However, executive political power was falling increasingly into the hands of two younger, truly professional politicians – Jawaharlal Nehru, born in 1889, a Harrow- and Cambridge-educated scientist who later read law before returning home, and Mohammad Ali Jinnah, born in 1876, another London-trained barrister. Nehru, who joined the Congress in 1918, was first imprisoned for political sedition in 1921 and spent eighteen of the next twenty one years in gaol, though he was always prominent in the nationalist movement and was several times president of the Congress. His homologue, Jinnah, led the Muslim League from 1916. It would be their hands that would shape Indian independence during and after the Second World War.

Dyer's murderous assault was one of the last acts of arrogant brutality performed in the name of the British Empire. At home, people were more concerned with putting their own house back in order after the war, and coping with austerity.

By 1925 the British coal-mining industry was in crisis, which had a knock-on effect on other sectors of industry. The First World War and the heavy domestic use of coal during it meant that mines were depleted; at the same time, Britain had exported less coal between 1914 and 1918 than it normally did in peacetime. Other countries, notably Poland, the USA, and, ironically, Germany, quickly filled the demand left by this gap. In addition to this, productivity in general was at a low ebb. Output per man had fallen to 199 tons in 1920–4, from 247 tons in the four years before the war, and a peak of 310 tons in the early 1880s. In 1925, Winston Churchill reintroduced the gold standard, which had the effect of strengthening the pound, making export trade more difficult, raising interest rates, and squeezing all manner of businesses.

Most notoriously of all, private mine owners wanted to maintain their profits and to do so proposed paying their men less, for more time. This led to a confrontation which was dispelled by the government under Stanley Baldwin, which offered to provide a nine-month-long subsidy to protect the miners'

IMPERIAL WELCOME

Another cartoon by David Low, this time from 1943 and featuring his famous empire-throwback character, Colonel Blimp. The story here is self-explanatory.

wages while a Royal Commission investigated the industry's problems. Initially this seemed like a victory for the workers, but in fact the subsidy bought time for the mine owners to prepare their ground. The Commission delivered its report in March 1926, acknowledging that certain improvements should be made in the industry but crucially rejecting any idea of nationalization. The report also recommended that the government subsidy should be withdrawn and that the miners' wages should be reduced to save the industry's profitability – a real blow in the face for the workers.

The mine owners duly published new terms of employment, which included an extension of the seven-hour working day and a reduction in wages, which were to be cut by between 10 per cent and 25 per cent. The mine owners declared that if the miners did not accept the new terms then from the first day of May they would be locked out of the pits.

Under the leadership of Arthur Cook, the miners' union rejected the new terms, adopting the slogan, 'not a penny off the pay, not a minute on the day'. They went on strike early in May and asked the TUC for previously promised support from other industries. Eventually 2 million people downed tools, and

Baldwin was obliged to use troops and special constables to maintain essential services, taking a monopoly control of information services, including the BBC. But after only nine days the TUC ended the general strike, leaving the disappointed miners to carry on alone until November, without succeeding in their aims. In 1927, the government introduced a Trades Disputes Act, which made general strikes illegal.

The Depression heralded by the Wall Street Crash of 1929 meant that the 1930s saw little relief in the living and working conditions of ordinary people, and from 1933 the shadow cast over Europe by German Nazism grew ever longer. But in Britain the working classes were finding a voice, and ceasing to be happy to 'know their place'. The First World War had indirectly started a social revolution that would be accelerated after the Second. The Establishment was now satirized and mocked. In 1930, the thirty-nine-year-old political cartoonist (born in New Zealand) David Low created Colonel Blimp, a type of the reactionary colonial Briton, by then an easily recognizable figure of fun – though it would be a long time before he would lose his serious support, which in some cases was sinister. In 1954, the League of Empire Loyalists was founded. This was a group drawn from right-wing Tories and former members of the British Union of Fascists, which campaigned against the dissolution of the Empire. Originally, they were no more than a collection of blimps, but with the passing of time the League associated itself increasingly with attempts to block black

GOOD MORNING! Have you used PEARS' SOAP?

An advertisement for Pear's soap from the 1890s. Pears was one of a number of companies to use the Empire frequently as an inspiration for its publicity campaigns. The theme here is skin-lightening; a lot has changed in a century or so.

and Asian immigration and some of its members were involved with other groups in the establishment of the National Front in 1967.

But it was not easy for non-European foreigners in Britain in the period between the two world wars. Already Africans and Afro-Caribbeans had been maligned in the war. Indians, especially Sikhs, were acknowledged to be brave fighters, but as far as Africans were concerned, the British view was that they were unreliable and even cowardly. How quickly the bravery of the Zulus in their wars against the British only half a century or so earlier seemed to have been forgotten. Certain regiments, the Coldstream Guards for example, were singularly reluctant to recruit black men. The comical black man was a music-hall staple. I can think of at least one public house which as late as the 1970s was called 'The Labour in Vain', its sign depicting a white laundrywoman scrubbing a black child in a bath full of suds. Cartoons in the papers often made fun of burlesque 'Negroes', and some black entertainers of the period, and much earlier, played up to this image.

Part of the propaganda was that white culture was superior; but as the First World War came to an end non-whites increasingly doubted this. Japan, after all, had absorbed much from Europe without surrendering its own culture (though, of course, Japan was not colonized). But the crunch came when educated black people were cut out of white society by their white peers and their white inferiors.

A West Indian cricket team toured England in 1933, the centenary year of the abolition of slavery. It was composed of men who in professional life were teachers, businessmen and accountants, yet this growing educated middle class was disregarded by Britain on the whole, which clung to the past and would not acknowledge that these people were more than well enough equipped to govern themselves. The peoples of the Caribbean supported Britain in both world wars, yet experienced great difficulty after each when they tried to live in the mother country. Between the wars, young black people were debarred from studying at institutions as diverse as St Mary's Hospital and the Royal Academy of Dramatic Art. Liverpool and Cardiff had large black populations derived from seafaring communities, but 1919 saw race riots in both cities. Not all interwar racism can be laid at the door of competition for employment, either. Almost all immigrants were self-sufficient, and India was already becoming a forceful presence in the mother country. There was an Indian Chamber of Commerce by 1927. The Bombay Emporium, the first Asian shop, opened in Tottenham Court Road in 1931. Veeraswamy's restau-

rant had opened in 1926 (though admittedly its founder was an Englishman), and other Indian restaurants soon appeared. And the food, so much more interesting than the average English fare of the day, quickly became popular. And there were Indian lawyers, teachers, and a few doctors as well.

Interracial relationships were at this time seen as complete sexual taboo and such prejudice would be a long time in the dying (and probably is not quite

An aerial view of the British Empire Exhibition at Wembley, London, showing the boating lake and football stadium, 30th June 1924. India's pavilion is seen at the bottom right.

dead yet). As late as 1948, the then Secretary for Commonwealth Relations wanted to ban interracial marriages, and in the same year Seretse Kama, heir to the throne of Bechuanaland, was blocked from his inheritance as a result of his marriage to a white Englishwoman. The couple were not even allowed to live in Bechuanaland, though in 1956 Westminster relented, and they were permitted to return as private citizens. Kama entered politics in 1961, and rose to become prime minister, presiding over his country's independence struggle, and emerging as the first president of an independent Botswana in 1966.

King George V, who reigned from 1910 to his death in 1936, did all he could to keep up the image of the Empire, perhaps seeing in it the only way to maintain Britain's ever-shakier role as a leader in world affairs. During his reign, he also saw the monarchies of Austria, Germany, Greece and Spain fall. He was himself an innovator and gave the first royal Christmas broadcast in 1933. He was personally appalled at Lloyd George's brutal policies in Ireland, and he was sympathetic to the strikers of 1926 – 'Try living on their wages before you judge them,' he said.

He sent his son on a world tour of the key Empire territories, where the future Edward VIII (who abdicated before his coronation) evoked a lot of popular support, and he instigated a British Empire Exhibition at Wembley in north London in 1924–5. Nothing now remains of this grand fête, although until very recently there was one famous surviving building: Wembley Stadium. The exhibition opened to the public on St George's Day. The site covered about 100 hectares, Kipling chose the names of its streets, it cost £11 million and was visited by 27 million people. Most countries of the Empire were represented and their pavilions were resplendent reflections of what it was thought those countries had to offer. In an age when newsreel was just beginning and photography was still the preserve of the few, George V wanted to bring the Empire to his local subjects in an attempt perhaps to rekindle interest in it. But it was also a trade fair.

For all the pomp, it was somehow already out of its time, as many contemporaries perceived. Few took it very seriously, and the trade fair element could be downright dull. P. G. Woodhouse imagined Bertie Wooster's visit:

I mean to say, millions of people, no doubt, are so constituted that they scream with joy and excitement at the spectacle of a stuffed porcupine fish or a glass jar of seeds from Western Australia – but not Bertram... By the time we had tottered out of the Gold Coast village and were looking towards the Palace

⊠
KING GEORGE V DID ALL HE COULD TO KEEP UP THE IMAGE OF THE EMPIRE, TO MAINTAIN BRITAIN'S EVER-SHAKIER ROLE AS A LEADER IN WORLD AFFAIRS.

PREVIOUS PAGE:
A Scottish regiment to the rescue! The Black Watch, or possibly the Argyll and Sutherland Highlanders, in action in the film *Gunga Din*, 1938.

⊠

**THE EMPIRE
EXHIBITION WAS
NOT AN
UNQUALIFIED
SUCCESS – OPEN
FOR TWO YEARS, IT
SUSTAINED A NET
LOSS OF £2
MILLION.**

*of Machinery, everything pointed to my shortly executing a quiet sneak in
the direction of that rather jolly Planters' Bar in the West Indies section.*

Another point of view came from African students in London, who
objected to some of the exhibits showing their countrymen in an idealized
village environment, as if they lacked all sophistication and were to be viewed
rather as 'objects in a raree show'. At the time, there were only about 125
African students in the whole country, but they tended to be the children of
affluent and influential parents, training to take up positions of responsibility
back home. However, they benefited wisely from the good education they got,
formed political clubs and debating societies, and began to become interested
in the question of independence.

All in all, the Empire Exhibition was not an unqualified success. It stayed
open for two years, but sustained a net loss of £2 million.

If, however, the Empire did not sell well as an exhibition, it would soon be
doing much better at the box office. Cinema was in the ascendant. There was
no television yet, and this was the golden age of the still very young movie
industry. Throughout the 1930s and into the 1950s a number of films were
made which used the background of the British Empire. In 1935 alone there
were at least three notable ones: *Lives of the Bengal Lancers* with C. Aubrey
Smith, *Clive of India* with Ronald Colman, and *Sanders of the River* with Paul
Robeson and Leslie Banks. *Sanders of the River* (made, incidentally, by
Hungarian immigrants) attempted to be more than a straightforward adventure story, though it shows in Sanders the type of the benevolent lone British
administrator, supporting Paul Robeson's good local chief Bosambo, who
appreciates the benefits of Empire, and Tony Wane's bad one, Mofolaba, who
prefers to stick to the traditional ways, characterized here by very primitive
animism and tribal warfare. Ultimately, of course, the Empire's candidate tri-
umphs, and the film underpins the validity of British rule. Another attempt to
delve below the surface of Empire was made in 1938 with the film *The Drum*,
starring Sabu, Roger Livesey and Raymond Massey. Here the British
Resident, Captain Carruthers (Livesey), foils the conspiracy of the devious
Prince Ghul (Massey) to declare a jihad on the Raj with the help of the
Russians. Sabu is the good prince who sides with the paternalistic empire,
embodied in Livesey's reassuring character.

There were some Hollywood howlers, too: *Storm over India* (1939) sees
Kabul as the capital of Burma; and *Gunga Din* with Cary Grant, and Sam Jaffe
in the title role, is extremely loosely based on Kipling's poem and deals with a

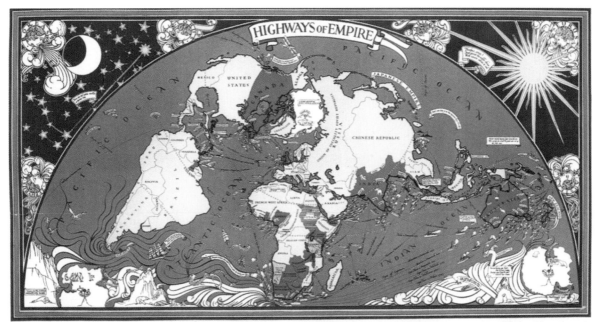

British effort to stamp out a revival of *thagi*. *The Four Feathers* re-enacts the Battle of Omdurman, and *Rhodes of Africa* (Walter Huston in the title role; Oskar Homolka as Kruger!) is a biopic stablemate of *Clive*. A film telling the story of the relief of Lucknow was blocked by the Secretary of State for India in 1938 on the grounds that it might antagonize the Indians, whose help we were about to depend on in war once again.

After the Second World War there was still a trickle of such films. Errol Flynn appeared in an awkward adaptation of Kipling's *Kim* in 1951, while 1959 saw the rather more interesting *North-West Frontier*, which while still a ripping yarn also does have Indians playing the Indian characters. More recently there have been more Kipling adaptations, for example *The Man Who Would Be King*, let down by stolid performances from its stars, and more profound reflections in *Heat and Dust*, the adaptation of Forster's *A Passage to India*, the biopic *Gandhi* and, above all, Satyajit Ray's *The Chess Players*. No doubt the Raj will continue to be an inspiration for some time to come, though as time passes and it slips further and further back into history, the appeal will be less immediate.

ADRIAN LESTER

JAMAICA

Adrian Lester has an award-winning career on TV, stage and screen. Trained at the prestigious drama school RADA, he first achieved fame as the campaign manager 'Henry Burton', in Mike Nichols's film *Primary Colours* starring alongside John Travolta and Emma Thompson.

His critically acclaimed theatre career has included Henry V at the National Theatre, directed by Nicholas Hytner. Perhaps he is best known for his starring role as the elusive conman Mickey Stone in the BBC TV series *Hustle*. Adrian is soon to star in several more Hollywood movies including *Spiderman 3* and *Case 39* alongside Renée Zellwegger.

Adrian was born and brought up in Birmingham. His mother, Monica, came to Britain from the British colony of Jamaica in 1960 when she was just fourteen. Adrian took his West Indian roots for granted as he was growing up but now that his own children are asking questions, he wanted to find out more about why his grandparents left Jamaica for a new life in Britain and how his story fits in with that of the British Empire as a whole.

Growing up in the 1970s, Adrian was aware of the differences between him and his school friends. Living with his mother and grandfather James Lester the voices he heard at home were Jamaican patois, not Brummie. He says as a child he remembers feeling like someone on the outside looking in. 'Everything that represented anything to do with my heritage was never shown on television. We didn't read about it in books and it was never taught in any classroom I went into. There was a lack of knowledge and awareness of everything that made me different.'

Adrian's journey began at his mum's house in Birmingham. Poring over family photo albums, Monica explained how she arrived aged just fourteen, wearing a smart, pale blue suit. Her father, James Lester, had come over six years earlier to establish a life in England. In the 1930s following the great depression, Jamaica's economy, based on the export of crops, crashed. James was working as a tailor but work was scarce and like many other Jamaican men he had been forced to look to America for work. He often went over to the US for short periods to earn extra money for the family. But an act passed by the American government in 1952 imposed tighter immigration controls on West Indians who wanted to come to the US to find work. At the same time, Britain was experiencing a mass labour shortage, and began to advertise for workers to come and fill these gaps from all over the Commonwealth and remaining British Empire. James decided to take a gamble on the mother country.

Adrian aged 3–3½, 1972–3.

Monica, Adrian, Mark
Lester (cousin) and brother
Scott Harvey, 1972–3.

JAMES DECIDED TO TAKE A GAMBLE ON THE MOTHER COUNTRY. ADRIAN'S GRANDFATHER HELD THE KEY TO FAMILY HISTORY.

Monica told Adrian that his grandfather held the key to the family history. James, now eighty-nine and no longer living in Birmingham, had fulfilled his wish to return home to Jamaica nearly twenty years ago. Aware of James's old age and frail condition, Adrian was conscious that time was of the essence and he decided to return to Jamaica to find out all he could from his grandfather. Adrian had only been to the island once before and this time he was looking forward to hearing his grandfather's stories and uncovering the family history.

When Adrian arrived at his grandfather's house, he was shocked to find that James was seriously ill and had to be rushed to hospital. A complication with an operation he had had a few years before meant that he had suffered internal bleeding. After settling James in hospital, Adrian had no choice but to

Adrian's grandparents,
James and Mabel, on their
wedding day, August 1944.

continue his journey alone. He headed for the rural parish of St Mary, in the
north-east of the island, where James was born. It's far off the tourist trail,
remote compared to the bright lights of Montego Bay, but Adrian immediately felt at home in this rural and lush environment.

In 1944 James Lester married Mabel Frazer and the couple moved to the
village of Forty-One. Monica, Adrian's mother, was born here in 1946. Their
house still stands, although it has been largely rebuilt. Seeing the house where
his mother spent her childhood, Adrian was struck by how basic it is and how
hard life must have been. He began to understand why James made the decision to move his entire family to a country that was propagated as 'the land of
opportunity'. It also gave him an insight into the origins of the pragmatic and
hard-working attitude that has always followed him as a second generation
Jamaican. Monica called it 'a kind of Jamaican stiff upper lip' and says it is how
most West Indians endured the racist attitudes they encountered when they
arrived in Britain.

ADRIAN LESTER
JAMAICA

In 1655 Britain had seized Jamaica from the Spanish and for centuries sugar was cultivated by slave labour brought over from Africa. Today most Jamaicans are descended from those slaves who were once traded as a commodity until their emancipation in 1834. Adrian acknowledges that he wouldn't be where he is without slavery, and has always associated the Empire and indeed his own heritage with slavery. But he wanted to know more about how being part of the Empire impacted directly on his mother's life. He went to visit May River Primary School, which his mother attended from the age of six. As a child the syllabus Monica followed was largely British. Adrian met Miss Bendor, the Principal of May River, to talk to her about what she remembered of her education when the British ruled Jamaica. The books she learned from were schoolbooks from England and they didn't have local stories as they do today. Children didn't learn about Jamaican history. Very little was taught about sugar and slavery, the very foundations of the Empire in the West Indies. Miss Bendor remembers learning archetypal British songs such as 'London Bridge is Falling Down', 'London's Burning', and 'Rule Britannia'. She didn't know what the songs meant as a child. Neither she nor her classmates had ever seen London Bridge.

Adrian went to the National Archives in Spanish Town to find out more about the thousands of Jamaicans like his grandfather who were making the journey to Britain. He discovered a leaflet issued by the colonial authorities called 'Bound for England…Some Hints for You!' It contained useful nuggets of advice such as 'Be sure to take warm clothes with you' and 'If you are a skilled workman do not sell your tools. Take them with you.' The leaflet also had advice for Jamaican women planning the trip. 'If you are a young girl, ask an older, trusted friend to meet you. If you are expecting a baby and your mate is in England be sure that he wants you to come before you go. Be sure you know his address. Be sure that he will meet you. Otherwise you should not go.'

As each ship docked, representatives of the Colonial Office in Britain met the new arrivals. Adrian went to meet Raphael Carl Rattray who as a young law student in 1950s London was drafted into the West Indies Welfare Division to help the immigrants find their feet. Despite the exhortations to take warm clothes, not all the Jamaicans were prepared. Few of them knew what they were going to find. When he went to meet the boats Raphael took overcoats and other clothing for the shivering new arrivals. He describes how they would wear terry cloth towels on their head and bathrobes to keep warm. Raphael and the Colonial Office would help them find jobs and places to live.

Despite many being skilled workers like James, most were sent to the labour exchange where they were deemed only fit for unskilled jobs. Many ended up in industrial centres like Birmingham where jobs in factories were plentiful.

After a week finding out about his grandfather in Jamaica it was time for Adrian to return home. Sadly James was still in hospital but the people and places he had seen had had a profound impact. He now understood why his grandparents decided to risk everything on a new life in Britain. But what lay ahead of them there? What sort of welcome did they receive?

By the time James travelled to Britain in 1954, thousands of islanders had already made the same journey since the *Empire Windrush* first docked in 1948. A huge labour force was needed to rebuild post-war Britain and, as colonial subjects and with British passports, Jamaicans were entitled to work and settle there. Uncertain of what he might find, James left his wife, Mabel, and three small children behind. After a brief spell in London James arrived in Birmingham after hearing about the job opportunities there from fellow Jamaicans. A year later Mabel joined him and for the next five years they struggled to make a new life, sending money back each month to their children who were still in Jamaica, being cared for by their grandparents. In September 1960, nearly six years since she'd last seen her father, Adrian's mother, Monica, arrived in Britain. Back home in England, Adrian wanted to explore her journey.

Adrian went with Monica to visit the house in Edgbaston that she lived in when she arrived aged fourteen. Many immigrants found it difficult to find accommodation. The signs in the bed and breakfast windows that said 'no dogs, no Irish, no coloureds' have become symbols of the colour bar that existed in Birmingham in the 1950s and 1960s. Many West Indians clubbed together to buy property and lived in very poor conditions. Adrian's grandfather bought a house with a fellow Jamaican and rented out rooms to cover the costs and help out other immigrants. There were often as many as a dozen people living in the house. For Monica England brought its own culture shocks. She was unused to spending so much time inside and sharing a home with so many other people.

By this time Birmingham had one of the largest West Indian communities in Britain. At Handsworth New Road Girls School Monica was only one of six black pupils in a school of over 200. Adrian met Maxine Taylor, a prefect at the school when Monica arrived. She remembers feeling awestruck by these girls from Jamaica, a country that she had never even heard of. She remembers that they spoke better English than she and her friends did with their

TOP:
Adrian's mother Monica as a teenager, 1960 (aged 14).
ABOVE:
Mabel, Adrian's grandmother, in 1975.

Adrian's grandfather James, standing by his Austin Cambridge car in Birmingham, 1964–5.

Brummie accents. But if the new arrivals were a novelty for them, Britain held its own surprises for Monica and her friends. Adrian had lunch with his mother, younger brother Jude, sister Yvonne and cousin Alfia to talk to them about what they had expected of England.

Monica's cousin Alfia explains that when they arrived seeing white people doing manual and agricultural work shocked them. This was something they had never witnessed in Jamaica. They couldn't believe that women were allowed into pubs, which also never occurred at home. They assumed they must be prostitutes. They also recall experiencing racist attitudes. Alfia was once in a bus queue with her friend and a white woman pushed in front of them. Her friend told her not to push in and the woman responded, 'Why don't you just go home!' Eventually the woman refused to board the same bus as them.

By the 1960s more and more colonies were winning their independence but faced with economic and political uncertainty thousands more former colonial subjects seized the opportunity to migrate to Britain. They were not met with the welcome they hoped for. In the Birmingham City Archives Adrian discovered some of the campaign leaflets produced by the Birmingham Immigration Control Association. He was shocked and dismayed to uncover the extent of the hatred towards immigrants that some people held. The archive also holds a collection of photographs by the acclaimed photographer Vanley Burke. In 1965 Vanley, like Monica, came from Jamaica as a teenager to join his parents who had already settled here. He was given a camera and began to photograph what he saw around him. His collection of photographs chronicles Jamaican life in and around Handsworth. He told Adrian of stories he had heard over the years. In some pubs the landlords had separate glasses for black and white people, and would break the glasses after their black customers had drunk from them. Some shopkeepers wouldn't touch a black person's hand when giving them their change. Vanley still records what he sees in Handsworth, like the new groups of immigrants arriving from Eastern Europe.

In July 1962, one month before Jamaica gained its independence, the Commonwealth Immigrants Act came into force. It laid down new conditions for entering the country. Being an imperial subject was no longer good enough. Britain's open doors had closed. 1962 saw the highest rate of immigration to Britain from the West Indies ever, as people rushed to get their wives and children over before it was too late.

Having retraced the journey his grandfather made from colonial Jamaica to Birmingham, Adrian felt he had satisfied his quest to find out more about how

James as an older man,
Jamaica, 1996–7.

he came to be a Jamaican Brummie. But his memories of the experience will always be tinged with sadness. Eleven days after Adrian said goodbye to his grandfather, James Lester died aged eighty-nine. Adrian now understands just what his grandfather had done for him. 'Everything I've learned has planted my feet more firmly in the place where I stand.' Adrian was thankful that he had had a chance to express his gratitude to James – and to acknowledge how he had done something so remarkable. 'The best lesson any young man could have is learning what he did,' Adrian concluded.

PART THREE

'TIS NOT TOO LATE TO SEEK A NEWER WORLD'

ALFRED, LORD TENNYSON

CHAPTER SIX

THE SECOND WORLD WAR AND ITS AFTERMATH

The last thing Britain wanted at the end of the 1930s was another war.

ABOVE:
Prime Minister Neville Chamberlain. His father, Joseph Chamberlain, was Secretary for the Colonies.
OPPOSITE:
Sir Winston Churchill in one of his informal uniforms, 1943.

The country had barely recovered from the last one; and against the same country, which was now rearmed – partly by our consent – and led by someone just as anachronistic as the Kaiser but with even greater ambitions, coupled with a dark, criminally psychopathic mind. Initially, Adolf Hitler was full of admiration for Britain, and for her Empire. He professed no territorial ambitions against Britain and would have much preferred to have had the British as allies – though he could not for a moment imagine why they did not just take troublemakers like Gandhi out and shoot them.

The British took a contrasting view. Taking tea with the Indian leader at Buckingham Palace, George V had said to him a few years earlier, 'Remember, Mr Gandhi, I can't have any attacks upon my Indian Empire.' And although Churchill, who grew to manhood under Victoria and never quite lost his ferociously proprietorial attitude to Empire, took a less diplomatic view, proclaiming himself in 1931 revolted 'by the nauseating and humiliating spectacle of this one-time Inner Temple lawyer, now turned seditious *fakir*, striding half-naked up the steps of the Viceroy's palace... to negotiate and parley on equal terms with the representative of the King-Emperor', it is unlikely that he would have had him killed. (Or would he? Jan Morris reminds us that Churchill later privately warmed to his theme, and declared that he would like to see Gandhi bound hand-and-foot, laid in the dust outside the gates of Delhi, and trampled to death by the Viceroy, riding an elephant!)

Much had changed in the few years since Churchill's outburst. A new war was inevitable, despite Prime Minister Neville Chamberlain's efforts. In the end, despite the fact that Britain quaked at the prospect of the price of such a thing on top of her shaky economic state, a stand had to be made. Most people had a very good idea of what the war would be like, too. This time it would be even deadlier and even more widespread. During the First World

THE SECOND
WORLD WAR WAS
AMONG THE MOST
COMPLEX EVER
FOUGHT, AND ITS
GEOGRAPHICAL
SCOPE WAS
LARGER THAN
THAT OF ANY
PREVIOUS
CONFLICT.

War, life for many people could go on much as it always had. For example, in 1917, the Astronomer-Royal, Sir Frank Dyson, could write to Einstein in Berlin, it being tacitly understood that the war could not go on for ever, and suggest that the eclipse of the sun due on 29 March 1919 would prove an excellent chance to prove the Theory of Relativity, 'since the darkened sun would pass through an exceptionally bright group of stars, the Hyades'. The point being that the First World War for all its horror never became what Josef Goebbels would dub 'total war' – war that involved everybody, soldier and civilian alike. Technological advances, especially in communication and aerial bombing, culminating in the ultimate destructive force of the atom bomb, drew everyone definitively into a dark age.

The battle lines this time were different, too. Britain, with its Empire (the colonies were still automatically included in the declaration of war), stood against Germany, Italy and Japan. The USA, though already supportive in terms of materiel, would not weigh in militarily until after the Japanese attack on Pearl Harbor in December 1941.

In the summer of 1941 Churchill boarded HMS *Prince of Wales* at Scapa Flow to cross the Atlantic, meet President Roosevelt and agree what would become the Atlantic Charter. Though the ship had to make many changes of course to avoid U-boats, and lost her escorts to bad weather, Churchill found the voyage restful, reading novels and watching films.

On the morning of Saturday 9 August 1941, the *Prince of Wales* sailed into Placentia Bay, Newfoundland, down a line of US ships, to the USS *Augusta*, where Roosevelt, his son, and his chiefs of staff were waiting. On meeting, Churchill and Roosevelt were silent for a moment until Churchill said: 'At long last Mr President', to which Roosevelt replied: 'Glad to have you aboard, Mr Churchill'. Churchill gave a letter to the President from the King and made an official statement which, despite two attempts, an attendant film crew failed to record.

Essentially the two leaders made a joint statement which covered their countries' broad strategy and war aims. It was chiefly a propaganda exercise designed to promote solidarity between the two nations. The charter presented a properly principled vision of a post-Second World War world, and the participants hoped that the Soviet Union would sign up to it as well, after having been attacked by its former ally Nazi Germany in June 1941 in defiance of the Molotov-Ribbentrop Pact. Its eight points were:

1. No territorial gains were to be sought by the United States or the United Kingdom.

2. Territorial adjustments must be in accord with wishes of the peoples concerned.

3. The nations had a right to self-determination.

4. Trade barriers were to be lowered.

5. There was to be global economic cooperation and advancement of social welfare.

6. Freedom from want and fear was to be enforced.

7. There was to be freedom of the seas.

8. Disarmament of aggressor nations and post-war common disarmament was to be effected.

The points of the charter were, on balance, fair, if not, in the real world, enforceable. They were also designed to ensure that there would be no post-war expansion by Britain or the Soviet Union. The USA had never had pretensions to an empire, though the Monroe Doctrine basically reserved to it the right to protect its own territorial interests and those of its immediate neighbours.

Matters were complicated. The British fleet was not big enough to watch Italy's ambitions in the Mediterranean and Suez and at the same time sufficiently guard farther-flung bastions such as Singapore, with the result that Singapore was left relatively (and, in the event, fatally) vulnerable. Japan, no longer a friend, had imperial ambitions of her own in the East, which made India and Australia interested parties in the combat. India, a colony still, joined in the war as a matter of course, though not unequivocally and with much internal dissent. The white-settler dominions, now able to make up their own minds, and with the depredations of the last conflict still more than within living memory, nevertheless supported Britain once more. Certainly Australia and New Zealand would be fighting this time in their own interests as much as in those of the mother country; Canada declared war on Japan (the more immediate foe) before Britain, and on Germany soon after. South Africa joined the British side only after bitter dispute. The Kaiser had supported the Boers, at least morally, and there was a strong admiration among many white South African politicians for Hitler's dogma. But the colonies did rally round and support was more voluntary than involuntary. Barbados famously sent a message of support to Westminster: 'Don't worry. Barbados is with you.'

The Second World War was among the most complex ever fought, and its

RAF recruits from the Caribbean arrive in Britain, 1944.

geographical scope was larger than that of any previous conflict. As far as the Empire was concerned, it saw two successive renegade Indian armies come into being within that country in support of the Japanese, led by Indian nationalists reduced to such a state of desperation and frustration that they were prepared to do anything to get the British out. Burma sided with the Japanese before returning to the Allied fold towards the end of the war. Malta, a vital naval base, was pounded relentlessly by Axis bombers, but never taken. On the other hand, Singapore crumbled too easily, surrendering to an inferior Japanese force – an action which resulted in considerable loss of face for the British and their Australian allies, and a great loss of standing and prestige in the eyes of the local population. Egypt, never officially part of the Empire but always bound up with it on account of the Suez Canal, faltered under its young king, Farouk, and inclined towards the Axis powers. Only the timely and firm intervention of the British ambassador, Sir Miles Lampson, secured the situation for the Allies.

But at the end of the war, the Empire, though it still existed, was entering its last twilight, and at heart even veteran imperialists, such as Churchill, who had grown up with it and loved it for all its faults, realized as much. If the First

World War had broken the British lion's legs, the Second had broken its back. From being one of the richest countries in the world, Britain had become one of its great debtors, saddled with a debt to the USA (the total, including aid to the dominions and the colonies, would total well over $30,000 million) that would not be expected to be fully paid off until 31 December 2006 and faced with crippling military overstretch. Britain could not, of course, have won the war without it. Nor could Western Europe – including West Germany – have rebuilt after the war without further aid under the Marshall Plan. But it was also in the interest of the United States to form as strong a bulwark as possible against the USSR, as post-war Europe quickly divided into east and west, Germany was split, and the world realigned for another war – the Cold War, which was to last about another forty-five years.

Even if Britain had not been so severely overstretched and had wanted to keep her Empire, she could not have enforced that desire. The old guard imperialists knew that the time had come for change. The country did, too, and looked towards a New Jerusalem. Soon after the end of the war Churchill, a redoubtable leader during the war, lost the general election in July 1945 to Clement Attlee. Churchill would come back again, in his mid-seventies, to

IF THE FIRST WORLD WAR HAD BROKEN THE BRITISH LION'S LEGS, THE SECOND HAD BROKEN ITS BACK.

Clement Attlee, arguably the greatest post-war British prime minister, seen here addressing the Labour Party Conference in 1939.

INDIA HAD BEEN NEGOTIATING ITS INDEPENDENCE FOR A LONG TIME NOW AND WAS BEGINNING TO RUN OUT OF PATIENCE.

run the country from 1951–5; but it would be under Attlee and his Foreign Secretary Ernest Bevin, that Britain was forced to engage in the process of decolonization and retreat from Empire.

India had been negotiating its independence for a long time now and was beginning to run out of patience. Lord Linlithgow, the viceroy, had declared war on India's behalf without consulting any one of its 400 million citizens, let alone the Congress, and that insensitivity led to great discontent, but constitutionally he was within his rights. The African colonies reflected a great variety of cultures, traditions and languages, which had been brought together willy-nilly under the imperial umbrella. The Caribbean, whose population was composed largely of the descendants of slaves, who had long lost cultural connections to their original homelands, tended by religion and tradition to identify more closely with Britain than did India. India had, in short, a more coherent identity of its own, and it had had a longer experience of the British presence, and, among the upper echelons at least, a more intimate contact with it. India was aware that it was the jewel in the crown of the British Empire. The dramatic fall of imperial possessions in the East Indies to the Japanese did not help matters. And it was not only Gandhi and the Congress who were fighting for Indian independence. Another group, the Indian Independence League, was formed after the fall of Singapore, under the benevolent eye of the Japanese victors. Indian prisoners of war, and, later, defectors from the British Indian Army, joined a new force under the aegis of the League, called the Indian National Army, led by the renegade independence activist Subhas

Lord Linlithgow, Viceroy of India 1936-1943, carried along a road in Simla in 1939, shortly before the outbreak of the Second World War, to which he committed India without any consultation with Congress.

Chandra Bose. The INA was a constant thorn in the side of the British from 1942–5, though its effectiveness was reduced by internal disagreement, and a growing suspicion that the Japanese were not entirely disinterested as far as Indian independence was concerned. (Bose himself died in possibly murky circumstances in an air crash in 1945.)

Perhaps more serious politically for the British was the Quit India Movement, which was another campaign of civil disobedience instituted by Gandhi, who in 1942 called for immediate independence. It came about as a result of British intransigence over independence negotiations, even though Churchill had sent a representative, Sir Stafford Cripps, to India. But Cripps was only empowered to make an offer of full dominion status when the war was over, with the option of leaving the Commonwealth altogether.

The Quit India Movement was endorsed by the Congress, by now a powerful political machine, and led, as after the First World War, not only to peaceful, but extremely violent and disruptive demonstrations. There were terrorist bomb attacks, British government buildings were set on fire, railway and telegraph lines were sabotaged, as well as electricity supplies. The British still maintained a powerful army and police service in India, and reacted by making mass arrests – of over 100,000 people – and isolated the Congress, imprisoning its leaders. Britain was helped by the abstention from the movement of the Muslim League, representing the Muslim voice in the Congress, which under its leader Muhammad Ali Jinnah condemned it, but the crisis did not die down until 1944. By then the end of the war was in sight, and Britain realized that it could not retract the offer Cripps had made on her behalf. In 1943, it made a half-step forward by replacing the lordly Linlithgow as Viceroy with Field Marshal Wavell, sidelined by Churchill as unfit for military service (though Feldmarschall Rommel always carried Wavell's own brilliant *Generals and Generalship* with him). Wavell was a more congenial and sensitive figure than Linlithgow, and as the penultimate Viceroy did much to pave the way for the independence, which would finally come in 1947.

Meanwhile, for the ordinary non-white colonial fighting man some of the same prejudices as had existed in the First World War were there to contend with again. In passing one should mention that only one black Briton (his father was black, his mother white), Arundel Moody, received a commission during the Second World War. Major Moody was born in England and had been to a British public school, but still, according to one account, was turned down by the RAF because he was not of pure British descent.

Flight Sergeant L. O. Lynch from Jamaica, a rear gun turret operator on Lancaster bombers, photographed in 1944 on the occasion of his winning that year's air gunners' trophy.

⊠

**THERE WERE
ABOUT 130,000
BLACK AMERICAN
TROOPS
STATIONED IN
BRITAIN, AND THE
BRITISH DISLIKED
THE PREJUDICE
SHOWN TO THEM
BY THEIR WHITE
COUNTRYMEN.**

Overall, against Britain's 4,650,000 fighting men, India committed 1,800,000, and the African colonies about 450,000. In the British forces there was less racial tension than in the American. There were about 130,000 black American troops among the GIs stationed in Britain, and they were segregated from their white comrades. On the whole the British disliked the prejudice shown to the black soldiers by their white countrymen. Later, when America criticized British behaviour in India, Britain responded with some asperity by pointing out their poor record in race relations. Black Americans were found to be more courteous and generally better behaved and less patronizing than white ones, though black GIs did encounter prejudice now and then. In his book, *Bloody Foreigners: The Story of Immigration to Britain*, Robert Winder mentions the Tory MP Maurice Petherick, who urged 'the Foreign Secretary to send the black troops to North Africa, perhaps, or "to go and fertilise the Italians, who are used to it anyway"'. Winder also cites a *New Statesman* story of a 'society lady who decided, in the spirit of doing her bit, to invite some American GIs to lunch. She wrote to the commanding officer, suggesting he send six men, adding "No Jews Please". On the appointed day she opened her door to find six large black soldiers on her doorstep. There must, she stammered, have been some mistake. "Oh no, ma'am," said one of the soldiers. "Colonel Cohen makes no mistake."' General (later President) Eisenhower wrote that 'The small-town British girl would go to a movie with a Negro soldier quite as readily as she would go with anyone else, a practice that some of our white troops could not understand. Brawls often resulted, and our white troops were further bewildered when they found that the British press took a firm stand on the side of the Negro.'

Invited over to American bases, black British servicemen were amazed at the luxury and no less amazed at the segregation. It could not apply to them, although white American troops and military police could cut up rough if they saw a black soldier in what they regarded as a white preserve. As William Naltey relates in an interview recorded by Mike and Trevor Phillips:

I was in Glasgow going to a dance-hall and I was going up in the lift with this American black serviceman, we're chatting away and suddenly he disappeared: I'm talking to myself. Then I notice that two American officers had come into the lift. Now I'm still in the lift. They haven't said anything to me. But they were laughing at the way this fellow suddenly jumped out of the lift and disappeared when they came in. You know, they had great

fun thinking, 'Oh, see, see that bastard jump out?' I couldn't understand it you know, it was something new to me until then. It took a lot of getting used to, I can assure you.

Many Caribbean men joined the RAF, and women served in the WRAF and WRNS. The RAF was reluctant, at least at first, to take Caribbean men on as pilots and they became ground crew and gunners. Black pilots tended to come from mixed-race and/or middle-class, educated backgrounds. However, once in the RAF, they found that they encountered little prejudice, protected as they were by their uniforms, status and rank. Many were killed in action; many were decorated. Some were taken prisoner, and found that the Germans exhibited no race prejudice, only experiencing it from white American prisoners of war. Ironically, during the war the Germans distributed as propaganda photographs of starving concentration camp inmates, passing them off as 'Indian victims of savage British rule'.

Factory worker Constantine Higgins fitting a wheel to a tank during the Second World War. Higgins was one of many skilled workers recruited to Britain during the war.

There was plenty for the colonial serviceman and woman to get used to. Eric Ferron was an infantryman in the Second World War who settled here and eventually became a social worker. The last word here should go to him, from his masterly memoir *Man, You've Mixed: A Jamaican Comes to Britain*:

Up in Cumberland [in the 1940s] the camp was near a small town by the sea. There were only a few Jamaicans there. One hot afternoon four of us were lazing around on the beach when two children came by, a boy about eleven and a girl a few years younger. They stared at us very hard but didn't say anything... The little girl was obviously longing to speak, but the boy took her hand and pulled her away. Then they passed by again; this time they stopped and she said: 'Hello.'

'Hello' I said.

'You see!' She turned to the boy: 'He does speak English.'

'Yes' I said.

'And you wear clothes.'

'Yes.'

'And you wear shoes.'

My friends got impatient. 'Why do you answer all these questions?'

'Well if she thought we didn't wear clothes and didn't speak English now she's finding out it was wrong and she's learning something. I don't see why we shouldn't help her.'

'Our teacher told us that black men live in trees and they don't wear shoes and they don't wear clothes and they don't have houses.'

I went back to camp and I thought about ignorance and innocence. It was difficult to distinguish between the two. Our expectation of the English was higher than the reality. We expected them to know their own history. When they showed us they didn't, we felt disappointed in them, and angry to be asked such stupid questions... They knew nothing about Jamaica, yet we knew so much about England... But they seemed to know nothing about the Empire. They forgot there was a war on and we were in it with them because it was our war too. Years later I began to understand the difference between ignorance and innocence. With the ignorant, prejudice is a way of life. They don't like the Scots, or the Welsh, or the Irish, or the Jews. They don't like the rich or the poor and they don't like the clever. They are far more dangerous than the innocent... Inside myself, I searched for the reasons for the violence, for the state of the world.

Apart from the war's military losses, about 11 million civilians including French, Poles and Germans (among whom were many decorated veterans of the First World War) had died in Germany and Poland as a direct result of the ignorance and prejudice Eric Ferron is talking about. Just over half the number died because they were Jews. The rest counted among them gypsies, homosexuals, criminals, religious dissidents, political dissidents, members of the resistance, the disabled and the mentally ill. Ironically Hitler, in keeping with Germany's demented mysticism of the time, had taken one of the great ancient symbols of the East, the swastika (from the Sanskrit word *su-asti*, meaning 'well-being') as his own.

In 1945 the League of Nations transmuted into the United Nations, of which there were originally fifty members. There are now 192, including all the previous member-states of the British Empire. Britain shed its responsibility for several states with relief. The occupation of Palestine, for example, had never been a success. This ancient land along the eastern coastal strip of the Mediterranean was the traditional first homeland of the Jews, but it was also the birthplace of Christ; from here, too, the Prophet Muhammad ascended to heaven from the crag now contained within the great mosque known as the Dome of the Rock. It had been the scene of Christian–Muslim wars at the time of the Crusades. By the twentieth century, the bulk of the population was Arab, but the Arabs lived peacefully with their Jewish and Christian fellow citizens under Ottoman rule. But it was not without stress, and the Balfour Declaration of 1917 ensured trouble ahead, by effectively making promises it could not hope to keep. But in 1917 the British needed control of Palestine to protect Suez, and the Zionists – the Jewish movement lobbying internationally for a Jewish state – wanted a homeland. The two could help each other. But the Arabs were also enormously helpful as British allies. After the First World War, the problem had been how to please both camps.

The problem also was that we thought we could. As Brian Lapping has pointed out in his *End of Empire*, 'nothing pleases a politician more than a coincidence of morality and interest'. The Jews had suffered at the hands of the Europeans in the Middle Ages, and at the hands of the Russians during the pogroms of the late nineteenth century. How better to make amends than by helping the Jews of the Diaspora (and, quite coincidentally of course, influential Jews had deep pockets) in their search for a land of their own? Jewish immigration to Palestine in the interwar years proved ill-advised, however, in the sense that, from a population of about 70,000 Jews in 1918, it grew

IN 1917 THE BRITISH NEEDED CONTROL OF PALESTINE TO PROTECT SUEZ, AND THE ZIONISTS WANTED A HOMELAND – BUT THE ARABS WERE ALSO ENORMOUSLY HELPFUL AS BRITISH ALLIES.

quickly. In 1925 alone, nearly 34,000 Jews arrived. The native Arab population quickly became nervous, and a series of bloody riots ensued.

The whole interwar and wartime story of Palestine is a vastly complicated one, but what concerns us here is the situation at the end of the Second World War, given the tension that already existed. A difficult relationship between the Jews in Palestine (and the Arabs, who regarded them as interlopers) and Britain already existed. Now there was the added burden of responsibility for those Jews who wanted to emigrate from the lands of their birth on account of the Holocaust. To make matters more complex, there was added pressure from the USA, as President Truman paid heed to the influential American Jewish lobby (which now represented the biggest population of the Diaspora).

The 'Haviva Reik', a small ship containing some 450 Jewish refugees, on arrival at Haifa on 8th June, 1946 after a dangerous journey across the Mediterranean. The banner in hebrew reads 'Keep the gates open, we are not the last.'

EMPIRE'S CHILDREN

On the day after the Labour government came to power in July 1945 the new prime minister, Clement Attlee, received a letter about Palestine from President Truman, pressing him to lift the quotas set on Jewish immigration in Palestine. A month later Truman virtually demanded that 100,000 Jews be allowed to go there. Attlee replied, pointing out that such a move would ignite tensions among the Arab population, which already felt threatened. Diplomatically, too, as Attlee also mentioned, it would be inadvisable to alienate Arab goodwill, given their control of oilfields which we had to keep out of the hands of the Russians.

However, the displaced persons camps of Europe were overflowing, and Truman, under pressure himself, was not about to be contradicted. At the same time Britain was beginning to realize that it had to do as it was told by the USA. The result was a tragic mess which has still not been cleared up today.

Jewish terrorist gangs, led by men who would later become respectable Israeli politicians, fought hard to assert their not unjustifiably perceived right to an independent state. The King David Hotel in Jerusalem was blown up, among other atrocities. The British turned back tramp steamers from France and elsewhere overloaded with would-be immigrants. Leon Uris immortalized one, the *Exodus*, in his eponymous novel. The Jews who were turned back were settled in camps in Cyprus, or, infamously, as in the case of the *Exodus*, returned to Germany.

These measures meant that world opinion swung against Britain as heartless, whereas in fact she was acting as a pretty well hopeless peacekeeping force without the authority to intervene. It was an expensive business, too – Britain had 100,000 troops based in Palestine. The British public wanted Britain out. Westminster longed to be rid of the mandate there. Early in 1947 Britain passed responsibility to the UN. The UN devised a partition plan, the only means of ensuring an at least partially peaceful solution to the problem. Britain pulled out, leaving chaos in her wake, on 15 May 1948. 'Final' partition was sorted out after the Arab-Israeli War which followed immediately, but the wound has never healed, and the future of Israel as a state remains uncertain, while at the same time, especially in terms of the advent of Islamism, it remains the fulcrum of an important aspect of present international tension and polarization.

Cyprus had been a British possession since 1878 – traded with the Ottomans in exchange for our support in a war against Russia. It was one of the four important Mediterranean outposts of Empire, along with Gibraltar, Malta and Palestine. The island-state had a Turkish-Greek population, which lived in relative harmony, though the Greek majority in the twentieth century wanted union with Greece – *enosis*. The leader of this movement was Archbishop Mihailis Makarios III, who as spiritual leader of the island was at the same time its temporal leader. In his fight to establish Greek hegemony, he made a political bedfellow of Colonel Grivas, a war veteran and a leader of 'freedom fighters', whose terrorist tactics led him into dangerous waters politically.

The Turkish population naturally resisted this impulse, and once again Britain was faced with a problem. After extensive negotiations, independence was achieved in 1960, but the Turkish-Greek differences were not resolved. Britain retained two military bases, but otherwise tried to keep a low profile. Once again, local differences had been totally disregarded by Empire, and now she had to pay the price, leaving mayhem in her wake. Even today, Cyprus is a divided island, with so much tension between the two sides that the capital, Nicosia, is still divided by a barrier akin to the Berlin Wall. A United Nations mission has been deployed there for four decades at the time of writing, and the existing British bases have not kept out of trouble in that time.

Malaya presented a different set of problems. The Allies had chased the beaten and chastised Japanese out of the East Indies, where their vainglorious emperor and his advisers had hoped to lay the foundations of a Japanese empire (the Japanese were to find success in other directions – those of manufacturing and commerce). The Japanese had been cruel and vicious overlords in their temporary victory, but they had left a difficult vacuum behind. In June 1948 three rubber plantation estate managers were murdered in Perak by members of the Malayan Communist Party, whose existence was a result of Malayan-Chinese-inspired resistance to the Japanese. After the Empire had retaken Malaya, the British had not taken steps to ensure that the local Chinese immigrants should enjoy full Malayan citizenship. Thus another problem was born. The killings reflected the disaffection of the local Chinese population. On the other hand, the largely Muslim Malayans felt themselves in danger of being marginalized in their own country by the opportunistic, relentlessly hard-working Chinese immigrants. The Chinese for their part wanted to be accepted as citizens in their own right: they were mainly poor, and had no voting rights. The Malayans, fearful of an ethnic takeover, resisted this. Once again the British had to become aware of and react to interracial tensions which hitherto had not been the concern of imperial administrators.

To the British, Malaya was a very important source of raw materials. Plastic

Turkish demonstraters on the streets of Nicosia in Cyprus, 3rd February 1958. Five Turkish Cypriots were killed during the disturbances when British troops opened fire on crowds protesting in favour of Cyprus' partition.

was still in its infancy, and we still needed rubber and tin from the East Indies, both valuable commodities in the international field. Malaya also remained an important strategic base in the Far East. In the event, the communist uprising, taking the form of an efficient guerrilla war, was one of the most effective against the Empire, but it was defeated.

The war against the British was run by the so-called Malayan Races Liberation Army (MRLA), the creation of the Malayan Communist Party, but, despite its name, largely manned by Chinese. Up to 500,000 Chinese were involved in the Party, out of a total Chinese population of just over 3 million. The MRLA, which numbered about 30,000, grew out of the Malayan People's Anti-Japanese Army, which had fought a guerrilla war against the Japanese, and had been trained and equipped by the British themselves; and it was the British who had declared communism legal after the end of the Second World War in recognition of the MPAJA's contribution to victory. Unknown to the British, however, the MCP had secretly stashed much of the wartime weaponry for use in an insurgency against the British if they were unable to gain power by any other means.

Fighting started when the MCP, under its new leader, Chin Peng, opposed the proposal of a Malayan federation, correctly guessing that the aim of such an organization would be to squeeze out communism. Chin Peng realized that the only way he could establish a communist state would be by force of arms. The word 'Emergency' used to describe what ensued is something of a misnomer. It was, in fact, a full-scale war, which some describe as a civil war. But it was not an accident that the euphemism was applied. If the conflict had been called a 'war' officially, the rubber and tin industries would not have been covered by their insurers; and naturally it was the rubber and tin industries which the MRLA struck at most frequently.

At the start of the Malayan Emergency, the British had a total of thirteen infantry battalions, comprising seven partly formed Gurkha battalions, three British battalions, two battalions of the Royal Malay Regiment and a British Royal Artillery Regiment being utilized as infantry. This was far too small a force to contain the enemy, and Australian and New Zealand troops and airmen were drafted in, as well as detachments from the Royal Worcesters, the Royal Marines and the King's African Rifles. The SAS (Special Air Service) was used for reconnaissance and quick strikes.

The Malayan Emergency. During fighting with Chinese Communist guerillas, an injured SAS soldier is stretchered to a helicopter, 1953.

It was hard to combat an army used to conducting guerrilla warfare in dense jungle, so the British used a plan which had worked in the Second Boer War. Hundreds of thousands of jungle-dwellers who might have been sympathetic to the MRLA were rehoused in fortified villages under guard. Such treatment was resented at first, but, in fact, living conditions in the villages were much better than they were in the jungle, and the British, therefore, had the unexpected benefit of winning the confidence and sympathy of the people they had resettled. Additionally, the British distributed food and medicine among the Malays and local tribes as part of a 'hearts and minds' campaign, whereas the MRLA, as they were pushed further back into the jungle, had to raid villages for supplies, thus earning the enmity of those local people not already under British protection. The British were at pains to be merciful to prisoners of war, who frequently changed sides. The MRLA, by contrast, took no prisoners.

They also made a bad strategic error by assassinating the British High Commissioner, Sir Henry Gurney, as he drove to a hill station in his Rolls-Royce in October 1951. Malays reacted by siding more closely with the British for protection, though it has to be said that at the same time there was a widespread fear that if the MRLA could kill the High Commissioner, who then could feel safe?

Gurney was succeeded by General Sir Gerald Templer, a tough customer who was, however, instructed by Westminster to intercede with the Malays to allow Chinese residents the right to vote. He also ensured that more Malayans were involved in the national executive, and he boosted the formation of a national army. Most importantly of all, he was authorized to hold out the promise of independence once the Emergency had been brought to a close. In the meantime, Templer was able to improve his intelligence of MRLA activities by deploying members of Special Branch from England and offering rewards for any useful information brought to him by the public in general.

By 1955 Chin Peng realized that a military victory was out of the question for him, so he sought a political solution instead. However, at talks held with the Malayan government at Baling, Chin found all his demands rejected and so the conflict continued for another two years. Malaya was declared independent at the end of August 1957, however, and Chin's war of liberation lost its raison d'être. Fighting gradually petered out over the next year or so, and the Emergency was finally declared over at the end of July 1960, having lasted twelve years.

In September 1963 Malaya joined with Sabah, Sarawak and Singapore to form the Federation of Malaysia.

AT THE START OF THE MALAYAN EMERGENCY, THE BRITISH HAD A TOTAL OF THIRTEEN INFANTRY BATTALIONS – FAR TOO SMALL A FORCE TO CONTAIN THE ENEMY.

Between 1922 and 1932 Iraq was governed under a British mandate. It was then granted independence but the British retained military bases, taking the country over again in 1941 to pre-empt a pro-Axis prime minister, and staying until 1947. The reinstalled Hashemite monarchy lasted until 1958, when it was overthrown through a coup d'état by the Iraqi army, known as the 14 July Revolution, but Iraq remained friendly towards the West. This was not always the case of its neighbour, another client state important to Britain on account of its oil. Iran had been controlled by the British for a long time. We had set up its ruler in 1921, a former Cossack officer, Reza Shah, who quickly established himself as a strong and dictatorial leader, who soon showed an alarming degree of independence. By the time the Second World War started, however, his despotism had made him unpopular. He was removed and for the duration of the war Iran was under the control of Britain and the Soviet Union. It had a constitutional monarchy with a liberal prime minister and a tractable new ruler in the form of Reza Shah's son. However, after the war ended, a new prime minister came to power. Mohammad Mossadeq was another independent-minded figure who took exception to the huge amount of profit drawn from Persian oilwells by the Anglo-Iranian Oil Company (later British Petroleum). Mossadeq was in a strong enough position to nationalize Anglo-Iranian, and his histrionic and colourful character ensured his popularity with his people.

The British and the Americans felt differently. They had been relieved of an important source of revenue, and they were painfully aware that Iran shared its northern frontier with Russia. If Mossadeq chose to make an alliance with the communists, security in the region would be severely compromised.

What followed sounds like the plot of an espionage novel of the period. Mossadeq, in fact, was not a communist sympathizer. He did not even have any contact with the Iranian Communist Party. But he was anti-British, and he had to be neutralized. The British secret service concocted a plan to get rid of him, unsubtly codenamed Boot (when the CIA effectively took it over they renamed it Ajax). But the plan itself was the brainchild of two senior academics, the Persian scholar Nancy Lambton and the future professor of eastern religions at Oxford University, Robin Zaehner, regarded as a bit of a loose cannon. Nevertheless, Ajax went into operation, led from the US Embassy by Kermit Roosevelt Jr. In essence, the plan was angled to stir up popular support for the young Shah, who remained loyal to the West and showed little inclination to assert his country's independence, and by so doing dislodge Mossadeq.

Britannia gets a makeover - a cartoon from the *Evening Standard* by David Low, February 1943.

There was a series of violent protests involving clashes between the two camps, which left several hundred people dead. At last, however, Mossadeq was broken. He accepted defeat in August 1953, and after a trumped-up trial for treason he was sentenced to three years in prison.

The young Shah, Mohammad Reza Pahlavi, then took control, but his rule became increasingly autocratic. With the support of Britain and the USA, he certainly modernized Iranian industry, but he also crushed all forms of political opposition through his secret police organization, SAVAK. In this atmosphere, against the background of a deceptively westernized Tehran, Ayatollah Ruhollah Khomeini became a sharp critic of the ruler. Khomeini, a popular conservative religious leader, was arrested and imprisoned for eighteen months. After his release, he continued to be a vociferous critic, and was sent into exile, first to Turkey, then to Iraq, and finally to France, whence he returned home in the wake of the Iranian Revolution which deposed Pahlavi, who was obliged to flee the country.

In a referendum held in 1979, the Iranians voted by 98 per cent in favour of establishing an Islamic republic. Khomeini and his fellow religious leaders took control of the country and began the Muslim fundamentalist movement which has been gathering impetus ever since.

By 1979, the British Empire would be all but finished. The 1950s and 1960s would see the fastest shedding of former colonies. But it all started in 1947, with the greatest divestiture of all.

SHOBNA GULATI

Over the last few years, Shobna Gulati has firmly established herself as one of Britain's most prominent television actresses. She has appeared in *EastEnders*, *Coronation Street* and most recently *Where the Heart Is*. But it is for her inspired performance as the ditzy 'Anita' in Victoria Wood's hit BBC show *Dinnerladies* that she is most well known. In real life she could not be more different.

She speaks six languages, including French, Hindi, Urdu and Punjabi, and has a degree in Arabic and Middle Eastern Politics. She has also trained as a classical Indian dancer. She describes herself as a 'cultural magpie', absorbing different aspects of the many cultures that she has been exposed to over the years. Shobna wanted to discover why her parents decided to make the move from India to Britain, and how that has influenced the person she is today.

Shobna was born in Oldham, Lancashire in 1966. Oldham is well known for being a particularly multicultural area. In 2001 it experienced some of the worst racially motivated violence seen in Britain for fifteen years. Shobna began her journey by visiting the pub where the riots began. She remembers feeling sadness that racial tension could create such a social divide. But how did Oldham come to be so ethnically diverse, and did her parents suffer the same sort of racist attitudes when they arrived from India in the 1950s?

Shobna's parents, Kulbhushan (aka Joe) and Asha Gulati were part of a mass wave of immigration from all parts of the Commonwealth in the 1960s. The reign of the British Empire was all but over, and the labour shortage in Britain (a residue of World War Two) led to a call from Health Minister Enoch Powell for Britain's former subjects to come and pursue a better life working for the NHS in the mother country. (Ironically it was Enoch Powell who would later deliver the famous anti-immigration 'rivers of blood' speech.) Shobna's parents, who were married in Bombay in 1958, were just two of the thousands of immigrants who made the trip from India to find work.

Joe has sadly passed away, so Shobna went to see her mother Asha, to find out what it was like for them when they first arrived in Britain. Asha remembers arriving in grey and wet Oldham in 1961 and being disappointed to find that the streets were not paved with gold, only rain. She tells Shobna that Joe, a trained doctor in India who had arrived a year earlier, came over to Britain with the hope of advancing his medical career. She remembers that he did everything possible to integrate himself into Western life, and although a subtle undercurrent of racism could always be felt, they just got on with life as best

TOP:
Shobna and her father Joe.
ABOVE:
Shobna's parents on their wedding day, November 1959.

they could. By the time Shobna and her siblings were in their teens, the family was living in the affluent village of Shaw. Dr Gulati had by then become a well-respected GP in Oldham.

Shobna wanted to find out what making such a transition might have been like for her father, so she went to see Dr Rekha Patel. Dr Patel studied medicine at the same college as her father in Bombay, and also came to Britain in the 1960s. She told Shobna that she came to the UK because she respected the NHS, but when she and other Asian doctors arrived they could only get jobs in the less popular, inner city practices and career progression was made much harder by racist attitudes.

To understand why her mother and father would make the choice to move from their relatively well-to-do and happy life in India, to come and work in Britain, Shobna had to return to India, and talk to others who remember India at the time of independence. She began in Mumbai (formerly Bombay) where her father trained as a doctor, and met three of his old classmates. Two of them worked briefly in Britain, attracted by reports of 'a land of opportunity'. At work they were generally respected because of their qualifications, but on the streets anti-Indian feeling was strong. All three only managed to rise to a consultant position while working in India.

Despite this, the Gulatis' experience of life was very different from that of the Asians who came to work in the factories in northern England. When they arrived in England they were already well-educated, fluent in English

TOP:
Shobna's father in his GP practice.
ABOVE RIGHT:
Asha and Joe at a party in Oldham.
ABOVE:
Shobna's father as a student at Grant Medical College.

EMPIRE'S CHILDREN

and highly anglicized. Both Shobna's parents experienced a very Western upbringing. Her mother had been a pupil at Elphinstone College in Bombay. This was Shobna's next stop. She is not surprised to find something not dissimilar to an English public school. 'I can imagine my mum here,' she said. 'It's very Victorian – very Raj.'

Asha's father, J. D. Malhotra, moved from the hills of the Punjab to pursue a better life. After training as an electrical engineer in England, he moved to Bombay in 1942 to work on the railways. Shobna went to visit the old railway colony where her grandfather worked at the site of a railway power station called Chola. Chola provided power to the Great Indian Peninsular Railway. Railways were the veins and arteries of the British Empire in India, and were responsible for the smooth functioning of the Raj economically and strategically.

At Chola, Shobna met sevety-eight-year-old Gopal Rao Rani. He remembers that before independence, a strong hierarchy existed among the workers, and the British were always at the top. Despite this, he said the British were popular with the Indian workers, because they provided work and maintained a sense of law and order. This was an essential part of the British's success in India (and indeed all over the Empire). By ridding the country of corrupt local

SHOBNA GULATI

INDIA

Shobna's father and colleagues.

Chola Power
Station – 1942.

rulers, it enabled just 1,500 British civil servants to control a country with a population of over 300 million.

Gopal pointed out the bungalow, a once very upmarket house where Shobna's mother lived with her parents. According to Asha, her father, JD, was one of the first Indian superintendents. As a senior officer he led a very affluent lifestyle, with servants, bridge and tennis, taking tea at 4 p.m. and whisky and water at sundown.

Since the 1920s influential political activists such as Gandhi, Nehru and Jinnah had campaigned against British rule, and in 1947 India finally won its independence. Britain had lost her most valuable asset, 'the jewel in her crown', and it signified the beginning of the end of the British Empire. Gopal remembers Independence Day as being one of mixed emotions. He was happy that India had won her freedom, but sad to see the British go because they had undeniably improved life for the average Indian, and he said they always treated them fairly and with respect. It is dubious whether this was always the case, especially in light of the colour bar implemented in the social clubs.

But freedom from colonial control did not benefit everyone in India. While Shobna's grandfather, J. D. Malhotra moved to Bombay with his family, his brother Bihari Lal and his family stayed behind in the family's ancestral homeland in the northern Punjab, and endured a nightmare that began with the onset of independence. To find out more, Shobna went to Delhi to visit her second cousin Shanti, Bihari's daughter. Shanti was so traumatized by what had happened to her as a child that she has barely spoken of it since.

The fight for independence was accompanied by rising tensions between the Muslim, Sikh and Hindu populations in the Punjab. None of these groups wished to be under the control of the others once the British withdrew. The

Muslim leader, Mohammad Ali Jinnah, called for a separation of the states that had a Muslim majority, to form a new country. The British administration decided that the Punjab would be split in two. The western side would be part of Muslim Pakistan, and the eastern side would remain a Hindu part of India. Millions of Punjabis, like Shobna's great-uncle, found themselves on the wrong side of this border, and were persecuted for it.

Shanti recounted to Shobna the horrific ordeal that she went through. At the time her parents were living in a British-owned cement factory compound. After a while the British decided they could no longer protect them, and the family took a train along with hundreds of other refugees to try and get to safety by crossing the border into India. They only got as far as Kamoke when a gang of Muslim vigilantes ambushed the train and killed almost everyone on board. 340 passengers were slaughtered, and Shanti only survived by hiding under a dead body. She found her brother and sister alive, but she never saw her parents or two other brothers again.

Shobna travelled to Pakistan to retrace the steps that Shanti and her great-uncle would have taken in their attempt to reach safety. She began in Khewra, where Bihari worked until India was partitioned, and visited the cement compound where the family tried to take refuge. Shobna then managed to track down a local resident, Chaudhary Munir, who was one of the Muslim security guards appointed to protect Bihari's family and the other Hindu refugees on the train. He explained that he and the other guards were locked up by the vigilantes, and were unable to do anything but helplessly watch the massacre. Afterwards he was profoundly traumatized by what he saw. He holds the British partly responsible for failing to make adequate arrangements for a peaceful transition.

Shobna then bravely made the final stage of her ancestors' journey, and boarded a train from Khewra station heading east, just as Shanti and her family would have done over fifty years ago. On reaching Kamoke, the station where the Muslim attack took place, she marvelled at the lack of commemoration to a time when so many lives were lost, and that is obviously still so raw in the minds of those, like Shanti, who remember it.

Shobna wanted to try and make sense of a conflict that claimed the lives of over a million people, including her great-uncle and his family. How could independence have been positive when it resulted in so much atrocity? To what extent were the British to blame? Seeking answers, Shobna visited Dr Mubarak Ali, an expert on the partition, who explained that although independence and partition were ultimately the best thing for India, the way it was

SHOBNA GULATI
INDIA

Shola's grandfather
J.D. Malhorta in his office
at Chola Power Station.

Shobna's grandfather
J. D. Malhotra and his wife.

EMPIRE'S CHILDREN

Shobna's grandfather
J. D. Malhotra in England
where he trained as an
electrical engineer.

HAD HER GRANDFATHER NOT MADE THE DECISION TO MOVE TO BOMBAY, HE AND SHOBNA'S MOTHER COULD HAVE SUFFERED THE SAME FATE AS BIHARI LAL AND SHANTI.

implemented was tragically inefficient. Borders were hastily drawn with very little consultation and Britain's rapid withdrawal left India with inadequate time and support to adjust. As a member of the Indian Congress pointed out, 'Mountbatten did a great job for Britain, but a lousy job for India.'

At the end of her journey, Shobna reflected on what she has learned. Ultimately, she had discovered that had her grandfather not made the decision to move to Bombay before independence all those years ago, he and Shobna's mother could have suffered the same fate as Bihari Lal and Shanti. Strangely, after all her travels, Shobna felt it less important to be identified as Punjabi, Indian or any other nationality. If anything, she feels truly a product of Empire, and the transitory life that created for her family. For her son, Akshay, the legacy of Empire is even more complex. His father comes from a family of African-Caribbean immigrants to Britain so he will inherit an even greater breadth of cultural heritage. Which of his ancestors from around the fallen British Empire will he most identify with?

CHAPTER SEVEN

LETTING GO: INDIA

With the 1935 Act, which had extended Indian home rule prerogatives, Britain had already laid the foundation stone for Indian independence.

But the war was an interruption to the process, and reluctant as many were to see the Empire's greatest asset go, others recognized that an independent India, if matters were handled right, could become something better than a possession – an invaluable partner and friend.

At first, no one considered that what had been British India would be divided upon independence into several countries, nor that the process of division would involve such bloodshed and violence. Whatever the hugely complicated ins and outs of the matter were, it was clear to Westminster that India should be given her freedom as soon as was practicable after the war was over.

It was pretty clear that Wavell was not the man to handle it. It has even been suggested that when Churchill appointed him viceroy, it was because he thought that might obstruct progress towards independence. Wavell himself, though his powers as a military leader had waned, was entirely sympathetic to the Indian point of view, and did much to win their confidence and respect. But, in the depths of the depression and self-doubt to which he was prone, Wavell knew that he wasn't the man for the job. He was too hesitant, too reflective and too sensitive. He was ill at ease socially, taciturn to a fault, and knew it. He was also, probably, too much of a gentleman. In a diary entry on 1 January 1946 he wrote: 'I very much doubt whether my brain power or personality are up to it.'

Typically, he also wrote a spoof of Lewis Carroll's 'Jabberwocky', which reflected his mood:

OPPOSITE PAGE:
The Mountbattens - Louis and Edwina - flank Gandhi in the course of their charm offensive in 1947.

'Twas grillig, and the Congreelites
Did barge and shobble in the swope,
All jinsy were the Pakstanites
And the spruft Sikhs outstrope.

Beware the Gandhiji, my son,
The satyagraha, the bogy fast,
Beware the Djinnarist, and shun
The frustrious scheduled caste.

Not unexpectedly he was dismissed from office by Attlee, who – an indication of the urgency of things – did not even accord him the courtesy of the habitual six months' notice (though Wavell was given the sop of a peerage). His replacement was an interesting choice. At forty-six, nearly twenty years Wavell's junior, Lord Louis Mountbatten had none of his predecessor's shortcomings for the job. He was quite an acute choice. Built up as a war hero by Churchill and by his very close friend Noël Coward whose film *In Which We Serve* glorified a rather questionable act of naval recklessness which was propagandized as heroism during the war (Coward himself playing the Mountbatten role), Mountbatten did not suffer from the trammels of either reflectiveness or sensitivity. Nor was he, as many tacitly acknowledged, and notwithstanding his close family connection to the British royal family, remotely a gentleman. But he had been a brave commander during the war, and had more-or-less successfully managed the war effort in the East. In October 1943, Churchill had appointed him Supreme Allied Commander, South East Asia Theatre. He held the post (under American supervision) until South East Asia Command (SEAC) was disbanded in 1946.

Mountbatten was the last and possibly the briefest holder of the title of Viceroy of India. He was in office from March to August 1947. In that time, he achieved all that was expected of him, and although the debate still continues about whether or not he could have managed things better, the fact remains that in terms of the thinking of sixty years ago he was probably, though at the same time awfully, the right man for the job.

What happened was this. Lord and Lady (Edwina) Mountbatten brought with them to India a sense of style and confidence that had been lacking in previous imperial administrations there. They were brilliant diplomats, and sought to dispel any sense of British froideur. They gave grand dinner parties at which half the guests were always Indian, and they were accessible to Indians of all social levels. But the last viceroy faced a difficult task. He had to consider not only the still independent princely states, but the different interests of the Muslims, under Muhammad Jinnah, and the Hindus, under Jawaharlal Nehru (Gandhi remained an important spiritual leader, but the

political nitty-gritty had passed to his protégé). In a sense, it was a Gordian knot which had to be cut, and cut quickly. Jinnah (a Lincoln's Inn-trained lawyer of whom it was famously said that he subsisted on cigarettes, whisky and will-power) and Nehru (an Inner Temple-trained lawyer who may or may not have had an affair with Edwina Mountbatten) were redoubtable combatants, if not adversaries.

Independence celebrations on the streets of Calcutta, August 1947.

The ceremonial opening 10 February 1948 of Sri Lanka's first parliament six days after independence from Britain. Sri Lanka's first prime minister of independent Sri Lanka, then known as Ceylon, is seated on the extreme left while the Duke of Gloucester presides.

How successfully Mountbatten managed it is still a matter of debate, but manage it he did. He was sometimes two-faced, sometimes dangerously abrupt. He told the commander-in-chief, Sir Claude Auchinleck, that he had a month to sort out the withdrawal of the British Army – a task which Auchinleck had advised him would take years; he gave the hapless English barrister, Cyril Radcliffe, who had never been in India before, two weeks to draw up the frontiers which would separate India from Pakistan – the Muslim state upon which Jinnah now insisted. Vast migrations would ensue, of Hindus to India, and of Muslims to Pakistan, amid horror and violence, when old neighbours of long standing turned on one another. My friend Vijay Singh, a professor of political history at Delhi University, remembers a small but striking inci-

EMPIRE'S CHILDREN

dent when his family headed east out of what would shortly become Pakistan. His father entrusted many of his household goods to his Muslim neighbour. When later he got in touch to find out what had happened to them and whether he could reclaim them, the neighbour replied, regretfully informing him that all was lost. However, Vijay's father noticed, from the eccentricity of the keyboard, that the neighbour's letter had been written on *his* typewriter!

There was also the problem of what to do with the independent princely states. It has to be said that Mountbatten rode roughshod over them. They were confronted with a decision: join India or Pakistan. Most did so. Some did not. One, Kashmir, is still the centre of conflict between Muslims and Hindus as a result.

Pakistan was a divided nation, but East Pakistan (formerly Bengal), after many years, achieved its own independence as Bangladesh in 1971, following a bloody civil war in which 10 million Hindu refugees fled to India. It has since been the scene of terrible natural disasters, but the Land of the Bangla-Speaking Peoples has survived as an independent state.

Burma (Myanmar), under its leader Aung San, who had sided with the Japanese in his own bid for independent nationhood before switching back to the British, became an independent republic in 1948, and decided to secede even from the Commonwealth. Aung San and several members of his government were shot dead a few months before independence, and now a long-standing 'socialist' absolutist military regime remains in control of the country, keeping Aung San's daughter, the focus of dissent, a long-term political prisoner.

Ceylon (Sri Lanka since 1972) achieved independence in 1948. Since the early 1980s it has been in the grip of a civil war between the government and ethnic Tamil separatists in the north. My friend Sharmini Ashton-Griffiths remembers that, in her parents' experience, under the British, if you wanted to get on in your career, it was worth converting to Christianity.

Westminster had hoped to be out of India by mid-1948. Mountbatten brought the date forward to 15 August 1947. Thus a regime which had lasted over 250 years was brought to an end in the space of seventy-three days.

Mahatma Gandhi did not live long after his protracted dream had been achieved. On 30 January 1948 he was assassinated by a Hindu fanatic, one of a number who had found his demeanour towards the Muslims too accommodating.

Mountbatten was himself assassinated by the Irish Republican Army thirty-one years later. The death throes of Empire cast a long shadow.

NO ONE CONSIDERED THAT BRITISH INDIA WOULD BE DIVIDED INTO SEVERAL COUNTRIES, NOR THAT THE PROCESS OF DIVISION WOULD INVOLVE SUCH BLOODSHED AND VIOLENCE.

CHAPTER EIGHT

TO SEEK A NEWER WORLD

As we have seen, Europeans reached the Caribbean in the fifteenth century. The people who lived in the islands were the Arawaks, Caribs and Taiano who were quickly wiped out by disease and forced labour, since their military technology was no equal to the West's.

Hoeing a sugar-cane field
in Puerto Rico, 1899.

The labour deficit occasioned by their demise was filled first by the slave trade from Africa, and, when that was abolished, by the importing of hundreds of thousands of indentured labourers from British India. As had been the case with white deportees two centuries earlier, the South Asians were committed to a term of about five years, to work in the coffee, rubber and sugar plantations. Many of these Asian immigrants settled in the Caribbean and stayed there. Their descendants are the Asian-Caribbeans, some of whom have since settled in Britain.

Mass migration within the Empire could also mean mass migration across the globe, and the British Nationality and Status of Aliens Act of 1914 defined as British citizens 'any person born within His Majesty's dominions and allegiances'. This was a pretty broad sweep, meaning at least in theory that 400 million of the world's population could move or be moved freely throughout Britain's international domain. Vastly improved and quicker transport aided the process. The Indian indentured labour force mentioned above not only worked in the Caribbean, but in Mauritius, Malaya, British Guiana (Guyana), Fiji and Natal. By 1922 about 40,000 Indians, mainly from the Punjab, had gone to East Africa to construct and maintain the railway system of Uganda. And at their back were other immigrants (fellow countrymen and women) who provided services for them. There were white-collar workers, too. Indians filled many posts in the less elevated echelons of their own country's civil service during the Raj.

Britain was never able to supply all the manpower needed to run her African acquisitions, so she employed large numbers of English-speaking Indians in junior bureaucratic roles. This led to tensions later, especially in Kenya and Uganda, since a social structure emerged in which the British were at the top, the Indians in the middle, and the Africans at the bottom. As early as 1931 there were 39,644 Indians in Kenya (which had only belonged to the Empire since 1920), 23,422 in Tanganyika (now Tanzania), and 13,026 in Uganda. When the British left, the South Asian element of the population became vulnerable. As has been the case throughout history, and we need only use a quotation referring to Huguenot refugees to Britain in the sixteenth century to illustrate this, to the effect that incomers were 'hated if they failed, more if they succeeded'. In the late 1960s and early 1970s, Kenya and Uganda threw out their South Asian populations in a programme of Africanization. They were dispossessed of all they had before they were told to leave.

Despite the influence of leaders such as Marcus Garvey the Afro-Caribbean opposition to British rule was driven less by political consciousness than by agitation over labour conditions. Demand for constitutional reform came principally from a black middle-class minority. These middle-class people were driven by a demand for equal political representation and job opportunities. They were determined to find them or make them. Added to this raising of consciousness was the labour situation, which, owing to the Depression of the 1930s, had affected everybody. In Jamaica, Alexander Bustamente emerged as a spokesman for rioting workers in 1938. Bustamente became a leading light among anti-colonial activists, though he spent two years in prison for his efforts at the beginning of the 1940s. But the unrest and the rise of proper political leaders, among whom was Bustamente's cousin and rival, Norman Manley, made for a slow but generally sure change in the political administration of the islands towards the end of the Second World War. There was an attempt at a Federation of the West Indies, proposed in 1947 and established in 1958; but it was not a success. Jamaica and Trinidad could not accept economic responsibility for the group, a point of view which Britain had to agree with. As Iain Macleod accepted, after having conceded independence, 'when you are giving independence to a country the size of Gambia, to islands the size of Malta and Cyprus, it's a bit much to expect Jamaica or Trinidad to sink their sovereignty with a whole collection of islands, many of which they would have to help, almost as pensioners'.

Some people from the colonies who had served with the British forces during the First World War settled in Britain in the interwar period. But the significant wave of people to come to live here seeking a new life and fresh opportunities were mainly ex-servicemen from the Caribbean arriving after the end of the Second World War.

Most Afro-Caribbeans identified strongly with Britain – the war against

IN THEORY, 400 MILLION OF THE WORLD'S POPULATION COULD MOVE OR BE MOVED FREELY THROUGHOUT BRITAIN'S INTERNATIONAL DOMAIN.

Germany had been their war as much as that of the indigenous British. At home, Jamaican schoolchildren had even contributed a percentage of their lunch money to the war effort. Before independence, many Caribbean islanders whose homes formed part of the British Empire saw themselves culturally and historically as British. Their schooling was British (they sang 'Land of Hope and Glory' at school assembly), their history lessons were British, many of the products they used were British. And they were far from alone. Great leaders like Nehru and Gandhi appreciated aspects of the British education they had had; and Nelson Mandela wrote of his education in Natal: 'You must remember that I was brought up in a British school and that at the time Britain was the home of everything that was best in the world….We regarded [London] as the capital of the world.'

Since the people of the Caribbean were in the main descended from slaves uprooted from Africa and long since deprived of their original cultural origins, it was not until after independence that any sense of national identity began to establish itself. In addition, the Caribbean islanders were, as we have seen, by no means a homogeneous people. They came from various parts of Africa, and various parts of British India. Some were white settlers. Some were of mixed race. One of my friends, from Guyana, is part Irish, part local aboriginal Indian, part West African and part Spanish. A sense of British identity was a common denominator. However, under the British, people found their social level by how dark their skin was. The fairer you were, the higher up the social scale you could go. This could have a knock-on effect in the mother country. (Two friends of an acquaintance of mine, actually twin sisters, were looking for lodgings in West London in the early 1960s. The lighter-skinned of the pair answered an advertisement for a flat, went round to see it on behalf of them both, and was accepted as a tenant; when she returned with her much darker sister, the landlords changed their minds. Despite the sorting-by-skin-shade at home, such experiences could still come as a shock to immigrants who had every right to expect equal treatment.)

Immigration to Britain was, of course, nothing new. People from outside Europe had been coming to the island regularly to visit or to stay since towards the end of the seventeenth century, and even before then there had been a few. In the main they were sailors, and it was in the ports, including London, that you were most likely to find them. They were known as 'Black Jacks' by the nineteenth century, and many who had turned their back on the sea had humble occupations, such as crossing sweepers. But their numbers remained low.

UNDER THE BRITISH, PEOPLE FOUND THEIR SOCIAL LEVEL BY HOW DARK THEIR SKIN WAS. THE FAIRER YOU WERE, THE HIGHER UP THE SOCIAL SCALE YOU COULD GO.

Left-to-right: John Hazel, a boxer; Harold Wilmot, and John Richards, a carpenter. They were three of the immigrants aboard the *Empire Windrush*, dressed in their best.

The real starting point of the first wave of immigration – and to begin with very few came, and fewer still came with the intention of staying for ever – dates from the arrival at Tilbury in June 1948 of the former German cruise ship, the SS *Empire Windrush*. Among other passengers, the *Windrush* carried 492 people, nearly all men, nearly all trained tradesmen and craftsmen, from

RIGHT:

Enoch Powell as an angry racist mouse – cartoon for the *Guardian*, 18 November 1968, by William Papas.

OPPOSITE:

The *Empire Windrush* arrives at Tilbury, 22 June 1948, with 482 Jamaican immigrants ready to settle in the Motherland.

Theodore by Papas

Jamaica, the largest of the Caribbean islands, seeking a new life and work opportunities in the mother country. They had come because work at home after the war was scarce and poorly paid, and because Jamaica had been devastated by a hurricane. They came with the intention of making enough money to send back home, and with luck to save enough to return with sufficient capital to establish themselves.

The *Windrush* immigrants were still, in 1948, citizens of the British Empire, with every right to come to Great Britain. And they came because many of them as servicemen had already seen and experienced a different way of life and believed that they had been accepted as equals. They came too because of conditions back home. In the late 1940s, Jamaica and other islands were experiencing an economic slump. Sugar prices had dropped to the point that it had virtually become an uneconomical crop, and tourism was nowhere near developed enough to replace it. The rum and coffee industries provided some work, and there was some fishing and small-scale local farming. But the island had also been devastated by a recent and ferocious hurricane. The only viable export was labour. Some left for the USA, until it clamped down on its immigrant intake; others took the far longer journey to the mother country.

After the Second World War, no longer 'protected' by their uniforms, those former servicemen, and some women, who either elected to stay or returned here, found Britain much less welcoming than they might have hoped. If Britain in the 1920s had been a grim place, society had not been changed as radically by the First World War as it had by the Second. The 1940s and early '50s saw prolonged periods of austerity as the country, for the second time in only three decades, had to pick itself up again. At the same time, Britain had begun to take on a more cosmopolitan appearance, as not only people from the Caribbean, but white immigrants from Poland (many

Sugar-cane cutters in the
Caribbean, c. 1913.

Poles had also fought in the RAF, and did not want to return to a commu-
nist country), the Ukraine and even Germany came here to live and work,
among them were people who had survived the Nazi concentration camps.

There was no restriction on immigration, nor was there any colour bar (in
contrast to South Africa, where, ironically, Japanese people, on account of the
economic importance of their country, were classed as white; though Chinese
were classed as 'coloured'). There had been no need for any such measures in
the past, and even the passport had only been introduced in Britain in its
modern form after the outbreak of the First World War. The people on the
Windrush had already got an inkling that they would not be greeted with open
arms during their voyage. For some reason the captain had a brusque memo
posted on the ship's noticeboard, which read:

I [cannot] paint you a very rosy picture of your future. Conditions in
England are not as favourable as you may think... Hard work is the order
of the day. If you think you cannot pull your weight, you may as well decide
to return to Jamaica, even if you have to swim the Atlantic. No slackers
will be tolerated.

Maybe it was meant as a fair warning. Maybe someone had sent the captain
orders. But by then it was too late to turn back.

In any case, they had all been invited to take the passage, they had all paid
for their fares, and some had been paid for by friends, family and local communities clubbing together to send them, so they felt a sense of responsibility
to their sponsors. Each of them had paid £28. 10*s*. 0*d*., no mean sum in 1948,
the equivalent of six months' wages. There may not have been very many of
them, but there were enough to cause a ripple. A few days before their arrival
an internal Ministry of Labour memorandum noted: 'There is no logical
ground for treating a British subject who comes of his own accord from
Jamaica to Great Britain differently from another who comes of his own
accord from Scotland. Nevertheless... a political problem has been created.'
The Minister of Labour, George Isaacs, added his own nervous comment:
'They are British Citizens and we shall do our best for them when they
arrive... I hope no encouragement will be given to others to follow them.'
Significantly, the numbers of white European immigrants arriving in the wake
of the war aroused no such fuss.

When the *Windrush* docked, one of the Jamaicans, Oswald Denniston, raised his hat and gave a short speech of thanks, proposing three cheers for the Ministry of Labour. His reward was the first job offer, as nightwatchman at the wartime deep bomb shelter at Clapham South underground station, adapted, along with several others, as a temporary hostel for the new arrivals. The nearest big labour exchange was a couple of miles away to the east, in the once grand suburb of Brixton. It was here that the immigrants, most of whom soon found jobs, began to settle. Denniston himself later set up a fruit and veg stall in Brixton market, which he was still running fifty years later. To be fair, the British had made some effort by sending a black official to welcome the ship.

Ivor Cummings knew something of what to expect. His mother was white, but he had an African father, which meant that he had been refused a commission during the war. In his speech of greeting, he said: 'I am afraid you will have many difficulties, but [I] feel sure that with the right spirit... you will overcome them.' Another of the passengers, Sam King, later Mayor of Southwark, subsequently said that: 'Everything humanly possible was done to help us.'

Mad, cynical, or just out of hand? Enoch Powell in 1969.

After initial government hesitation following the arrival of early small groups on the *Windrush* and her sister ships, immigration was actively encouraged. By the 1950s there was a shortage of labour in Britain and, as we shall see, organizations such as London Transport actively canvassed for staff in the Caribbean, and the expanding National Health Service recruited nurses from the West Indies and doctors from India. The Minister for Health in the mid-1950s who was instrumental in this recruitment was Enoch Powell, who later on, when he decided to play the racist card in his political game, made a subtle distinction between 'educated' and 'uneducated' blacks.

Immigration up to the mid-1950s was still relatively small-scale with around 27,550 having settled here from the Caribbean. One of the factors that speeded it up from 1952 was the passing of a bill by two right-wing American politicians, Pat McCarran and Francis Walter, which severely limited the number of immigrants from the Caribbean to the United States, that is, 100 per island administrative group, or 2,500 per year. Great Britain may have been a lot further away, but it had strong links with the Caribbean. English was the common tongue, and there were job opportunities to be had. By 1960 immigration from the Caribbean had risen to 49,650. In 1961, on account of the imminent introduction of the Commonwealth Immigrants Act (1962) which was designed to limit the number of incomers, the number rose to 66,300, as people tried to beat the new Act. Thereafter the number fell to 31,800, and then to the very low figure of 3,241 in 1963. Although it grew again to nearly 15,000 in 1965, it dropped back again to an annual average of around 10,000.

The mood of immigrants was mixed. On the whole they were optimistic, partly by nature, and partly on account of the fact that most of them were young and keen to experience a wider world than the one that existed at home. They were by tradition adaptable. They also, as we have seen, associated themselves very much with the mother country, of which they knew considerably more than the British did of theirs. They did not expect the streets of Britain's towns and cities to be paved with gold, though for some of them it was still a shock to see white people who were poor, who did menial jobs and who struggled to make ends meet. They also suspected, because of their experience of being a colonized people, that they would be in some danger of being treated as second-class citizens. What also came as a bit of a shock was *quite* how cold and wet Britain was. They had all been warned about it – there was a brisk trade in secondhand overcoats during the 1950s in the Caribbean for those venturing to Britain – but the dank reality of the British climate was something else. In an interview recorded by Mike and Trevor Phillips, Connie Mark, a medical secretary in the WRAC in Jamaica during the war, recalled her shocked first impressions of 1950s London:

So many things horrified me when I first came here. I couldn't understand how all the houses in a street could almost be the same. There didn't seem to be any individuality. And when I saw things like bread being delivered, bread literally was left outside the door with your milk, and [sic] I was horrified. And then, what surprised me most of all was the child care, because at home, when we were fighting for self-government and independence, we talked about Britain, we said, you know, children taken care of, provisions are there. And then, of course, you had to take your child to a childminder, surprised me a lot, you know. And, of course, the cold, you didn't realise how intense that cold is, and I knew that there were a couple of people who came with me who went back the first Christmas. We just couldn't take it. And the unfriendliness of people, that surprised me, 'cos it's like a shock wave, you know. I couldn't believe the lack of humanity. And I don't even want to use the word 'prejudice' because it's a new word, you know, the unfriendliness and the coldness and the mask, like, is given for a smile. And deep down, there was this hatred that they have of you. I mean, I was just horrified of things like that, I couldn't believe it at all.

⊠
MOST CARIBBEAN IMMIGRANTS ASSOCIATED THEMSELVES VERY MUCH WITH THE MOTHER COUNTRY, OF WHICH THEY KNEW CONSIDERABLY MORE THAN THE BRITISH DID OF THEIRS.

Off the boat and onto the train: an Afro-Caribbean couple travel from Southampton to London Victoria on 9 June 1956.

So, cold, grey, grimy, depressed and hostile Britain was not perhaps the ideal destination of choice. There was far less street life, there was a different set of social rules to learn, and there was prejudice. That did not necessarily dampen everyone's enthusiasm. The Calypso singer who went by the stage name of 'Lord Kitchener' (Aldwyn Roberts) came over on the *Windrush*, and composed this buoyant song:

London is the place for me,
London, that lovely city.
You can go to France or America,
India, Asia or Africa,
But you must come back to London city.

The immigrants in the 1950s arrived mainly by sea, then increasingly by air from the 1960s onwards. The work they came to do initially fell into two main categories: for the men, work was available in public transport; for women, in the health service. There was a general labour shortage in Britain after the war, and it was especially hard to fill the lower-grade, poorly paid jobs which could be dirty and difficult, and could involve shift work and long hours.

At the outset in Britain, some people, even some companies, went to extraordinary lengths to prevent black people from getting work. The Bristol Bus Company in the early 1960s blandly announced that it would not employ black men as conductors on the grounds that they might upset white female passengers. At least in this instance the company was not allowed to get away with it. Led by a young local black schoolteacher, Paul Stephenson, a petition was got up to make them change their minds.

If men went initially to work largely in public transport, women went into nursing. They came for the most part from Jamaica, and they quickly learned that, whereas State Registered Nurses could look forward to promotion, State Enrolled Nurses could not. As most black nurses belonged to the latter category, many switched to midwifery, a branch of medicine still to a greater extent dominated by Jamaicans today.

Barbados especially supplied many public transport workers, since in 1956 the London Transport Executive came to an agreement with the Barbadian Immigrant Liaison Service. The deal was that recruits were advanced the price of their passage to Britain by the Barbadian exchequer, which they then repaid in stages over two years from their wages. Recruitment posters in the

Chandler McGhie, bus conductor from Jamaica – one of the first of many. Birmingham, 1955.

EMPIRE'S CHILDREN

Caribbean featured an attractive immigrant bus conductress on the platform of a double decker. By 1958, 118,000 people, mainly single young men, had been recruited to work for London Transport as bus conductors, drivers, mechanics, ticket clerks, tube drivers and catering staff. The scheme continued until 1970. In the mid-1960s, it was extended for a year to Trinidad and Jamaica. The catering trade, notably Joe Lyons and Company, also recruited largely from Barbados.

If you applied, things could happen fast. Keith Hunt was recruited as a bus conductor in 1961: 'I came in from cricket on a Saturday night, and on the radio London Transport wanted these people urgently, and I got up on Monday morning and went and registered. I was in Hackney Garage the following week.' It could also be rough. '[We] were not used to sharing five to a room,' Roel Moseley remembers; 'however poor you were in Barbados you were not used to sharing a room. You had to be in work by 06.30am. You had to keep your dignity ... you had to keep working ... a lot of boys came here and had mental breakdowns because of that stress.'

All immigrants had to get used to very basic lodgings, and to paying what was then a fair amount of money – £4. 10s. 0d. a week – for a room-share with two other countrymen. One of the ways in which racism showed itself was by landlords charging much higher rents to blacks than to whites, if they accepted black tenants at all. Typically, a white person might expect to pay £1. 5s. 0d. a

Not quite home from home. The kind of lodgings black immigrants could expect in England. This family was photographed in Brixton in the mid-1950s.

week for a flat, whereas a black person might have to pay £3. 5*s*. 0*d*. for a room. And it was not unusual to see signs in the windows of houses with rooms to let saying: 'No Blacks; No Irish', and even: 'No Dogs; No Actors'.

There was no law against this kind of bias and individuals could announce their preferences quite freely in this way. Cashing in were some ruthless customers. Among the most vicious and infamous was another immigrant, a Polish Jew called Peter Rachman. Born in 1920, he was building up an empire of slum dwellings in the 1950s in the then run-down Notting Hill and Notting Dale areas of London. Rachman's method was to evict the protected sitting tenants of the properties he bought, by violent means if necessary, and replace them with, according to his business plan, prostitutes (one of his mistresses was Mandy Rice-Davies, one of the central figures of the Profumo government scandal of 1963), or packed in black immigrants with no choice.

In the introduction to his memoir, *Man, You've Mixed* – a book I think everyone should read – Eric Ferron writes: 'I put this book together because I hope that young people who feel there is no hope may read it and that it may convey to them a strength that will enable them to withstand their difficulties... I hope the book will also be read by adults who will see how pain can be put to constructive uses.' In the memoir Ferron recounts his own early experience, in 1950, of looking for lodgings in Surrey:

> When I had just started work in a hospital in Surrey, I applied by telephone for a room advertised in the local paper, a front room on the first floor at two pounds ten shillings a week, which was as much as I could afford at this time. The lady asked me to come round and see it that evening after I had finished duty. I went round and knocked on the door. She opened it, looked a little taken aback and said, 'Oh! Was it you on the phone?'
>
> 'Yes,' I said.
>
> 'You're sure it was you? You sounded so different on the phone. I didn't know it would be you.'
>
> 'Who did you expect it would be?'
>
> She flustered. 'Well, I don't know really. I thought it would be a white man I suppose. It sounded like it on the phone.'
>
> I didn't respond but asked to see the room. Just a minute; and she shut the door. She could at least have left it open I thought. I also had a feeling that I wasn't going to get the room. She was back in a few minutes.
>
> 'I'm so very sorry but my husband phoned just this minute and told me

he has offered the room to a friend at work.' She was sorry I had wasted my time coming all this way and she hoped I would understand.

I said, 'If you'd known I was black would you have asked me to come?'

'Well, to tell the honest truth, no, I wouldn't.'

'Why not?'

'It's very difficult round here. I personally have nothing against coloured people but people round here are a funny lot. I believe there's black and white in all of us but people round here don't see it like that. I couldn't risk it.'

'What is there to risk?'

'It's not because of what they think. But you must understand how difficult it would be for me. No-one would speak to me. I'd go into a shop and no-one would speak.'

'Is it really as bad as that now?'

'Yes,' she said, and she seemed to be apologising.

'But surely you can stand up to what people say? You're your own boss in your own house.'

'And you're a very good talker,' she said. 'What is your language? Where do you come from? You speak English very well.'

I told her.

'I see. I thought you must have learned to speak English when you came here. I'm so very sorry about all this.'

She seemed a good woman and she was beginning to listen. I decided to risk it. 'Since I've been talking to you I've got the impression you are a kindly honest woman, yet you began by hiding something.'

'I'm not hiding anything.'

'You know your husband didn't telephone. You know when you opened the door that no-one else had taken the room. You knew you'd decided you wouldn't let it to a black man. Why couldn't you be honest with me?'

She thought for a minute, then she said: 'Would you like a cup of tea?' I said I would and she invited me inside.

'It seems so awful really. Of course my husband didn't telephone. I feel terrible about it. I've read about people rejecting coloured people and I never thought I'd do the same thing. But it's the neighbours. And my husband is very strict about who he has in the house.'

I said nothing.

'What about in Jamaica? Do you get on with the white people there?'

'Yes I do. There's no difference. But we don't seem to let rooms in Jamaica.

Girls waiting in the Customs Hall at Southampton Docks after disembarkation. Hope and optimism, May 1956.

Everyone has their own house.'

'What about in the towns?'

'I don't know. I've always lived in the country.'

We talked on. I felt that there was a woman for the first time trying to be honest about her colour prejudice. She was talking to a black man face-to-face and finding out that he was a human being who felt deeply about being rejected but who could take it, and discuss it. She didn't know what to do.

'You might like to see the room now you are here.'

It was just as she had described it over the telephone, a big room, well-furnished and warm. 'I provide meals because there's only one kitchen.'

We went back downstairs. She told me about her husband and her little boy who had just done well in his exams at school. And the time passed pleasantly. 'I could talk to my husband when he comes home. He might let you have the room.'

But I didn't want the room now. I had felt insulted, but I was pleased. I'd done my job. She would remember meeting a black man, finding he could talk English, and wasn't a monster.

How hard it is to face the fact that the British were cold-shouldering these warm-hearted people, and were in great danger of making enemies where it would have been in their interest to be making friends.

However, there was also a curious innocence that attached itself occasionally to the awareness that people were coming to this country whose skin was a different colour from white (or 'pale mauve'; as one wag chalked up in a tube station in the 1960s: 'Keep Britain Pale Mauve'). Paul Boateng, the son of a white mother and a black father, and now British High Commissioner to South Africa, remembers that people would come up to his dad in the street and touch him 'for luck'. But unfortunately there were more ugly incidents than innocent ones. Television was sometimes quick to pick up on this. An episode of *Coronation Street* in the early 1960s featured a scene in which the character Len Fairclough is angered when a black bus conductor touches his shoulder as he leaves the bus to remind him that he has not paid his fare. There were the sitcoms, too, which more than touched on the race issue – it featured in *Till Death Us Do Part* and *Rising Damp*, and formed the central thesis of *Love Thy Neighbour*. To watch some of them now, thirty years or so later, can be a toe-curling experience, however.

By 1961, there were 175,000 Afro-Caribbeans living in Britain, mainly in poor, working-class urban districts. As had often been the case with immigrants before, the voice of prejudice reasoned not that they were in such places because they were too poor to find anywhere else to live, but that they had themselves degraded the areas (similar accusations were made of the Irish in the nineteenth century). In Mike and Trevor Phillips's book *Windrush*, Ceri Peach, professor of geography at Oxford University, and author, gives a fascinating view of the Caribbean demography of London and elsewhere:

> *If you look at the area north of the Thames, you can pick out almost a kind of archipelago: Dominicans and St Lucians around Paddington, across the Montserratians around Finsbury Park. Chain migration and differentials in times of arrival produced this sort of differentiation within the Caribbean pattern. High Wycombe, for example, had a high proportion of St Vincentians. People from Nevis particularly concentrated in Leicester and also in Leeds. You can pick out these effects of family connections, village connections quite strongly still in the map. Of course it doesn't affect so much the children, but the first generation, people born in the Caribbean, still show the continuity from that very early settlement pattern. There were very, very good lines of communication between the Caribbean and Britain. The responses, for example, to shifts in the demands of labour were typically felt within about three months of happening, and people coming from the Caribbean who were questioned all had addresses of friends to whom they were going when they came. So it's quite clear that there was a very, very precise flow of information, and flow of money, particularly in the case of dependants coming. People knew where they were going, and so essentially what you had is sort of recreation of the family and village and island patterns. Of course, facing a fairly hostile environment, having support, having people who knew a little bit about the system, partner systems and so on, they were very important in facilitating finding accommodation and... work in Britain.*

Immigrants were often accused of coming here to live off the fat of the land (even though only a very small proportion of them have ever depended on social security). They were accused of accepting small wages and thereby keeping pay artificially low; of taking our jobs, seducing our women, even of being descended from cannibals. And white people often lumped the newcomers all together, as if they all shared the same culture or even ethnicity. Jamaica is as far from Trinidad as Britain is from Morocco. But the peoples of the Caribbean are diverse: each island state has its own personality and identity. The same differences exist between them as exist, say, between Spaniards and Swedes, or French and Poles. And they have the same class differences, too. And, sometimes, similar prejudices, though common cause as a result of the supranational experience of white prejudice has to some extent lessened these.

Africans, especially those from the upper and ruling classes, had been coming to Britain, for the most part for higher education, for many years. Ghana, which was the first African country to gain independence from Britain, in 1957, sent many young people over to study from that time on. In the 1970s Africans began to arrive in larger numbers representing a broader social spectrum. At the same time, those immigrants from the Caribbean already settled were seeing their children, born and educated here, growing up. This first generation to be born British was faced with a different set of problems from those of their parents. They were less inclined to treat the mother country with deference, and they were less inclined to accept the status quo or to compromise. Equally, they placed importance – and this was partly a question of establishing identity – in their Caribbean roots and culture. They were not foreigners, but they did not feel especially British either – thirty years ago,

Arrival at Victoria Station, London, May 1956. A lifetime in suitcases.

people had not yet grown accustomed enough to each other to reach a point of mutual acceptance; and in any case the black youth rebellion was not unlike the white youth rebellion – each new generation is bound to question what its parents accepted.

One problem was the divide as generally perceived between black culture and white, though a section of white youth very much wanted to embrace and associate with black culture (in general, and with music in particular). If there had to be a common denominator, a standard to rally to, it was perhaps most strongly represented by the interest that grew up in Rastafari. This movement centres on the cult of Emperor Haile Selassie of Ethiopia, whose name before his coronation was Ras (duke) Tafari Makonnen. The movement actually grew up in Jamaica in the 1930s around the Ethiopian emperor not just as a person-ification of God but as the leader of the only African state to maintain its cul-ture and its independence (except for temporary interruptions) throughout history. Rastafari has gained attention through reggae music (especially through the genius of the late Bob Marley) and also, in the Caribbean, through being championed by the political leader and activist Marcus Garvey, who saw the only answer to oppression for the black races of the world as lying in unification and solidarity, to which end he encouraged strongly an interest in the African culture of their forebears.

Some sections of the white community sought to deepen, not bridge, the racial divide. Following an outburst of racial violence in Nottingham, where local Teddy Boys, out for trouble, targeted black people in the summer of 1958 (they would declare that they were going 'black-burying'), thugs in Notting Hill, not to be outdone, went on the march themselves. They were aggressive young men without much hope or ability to express themselves who were eas-ily led by men such as Oswald Mosley, who remained an unrepentant racist even after the war. In his early sixties in 1958, Mosley saw another opportun-ity to feed his rabid political ambition. By means of rabble-rousing pamph-leteering – which included such subtleties as pictures of spear-wielding black men entering Britain – he managed to incite a tense atmosphere which led to violent outbursts by mobs. In late August 1958, nine white teenagers attacked five black men with crowbars and injured three of them grievously. The teenagers all pleaded guilty at their trial and were sentenced to four years each, but their action led some MPs to call immediately for immigration control, and they were not the only ones to see the violence as having been in some measure provoked by the immigrants themselves.

Oswald Mosley *(l.)* toasts the faithful at a neo-Nazi rally in a pub in Dalston, London, in January 1953.

In the wake of these racially motivated attacks came more violence. In May 1959, a thirty-two-year-old carpenter from Antigua, Kelso Cochrane, was set upon and murdered by a bunch of white youths not far from the flat he shared with his fiancée in Notting Hill. There was no apparent motive other than race hatred, though that was denied by the police, who failed to make any arrests. The investigating officer Detective Superintendent Ian Forbes-Smith said: 'We are satisfied that it was the work of a group of about six anti-law white teenagers who had only one motive in view – robbery or attempted robbery.' In fairness, the police interviewed over 900 people, though only 1 per cent of them gave any useful information. About the same time, the National Labour Party (nothing to do with the Labour Party) and the White Defence League merged to form the British National Party, the forerunner of the National Front, which fortunately has remained a minority interest in this country. Nevertheless, Kelso Cochrane's murder has chilling affinities with the murder of Stephen Lawrence in Eltham in April 1993.

From the shameful violence of the Nottingham and Notting Hill 'race riots' (mercifully rare occurrences in our sombre but generally tolerant society) came, as a reaction, something new – and something in which most of the peoples of the British Caribbean united. The Notting Hill Carnival was inaugurated in January 1959 in response to the rioting. It was held indoors for the first few years, and moved outside in 1965. It was a pretty small affair to begin with, but by the mid-1970s it had grown into a major event, with some 150,000 people participating as the floats and dancing progressed around Notting Hill and up Ladbroke Grove. Unfortunately, there was violence and there were clashes with the police which were decried in sections of the press. This gave the carnival a poor reputation and some called for its cessation; but there were other influential figures, including Prince Charles, who supported and saved it. Latterly, it has become a much more conservative affair, with racial tensions and non-associated criminal violence greatly abated.

The 1960s saw the rise of the civil rights movement in the USA and Martin Luther King, who was murdered in April 1968 at the age of thirty-nine, remains a powerful figure in all our minds forty years later. But at the same time the more aggressive Black Power movement had begun, and Black Panthers were established in Britain by the end of the decade. The word 'black' was adopted as an acceptable, and often preferred, form of description, Afro hairdos and wigs became first a political and then a fashion statement. Blaxploitation music and movies got a mixed reception from both 'sides' but

tended to be fairly vulgar, though there can only be a few people who do not remember Richard Roundtree as 'Shaft' in 1971 without a certain amount of wry affection. The anti-apartheid movement gathered strength, focusing on the appalling situation on South Africa, an old-fashioned police state (whose secret police, BOSS, was trained, ironically, by the Israeli MOSSAD) tolerated because of its wealth.

Meanwhile at home there was greater assertion by black people of their rights, sometimes resulting in clashes with the police, who retain a reputation for institutional racism. The Notting Hill Carnival became a more militant event and there were violent scenes in the late 1970s. This confrontation reached a peak with the Brixton riots of the early 1980s, followed by unrest in Toxteth. In the meantime, the redtop newspapers had given much publicity to the prevalence of black street crime especially in South London. And the police revived an ancient vagrancy Act which became known as the 'sus law', enabling them to pick anyone up on suspicion. Most of the targets were young

Left-to-right: John Lewis, Ronald Cooper, Alfred Harper and Peter Thomas, 'teddy boys' remanded at West London Police Court on 4 September 1958 on charges relating to the Notting Hill race riots. Fifty years on, where are they now?

Tiger Bay residents, Cardiff, 1950.

black men. I lived in Brixton and West Norwood between 1983 and 1996 and I can remember listening to young black men discussing being picked up and turned over by the police as a matter of course. Sometimes they might have been discussing the weather. But as time passed, slowly there was improvement.

Music, however, provided a popular cross-cultural bridge. From the start black music was embraced by white people, and would form the basis of modern pop music. Jazz clubs sprang up in places like London's Soho and there was a vogue for limbo and calypso, the latter gaining widespread fame through the contribution of the Guyanan actor-singer Cy Grant, who sang a calypso based on the day's news for a nationwide news magazine television programme called *Tonight* in the 1950s and 1960s, with the refrain:

We bring you the news you ought to know
With Tonight's topical calypso.

In the ensuing decades the impact of black music would provide some interesting anomalies. The term 'skinhead' derives from the Afro-Caribbean 'shine-head'. Mods loved Jamaican ska music; skinheads loved reggae, with the result that they were happy to have Jamaican friends, but took an entirely racist view of 'Pakis' (a generic derogatory term for all South Asians). Black people dominated the popular music scene and the first British generation created their own brand of it – Soul – made in Britain and with British references.

The other area in which black Britons were able to excel was sport – in particular football, cricket (which Afro-Caribbeans and South Asians have made their game), athletics and, to a lesser extent, boxing. In 1950 at the Test Match between the West Indies and England at Lord's, the West Indies trounced England. The Calypso singer Lord Beginner caught the moment, one of those few where 'we had the chance to get it over on the white man':

Cricket lovely cricket
at Lord's where I saw it
cricket lovely cricket
at Lord's where I saw it
Yardley did his best
but Goddard won the test
with those little pals of mine
Ramadhin and Valentine.

By the early 1980s the numbers of people arriving from the Caribbean had begun to die off, while at the same time the numbers coming here from decolonized Africa were increasing. Since 1991, about 250,000 people have emigrated from Africa, especially from Nigeria. These peoples do not have a great deal in common with the Afro-Caribbeans, and there have occasionally been tensions between them. The Africans have little to do with reggae or Rastafari; they have closer obvious cultural links with Britain – for example, they are used to a similar cuisine, so that Britain in many ways is a home-from-home. So many Africans have moved to Peckham in south London that the district has earned the nickname Little Lagos. Many of the Nigerians are vastly overqualified for the jobs they currently do. (I met one, Champion, who

⊠
FROM THE START BLACK MUSIC WAS EMBRACED BY WHITE PEOPLE, AND WOULD FORM THE BASIS OF MODERN POP MUSIC.

THE BRITISH
NATIONALITY ACT
OF 1948 WAS THE
FIRST STEP IN THE
PROCESS OF
DEFINING AND
LIMITING ACCESS
TO THE MOTHER
COUNTRY.

was working as a night-security guard in an office block and who was bored stiff, as he was a political refugee, having worked as a journalist at home. I used to lend him huge novels – Tolstoy, Cervantes, Dostoevsky, Dumas, Pynchon, Trollope, Musil – to help him get through the nights.)

One of the most recent waves of immigrants has been the one from (Muslim) Somalia. Their exodus, from a country ravaged by civil war for so long that it scarcely exists as a governed entity, began in the late 1980s. (Somalia has had no effective national government since 1991, though there is an internationally recognized government in Baidoa, which, however, controls only Baidoa. There are two breakaway states within the 'country', and the situation remains volatile.)

This chapter should properly end with a note on the legislation that has been carried through since 1945 to deal with the shifts in ethnic population Britain has experienced after the Second World War.

There has been a long history of legislation vis-à-vis incomers. In law, 'Calvin' is still cited, referring to a case of 1608 determining the rights of citizenship of Scottish subjects since James VI of Scotland became James I of England but did not quite thereby unite the two countries (that came a century later). Three hundred and forty years later, in 1948, the British Nationality Act attempted to define six categories of citizenship:

1. *Citizens of the United Kingdom and Colonies (CUKC)*
2. *Citizens of Independent Commonwealth Countries*
3. *Irish British Subjects*
4. *British Subjects without Citizenship*
5. *British Protected Persons*
6. *Aliens*

The distinctions, as can be inferred, were vastly complicated (see Bibliography for publications giving this more detailed attention than can be accorded it here), but most of the immigrants with whom we are concerned were contained within the first two categories.

The Act was the first step in the process of defining and limiting access to the mother country, but effectively access was still pretty much open to most people. My father, as a German and Undesirable Alien in 1948, was sent home in that year as a Category Grey Prisoner – the category given to specialized troops; (Category White was ordinary infantry; Category Black was the political branches of the SS including concentration camp staff, the German secret services and ideological Nazis). But he was able to re-enter Britain in 1951, change his surname (from Messerschmitt), and become naturalized in 1956. He was by no means unique. Plenty of Germans and Italians who had been prisoners of war in this country followed the same route when they, for sentimental or other reasons, chose to make their home here, just as British intelligence and other military personnel in post-war Germany married locals and made their homes there. In the same way as you cannot avoid prejudice, as a natural antidote to it, you cannot avoid the melting pot.

The racial paranoia was more striking. MPs who held the racist/nationalist card, such as Cyril Osborne, began to campaign against immigrants as early as 1952, and kept it up for years. Famously in 1964, the eminent Labour MP Patrick Gordon Walker (who was not entirely liberal in his views himself) lost his Smethwick seat to a Conservative called Peter Griffiths (who survived in politics until the 1990s), whose hustings slogan was: 'If you want a nigger for

Yvonne Connelly, the first Afro-Caribbean head of an Inner London Education Authority school: King's Cross Infants' School, February 1969. Photographed by James Jackson.

⊠

NEARLY SIXTY YEARS AFTER *WINDRUSH*, THERE IS STILL MUCH TO BE DONE IF WE ARE TO BECOME A TRULY EQUAL MULTIRACIAL SOCIETY.

a neighbour, vote Liberal or Labour'. Griffiths was unseated shortly afterwards by the actor-turned-Labour-politician Andrew Faulds, but the bad taste in the mouth has never really gone away.

After the race riots of 1958, the renewed pressure to enforce immigration control ultimately saw the arrival on the statute books of the 1962 Commonwealth Immigrants Act (whose effect many Caribbeans had sought to avoid by coming over before it came into force). This Act included an employment voucher scheme, and determined (basically) that there should be three categories of immigrant:

1) Those who had been promised a specific job by a specific employer.

2) Those individuals whose training and/or specific skills and/or level of education made them useful to Britain.

3) Those who were unskilled and sought entry without a guaranteed job here. This category was limited initially to 10,000 vouchers a year. The first two categories were also subject to a quota of 20,800 in toto.

Refinements and riders came in the form of the 1965 Race Relations Act – a response to the Smethwick debacle. There were further responses to the crises of the Kenyan and Ugandan Asians, and to Enoch Powell's inflammatory racist speech, known popularly as the 'rivers of blood' speech) of April 1968, which he gave in the cynical hope of furthering (or perhaps more accu-

Guardian cartoonist Papas sees Enoch Powell leading a trio of blind politicians through a graveyard of immigration legislation. Powell himself can see with one eye ('in the country of the blind the one-eyed man is king'). The politicians are, in order following Powell, Edward Heath, Iain Macleod and Lord Hailsham. Published 11 October 1968.

rately, resurrecting) his career, but which in the event he torpedoed, though for a time he enjoyed some minority popular support.

A predominantly South Asian crowd protests against the new Immigration Bill of March 1971.

Another, tougher Immigration Act was passed in 1971. There followed the Thatcher government's British Nationality Act of 1981, which placed further restrictions on the right to British citizenship in a simplistic response to popular opinion.

On the plus side, the Race Relations Act of 1976 provided that it is unlawful to discriminate against anyone on grounds of race, colour, nationality (including citizenship), or ethnic or racial origin. All racial groups, including white, are protected from discrimination in Britain. Under this Act the Commission for Racial Equality was set up in the same year. This will become the Commission for Equality and Human Rights in 2009. But nearly sixty years after *Windrush*, and despite many steps forward, there is still much to be done if we are to become a truly equal multiracial society.

CHAPTER NINE

LETTING GO: THE CARIBBEAN AND AFRICA

When the dominoes started to fall, they started to fall quite quickly. For many countries the road to independence had been a long one. In May 1933, on the centenary of the abolition of slavery, the Trinidadian writer C. L. R. James (who moved to Britain in 1932) gave a radio talk in which he argued that the way for his compatriots to better themselves was through education and ultimately the assertion of their own independence. James was a prophetic anti-colonialist who in later life saw his dream fulfilled.

As we have seen, despite the influence of pan-African nationalists like Marcus Garvey, the main impetus towards independence from Britain in the Caribbean was less aspirant nationalism than dissatisfaction with working conditions. The Depression of the 1930s affected the Caribbean just as much as it did the USA and Britain. It had always been touch and go in the relative-

A 1920s advertisement promoting colonial trade within the British Empire. A naïve and ironic pointer to the exploitation that was to follow.

ly small towns, but in the 1930s it hit the rural population as well, and they were in the majority. Wages went down as the population, the cost of living and unemployment went up. The discontent this mixture triggered led to strikes and riots throughout the region. Britain, embarrassed by this upset in its back yard, sent commissions of inquiry to find out how to improve matters, especially in view of mounting and often sanctimonious criticism from the increasingly powerful USA.

By 1943 a plan had been hammered out whereby the British Colonial Office declared its intention to 'guide colonial people along the road to self-government within the framework of the British Empire'. Colonies would earn their independence after a probationary period which, it was anticipated, would be long. Thus the plan looked suspiciously like prevarication. However, universal adult suffrage was gradually introduced – in Jamaica in 1944, in Trinidad and Tobago the following year; in Barbados in 1950, British Guiana in 1953, and British Honduras in 1954. It was not an entirely hands-off affair. The British did not like the government voted in by British Guiana in its first elections, believing it to lean too far towards the USSR, so they sent in troops and occupied Georgetown in October 1953, overthrew the government and suspended the constitution. Gunboat diplomacy cast a long shadow.

However, the clock could not be held back for ever – the Colonial Office itself knew that its days were numbered – and so in 1958 and 1959 Jamaica and Barbados were both granted free self-government. Independence in the British Caribbean went hand in hand with the development of trades union movements: better working conditions and self-government were political siblings. The Colonial Office initially saw independence as being achieved in the form of a federation of island states, and for a time it looked as if the plan might succeed. But then political leaders in the Caribbean realized that the federation idea would mean that the British could hive off responsibility for the smaller, less economically successful island states on to the larger ones, like Jamaica and Trinidad. Jamaica seceded from the federation in 1961 and the British Colonial Secretary, Iain Macleod, reaching the end of an extraordinary two-year term in office, during which he had overseen the groundwork for a total decolonization process, conceded that they had a point. The Prime Minister of Trinidad and Tobago, Eric Williams, also withdrew. Over the next twenty years independence was granted to most British Caribbean holdings: Jamaica formally seceded in 1962, as did Trinidad and Tobago. British Guiana (now Guyana) followed in 1966, as did Barbados. Grenada left in 1974, Dominica in 1978, and St Lucia

Kwame Nkrumah (arm raised) announces the independence of Ghana, March 1957. He is surrounded by (left-to-right) Caseley Hayford, Komla Gbedemah and Kojo Botsio. All wept during the speech.

in 1979. St Vincent and the Grenadines left later in the same year, and the last to leave were British Honduras (now Belize) in 1981, with Antigua and Barbuda following later in the same year, and St Kitts and Nevis in 1983. Most of the new states, unlike their counterparts in Africa, wanted to retain the Queen as head of state, though Trinidad became a republic in 1974. All remained within the nebulous but convenient (and growing) Commonwealth, which was originally called the British Commonwealth but was soon diplomatically renamed the Commonwealth of Nations. In the Caribbean, Britain retained within the Empire Anguilla, Montserrat, the Turks and Caicos Islands, the Caymans and the British Virgin Islands.

You could say that our departure from the West Indies was relatively smooth. In India it had left a bloodbath in its wake. In Africa, there was a mixture of the two. The British were, with the French, the major power left in Africa after the Second World War, and Britain should be proud of the fact that she handled her withdrawal better. But it was not by any means an immaculate withdrawal. Just as Britain had scrambled into Africa, so she scrambled out. There were two sources of pressure: the desire of the African states to achieve independence, and Britain's desire to let go of the financial and administrative responsibility for them.

The architects of disengagement were again Harold Macmillan and

Kenyans demonstrate for independence as early as 1950.

Colonial Secretary Iain Macleod. As early as February 1960 in South Africa, of all places, Macmillan made a brave speech, almost as famous as his one about how we had 'never had it so good'. He spoke to a somewhat silent South African parliament about how post-war Africa was changing: 'The wind of change is blowing through this continent, and whether we like it or not, this growth of national consciousness is a political fact.' Macmillan was trying to get the white South African regime to wake up to the fact that we in the West had better strive to keep emergent African nations on our side, and not let them go over to the East. But his relatively mild, though politically astute, observations did not cut much ice with the obdurate and intellectually isolated descendants of the Voortrekkers. The notorious but not uncomplicated South African Prime Minister, Henrik Verwoerd, merely commented in his response that it was as important to do justice to the white man in Africa as the black. Later in life, Verwoerd famously observed: 'I do not have the nagging doubt of ever wondering whether perhaps I am wrong.' The 'architect of apartheid' was assassinated, two days short of his sixty-fifth birthday, in Cape Town in 1966. ('One of the happiest days of my life', a South African friend said to me not long afterwards.) South Africa had been drummed out of the Commonwealth in 1961.

A central problem was that Britain had not in Africa, as she had in India, established over more than a century an infrastructure that would withstand the handover of power. It was no accident that the first and most stable regimes lay in the hands of people who had received an English education, usually in law. But the political instability in Africa which still exists today is, it could be argued, a result of Britain's abnegation of responsibility, and the fact that during the Cold War, African states became pawns of the great Eastern and Western powers, just as they had been pawns of the European powers under Empire. As China and India, the coming world powers, now move in, and as the Western powers attempt to counter that influence by cautious investment in health aid, we see that Africa, with its enviable natural resources and huge potential workforce, remains at the mercy of the rest of the world.

Egypt was never officially an annexed part of the British Empire, but because of the Suez Canal Britain needed, as long as sea power was the key to world control, to make sure her influence at least in the Canal Zone was incontestable. However, in the 1950s, everybody in the West was jittery about the rise of the Soviet Union – its influence, its oil wealth and its ability to do more than contend in the space race (it put the first Sputnik satellite into orbit in 1957) and to stand its ground in East Germany and show brutal muscle in Czechoslovakia in 1948 and Hungary in 1956. The West in general, but especially France and Britain, which had not yet fully adapted to the idea that the centres of power had shifted, viewed with dismay the rise of the thirty-four-year-old Colonel Gamal Abdel Nasser in Egypt. Here was a leader who managed at a stroke to get rid of the dissolute and invidious King Farouk, to assert Egypt's independence, to nationalize the Canal, and confidently to threaten Britain with the possibility of a political love affair with Russia. On top of that, he looked set fair to become the leader of the Arab League. If he could achieve the almost impossible task of unifying the League, then the Canal would be non-negotiable, as would oil; and the artificially created state of Israel – nevertheless already a political fulcrum – might not look forward to a very long existence.

In October 1951 the Labour Party under Clement Attlee gave way, with its tiny majority, to the Conservatives under the aged Churchill, with a majority not much larger. The next few years saw a massive balancing act, but little was resolved. Churchill left office in 1955, at the beginning of his eighties, retiring to give way to his heir and former Foreign Secretary, Anthony Eden, then only in his fifties. Eden was a sensitive and gifted orientalist but a febrile politician, in poor health, and confronting one of the great crises in the passing of Empire. The details and circumstances here are complex, but essentially

Enemy Mine: Sir Anthony Eden, a talented man but a deeply flawed prime minister, speaks to the nation on BBC television about the Suez Crisis, August 1956.

Nasser called the shots. In November 1954, two years after the military coup which had got rid of Farouk, Nasser took control of Egypt. Less than a year later, he reached an arms agreement with Czechoslovakia. But about the same time he was negotiating finance ($200 million) for the Aswan Dam with the World Bank. Nasser's confident double-dealing, allied to other troubles in the Near East, made the USA and Britain dither about the dam project by mid-1956. Then, in July of that year, without consultation (the USA was beginning to treat Britain with increasingly dismissive contempt), the US Secretary of State, John Foster Dulles, an unreflective samurai in the fight against communism, abruptly withdrew the loan for the Aswan Dam, using a minor diplomatic incident as his excuse. Britain was thereby internationally perceived as weak. Nasser capitalized. A week after the cancellation of the loan, he nationalized the Canal. Britain's interests were closely engaged as 30 per cent of the shipping that had passed through Suez in 1955 was British. Just as, owing to reckless privatization, Britain is held to ransom today by Russian oil and gas, so then she was dependent on the Canal for some of her power supplies. Matters soon came to a head.

The Israelis were no friends of the Egyptians. Something had to be done, according to the thinking of the time, to assert British interests. The French shared Britain's concern and interest in control of the Canal, and both nations,

Nasser blocks the Suez
Canal by scuppering ships
across it. November 1956.

though in possession of the moral high ground (though Germany and Italy were not exactly repentant), economically wrecked by the war, with national pride and standing at a nadir, wanted to assert that they were still powers to be reckoned with.

A plan was formed to bring Nasser down and at the same time assert European authority in the Near East. Israel had already developed a powerful and efficient army, which it euphemistically called a Defence Force. In collusion with France and Britain, it was agreed that the fledgling nation should mount a pre-emptive defensive strike against Egypt, to which Egypt would react. Britain and France would then intervene if their insistence that the two belligerents withdraw to about 15 kilometres' distance from the banks of the Canal was not observed.

This seemed pretty foolproof. Israel, party to the plot, would comply. If Egypt did, Nasser's standing would drop. If it did not, France and Britain would be able to go in to secure the Canal. As expected and hoped, Egypt took an aggressive stance. Britain went in with the French, bombed Egyptian airfields, and seemed in a latter-day moment to have succeeded with another bit of gunboat diplomacy.

But alas, the USA pulled rank. The United Nations, which by now included as members many former colonies of the British Empire which were by no means going to support the former mother country, weighed in as well. The General Assembly condemned the action and demanded a ceasefire by sixty-four votes to five. The only countries to support France and Britain (who, of course, voted for themselves) were Israel and Australia and New Zealand. Canada abstained. India, Pakistan and Ceylon supported the USA and the USSR in their condemnation – despite the fact that at precisely the same time as the Suez crisis (late October/early November), Russia was brutally stamping on Hungary's bid for freedom. No doubt Jesus would have wept, and Voltaire smiled.

But two wrongs did not make a right. The USSR got away with their repulsive action in Hungary for the time being, but Britain and France were vilified in the United Nations and it took years to live the ill-advised Suez venture down. Nasser gained prestige, the independence of his country was assured, and he ran it (with the help of a vicious secret service deployed against dissidents) successfully until his early death aged fifty-two in 1970.

Eden, who had been prime minister for under two years, resigned in January 1957. He was replaced by Harold Macmillan, who had been a hawk over Suez, but managed to survive the cleansing of the Augean stables in its wake.

Macmillan was a pragmatist. He knew Britain had to let go of her other African colonies fast, clamouring as they were for independence, and well aware of how effectively Nasser had shown the British the door. The thing was to keep them close diplomatically. No one wanted the African states to be successfully wooed by the Russians.

One obstacle to controlled withdrawal from Africa was the old white settlers who were used to ruling the roost, especially in the more congenial East African colonies like Kenya, where they still cling to the ghost of a lifestyle, and Zimbabwe (then Rhodesia), where they do not. Another was the mindset of some colonial governors. Ensuing and existing political instability across the board in Africa was often at least partly the result of borders drawn up by colonizers with no regard for tribal or other ethnic traditions.

The little, bitter war. Egyptian civilians traverse the obliterated streets of their town during the Anglo-French-Israeli offensive.

On the whole, Britain managed withdrawal quite well, though the speed of the process took many on both sides by surprise. In the enterprise, Harold Macmillan, prime minister from 1957 to 1963, the most significant period of letting-go in Africa, was aided by his agile Colonial Secretary, Ian Macleod, whose mental dexterity probably saved us from the messes left behind in Africa by such countries as Belgium, France and Portugal.

In a period of just twenty-three years Britain let go of a series of colonies and protectorates including: the Gold Coast (1957), which became Ghana under Kwame Nkrumah; Nigeria (1960) – sadly still impoverished today after getting through $280 billion worth of oil revenue; Tanganyika under Julius Nyerere in 1961 (which in 1964 merged with Zanzibar to become Tanzania); Uganda (1962); the Gambia (1963); Kenya (1963–4) under Jomo Kenyatta (né Kamau wa Ngengi; then John Peter, then Johnstone Kamau); Northern Rhodesia (1964), which became Zambia under Kenneth Kaunda; Nyasaland (1964) which became Malawi under Hastings Banda; and Rhodesia in 1980 (formerly Southern Rhodesia) which became Zimbabwe under Robert Mugabe.

Several of the leaders who stepped into British shoes had been away from home for a long time, improving their education or working in the West – and in some cases in the East – to use those points of the compass in Cold War terms. Jomo Kenyatta, an ethnic Kikuyu, came to Britain in 1929, then stud-

Harold Macmillan, then prime minister, inspecting a Guard of Honour of 1 King's Africa Rifles in Lusaka, then Northern Rhodesia, January 1960.

EMPIRE'S CHILDREN

ied in Moscow before returning to Britain where he spent the war years working as a farm labourer and marrying a local woman. Nkrumah spent a decade in the USA before coming to Britain in 1945. Banda was a medical practitioner who had been educated in the USA and Scotland, and spent the war years as a GP in northern England.

As early as 1948 Britain had stated its intention of getting out of Africa in the following terms: 'The central purpose of British colonial policy is simple. It is to guide the colonies to responsible self-government within the Commonwealth in conditions that ensure to the people concerned both a fair standard of living and freedom from oppression from any quarter' – the usual high-sounding political promises in other words. The new African leaders were not slow to accept the proffered hand, however, though they also had to lock horns with local tribal chiefs, who had by now settled into the role of Britain's traditional allies, and white settlers who lived a privileged existence in the occupied territories, but who had also contributed much to local economies.

These were difficulties the leader of the first country to secede, the Gold Coast, had to face. First of all Nkrumah had to gain political supremacy over the rival party in the Gold Coast which represented the interest of the chiefs. Then there were the rival interests of other parts of the country, the Ashanti and Northern regions, to be won over or neutralized. There were also the British themselves, who favoured the rival 'conservative' party, from which Nkrumah, who was impatient to gain control of his country, had split. Despite being imprisoned briefly by the nervous British Governor General, Nkrumah won convincingly at the 1951 elections and thereafter, despite bloody outbursts and strong ideological disagreement, managed to maintain his hold on power and became the country's president in 1957 and changed its name back to the pre-colonial 'Ghana'. Nkrumah, who had Marxist leanings, was later overthrown by a CIA-backed coup, but Ghana has maintained its independent and relatively stable status, and celebrates its fiftieth anniversary in 2007.

Kenya had a rougher passage. It originated as the East African Protectorate, created around a railway line. White settlers were encouraged, who duly took the best land, appropriating it from Kikuyu and Masai tribes who had hitherto used it seasonally. The settlers developed what had been highland grazing country into profitable farms, some of which they still hold tenuously today, and whites, for better or worse, still play a significant role.

The country has the mighty distinction of being regarded as the cradle of the human race, as the researches of a famous local white family of anthropol-

The brilliant Iain Macleod, Secretary of State for the Colonies, 1959–1961, and chief engineer of the independence of British colonies in Africa.

Kwame Nkrumah,
President of Ghana,
speaking at a rally in
Harlem, NYC, in 1960.
Nkrumah was later toppled
by a CIA-backed coup.

ogists, the Leakeys, have established over decades. Kenya was so named by the British when they formally took over in 1920. The name derives from *kinyaa* – the mountain of the ostrich, because of the shape of the summit of Mount Kenya – though in Kikuyu *kere'nyaga* means Mountain of Mystery.

Jomo Kenyatta returned to his native land in 1946, and became involved in a movement directed at attaining independence by peaceful means. There was a breakaway group, however, devoted to achieving independence whatever the cost. This movement developed into the Mau Mau, perhaps the first 'terrorist' group to achieve world recognition and press attention, unless you go back as far as the Boers. 'Mau Mau' is possibly a repeated acronym for the Swahili *mwafrika aparte uhuru*.

The Mau Mau originally directed their attention at fellow Kikuyus whom they regarded as collaborators with the British, and although Kenyatta's name was associated with the extremists for propaganda purposes, he himself always dissociated himself from them. The Governor General, confronted with what amounted to an internal revolt, declared a state of emergency in October 1952 and arrested Kenyatta and a number of other leaders. This action made things worse, not least because in press photographs the white prison guards' faces

Jomo Kenyatta, first
President of Kenya, under
armed guard during the
Mau Mau rebellion against
the British. 1952. Kenyatta
was sentenced to seven
years' hard labour, but
released into internal exile
in 1958.

EMPIRE'S CHILDREN

AT THE END OF THE TROUBLES IT WAS FOUND THAT THERE HAD BEEN THIRTY-TWO EUROPEAN DEATHS, WHEREAS THE BRITISH HAD KILLED OVER 10,000 KIKUYU.

19th November 1952: Future Kenyan president Jomo Kenyatta being led into a courthouse in Kenya, charged with leading the Mau Mau Rebellion against the British.

were blanked out to protect them from Mau Mau reprisals, but those of the black guards were not.

The Mau Mau extremists turned their attention to white settlers. Notoriously, and catching the firm attention of Britain's press, a settler was disembowelled in October 1952, and another three were killed in the following January, culminating at the end of that month with the murder of Dr Esme Ruck, pregnant at the time, and her husband Roger and their six-year-old son Michael. There followed in March the burning to death by Mau Mau of ninety Kikuyu women and children who were deemed to be 'loyal' to the British.

The British response was to crack down further. Kenyatta and his colleagues were sentenced to seven years' hard labour and then internal exile. British troops were brought in and 30 per cent of adult male Kikuyu were interned or imprisoned. The camps in which they were detained were so grimly and viciously run that now, fifty years later, former detainees are taking legal action to sue the British government.

At the end of the troubles it was found that there had been thirty-two European deaths, whereas the British had killed over 10,000 Kikuyu. One particular atrocity, in Hola internment camp in 1959, involved the beating to

THE STORY OF BRITISH DEPARTURE FROM AFRICA, THOUGH MESSY, HAS GENERALLY NOT BEEN AN UNSUCCESSFUL ONE.

Jomo Kenyatta in 1961, the year he became president of the dominant KANU party, and became an MP; photographed by Terence Spencer.

death of eleven inmates, and earned international press attention. Britain was still the black sheep of the United Nations after Suez, and this new 'blot' on the escutcheon caused Macmillan to speed up decolonization. Kenyatta became Prime Minister in 1963, and his country became a republic within the Commonwealth the following year.

Elsewhere in Africa, following a pattern it was also to attempt in the Caribbean, Britain tried to set up a Central African Federation of three states, Northern and Southern Rhodesia, and Nyasaland. Strategically these were buffer states between South Africa and the emerging independent countries, and it was hoped that a combination of white and black rule would exert a moderate influence. It was doomed to failure. Southern Rhodesia had a quasi-independent white infrastructure and was not about to compromise with its poorer black neighbouring states; while the African nationalists in the other two countries did not like the idea of playing second fiddle to the 'white' state, which made no secret of its admiration for the regime in South Africa.

The future president of Nyasaland (now Malawi), Hastings Banda, returned home in his early fifties, having been away for forty years and having forgotten his mother tongue. In a country where blacks outnumbered whites at a ratio of 300 to 1, he had little difficulty in persuading his fellow countrymen to work against inclusion in any white-dominated federation, though it is interesting that it took a man who had become an outsider to return and establish political leadership. Banda suffered the usual fate of political activists and was imprisoned in the dying days of British rule, but in the summer of 1964, six years after his return home, he led his country to freedom.

Later in the same year Northern Rhodesia, rich in copper, became Zambia under its leader, Kenneth Kaunda. The moves to independence were eased by pressures on Britain elsewhere – imperialism was frowned upon by the growing membership of the United Nations, the USA and the USSR had no interest in supporting their dying rival power, Algeria had turned into a powder keg for the French, and above all Britain wanted to wash its hands in as dignified a way as possible of colonies which had become expensive and ungovernable liabilities.

There remained Southern Rhodesia. This, under a new, youngish and bullish prime minister, Ian Smith, unilaterally declared itself independent of Britain in 1965. Despite various pusillanimous attempts to bring the country to heel over the next fifteen years, it was not until a black revolution from within that the illegal white hegemony finally crumbled in 1979–80, following an astute intervention by the mother country, just to mop things up, and introducing in Lord Soames the last of the African governors general. Power passed to the more successful of the local political groupings, under the (originally) Marxist Robert Mugabe, who is still, at the time of writing, in tenuous control, as a very old man, of a country he has managed to bring to the verge of economic ruin by his own vainglory.

But the story of British departure from Africa, though messy and leaving a far from perfect situation behind, has generally not been an unsuccessful one. In Nelson Mandela, Africa has given us the greatest statesman of modern history; and perhaps even Lord Lugard's hopes for the Empire when Africa was in the ascendant has a ring of truth about it today:

… We shall leave the land to those it belongs to, with the feeling that they have better business friends in us than in other white men.

Hastings Banda, aged 63, the first independent prime minister and President of Malawi.

CHAPTER TEN

AFTER THE RAJ: IMMIGRATION FROM SOUTH ASIA

The history of immigration from what had been British India, but was now, of course, a number of different countries, divided by both religion and political ideology, went back a long way. At the beginning of her study of Asian immigration, Rozina Visram cites a christening at St Dionis, Backchurch, in the East End of London, of an Indian youth, named Peter, in December 1616.

Between the beginning of the seventeenth and the middle of the twentieth centuries there was always an Asian presence in Britain, but it has become more pronounced since the end of the Empire. Indians, Pakistanis and Bangladeshis have integrated relatively smoothly, and on an everyday level are commonly associated with working as doctors, accountants, pharmacists, shopkeepers and restaurateurs, but are also well represented in computer sales and technology, business, the law (the current head of the Crown Prosecution Service is a Birmingham-born Pakistani lawyer), entertainment, the arts, and even the Royal Navy (Rear Admiral Amjad Hussain is head of the Royal Navy's Defence Logistics Department, and was born in Rawalpindi. He is the most senior Muslim officer in the armed forces). There are also several South Asian politicians, life peers and millionaires whose names appear regularly in the media.

South Asians in Britain, while inevitably inheriting from their parents and grandparents a cultural affinity with Britain, tend more than Afro-Caribbean and even more perhaps than African Britons to retain a sense of their own culture. This is something they share with the long-established British-Chinese community, and the more recently established Thai community. A much larger proportion of South Asians consider themselves to be inherently Indian/Pakistani/Bangladeshi rather than British, than do Caribbeans, for example. Interestingly, the very word 'Asian' as applied generally to people of the Indian subcontinent did not become current until 1948, following the end of the British Raj. Just as is the case with the Caribbeans and the Africans,

1968: Asian children arrive in England with their mother. They are refugees from Kenya, and they are the lucky ones. Following a flood of Asian immigrants into Britain, forced into exile from Kenya, a bill was hurried through Parliament to restrict annual arrival numbers.

there is resentment at the white incuriosity which tends to lump a vast assortment of races, cultures and religions under one umbrella.

The cultural heritage is deep. First names and family names remain South Asian; they are not former slave names inherited from the British in the seventeenth and eighteenth centuries as is the case for many Caribbeans. At home, many South Asians remain within their own communities and observe their own traditions, and this, especially in the case of some Muslim South Asians, and particularly in the wake of the rise of aggressive Islamism, has led to tension and mutual mistrust. At the same time we are painfully aware of the plight of the British Muslims held without trial for years at Guantanamo Bay. At the time of writing, there are nearly 1.6 million Muslims in Britain – a tiny proportion of the population, but one which has made a significant and positive impression on native culture and native economy. In many ways, native Britain has absorbed more popular culture from the Indian subcontinent than vice versa.

In Britain today a quarter of British South Asians are involved in the medical profession; 25,000 of them are doctors, of whom 10,000 are GPs. In the 1960 film *The Millionairess* the white actor and comedian Peter Sellers parodied the Indian doctor stereotype. During the decade that followed, thousands of doctors moved from India to Britain, recruited by Enoch Powell (whose

⊠

**MOST SOUTH
ASIAN DOCTORS
BECAME GPS, AS
THEIR CAREER
POSSIBILITIES
WITHIN SURGERY
AND CONSULTANCY
WERE BLOCKED.**

'rivers of blood' speech interestingly excludes, quite specifically, professional Asians – a section edited out of the speech as it appears on racist websites). Powell wanted to attract doctors in 1962, just as formerly he had wanted to attract nurses. By this time it was a two-way street, since Indian medicos were being trained at home in state-of-the-art facilities established by the British in competition with the Russians, who also needed doctors. The father of the popular Oldham-born actress, writer and dancer Shobna Gulati, a well-known star of *Coronation Street*, was one of the many doctors who came to Britain during the recruitment initiative.

Most South Asian doctors became GPs, as their career possibilities within surgery and consultancy were blocked, though I can remember when I worked as a porter at Whipps Cross hospital in the mid-1960s that there were, even then, South Asian consultants. That apart, it has to be said that 40 per cent of junior hospital grades were filled by professional Asian immigrant doctors, who did not even enjoy full job security. Even as GPs, they found themselves having to take appointments no one else wanted, in rough inner cities or remote rural districts.

One GP deserves a special mention, as he became the one-and-only doctor in the tiny town of Inveraray, Scotland – racially the whitest town in Britain. Dr Keral Singh Bijral has practised in the town from 1983, having fallen in love with Scotland (despite the midges!) while on holiday there ten years earlier.

After health came food. After the Second World War, British food reached a nadir. Except for a few London restaurants, most *plats du jour* tasted of cardboard. Indian food – actually mainly Sylheti food – enlivened British taste buds. The Indian restaurant was nothing new – the first one opened in 1809 – but it was not until after 1945 that the Indian restaurant became a fixture in British cultural life, and native Britons who probably had not even the haziest knowledge of the Empire happily accepted a culinary fillip which was a welcome change from the mince-and-mash doldrums plonked daily on the national plate.

The Sylhetis first came here in the nineteenth century, having served as ships' cooks and jumped ship in the ports because of their rotten labour conditions. They established cafés and restaurants in the ports for lascars, and the tradition spread from there. After 1971, when East Pakistan, following a series of political and natural disasters, re-emerged as Bangladesh, many fled that proud but challenged country and established 'Indian' restaurants throughout the land.

And today, for the real South Asian gastronomic experience in London you mostly have to go to Brick Lane, near Aldgate and not far from the Mile End Road mosque. Bangladeshis have replaced Jews in this part of London (even the famous Jewish café Blooms has gone) in the course of the last few decades. Another confirmation of the multi-ethno-cultural melting pot we are privileged to live in. In the same district, in Princelet Street, is a building which started life as a church, became a synagogue, and after that a mosque. Now it is the fledgling Museum of Immigration.

The doctors and the restaurateurs were followed in the later 1960s and early 1970s by Asian refugees from Kenya and Uganda, and many of these people took over and developed the small corner shops and supermarkets, which have become indispensable. Individual white traders became rarer after the advent of supermarkets such as Fine Fare in the late 1950s and early 1960s pushed them out of business. But the corner shop industry today rivals the big chains. The Patel clan, from Gujarat, a wealthy farming family with roots in six villages, now runs most corner shops in Britain.

Immigration was not any easier for the South Asians than it has been for the Caribbeans and the Africans. In each case, the lucky ones always had pre-settled relatives or friends to take them in; otherwise, it was a question of the hostel or the shared room. Many early immigrants from Mirpur and other regions of Pakistan took on bleak work in the factories of the Midlands and north of England. Some did well, and – a weakness perhaps, but also maybe a bolster –

October 1955: A Sikh doorman at work outside one of the first Indian restaurants in London.

Immigrant worker at Repton Foundry, Bradford, 1967.

needed to advertise their success by material means. There is a running joke in Leicester about the *wa'benzi* – the people of the Mercedes-Benz! For most it was a grim, sixteen-hour-day life living in quasi-slums. And there was no happy ending, since towards the end of the 1970s a slump in the textile and steel industries meant great unemployment. But by then the immigration boom was over.

The first generation of South Asians born here are mainly high achievers, now middle-aged, who through the influence of their parents have proved themselves to be highly competitive both in education and career, and their children follow suit. Careers of choice are medicine, the law, dentistry and accountancy. But this is nothing special. Immigrants and refugees traditionally work hard to establish themselves in their host country. That, for example, is in a nutshell the history of the Jewish Diaspora. And as always there have been repercussions. The actress Meera Syal remembers that she hated going to school on days following sitcoms that played the race card. To return briefly to a subject touched on earlier, one of the Indian characters, Ranji Ram, in *It Ain't Half Hot Mum*, a sitcom of the late 1970s, was played by a white British actor, Michael Bates. At least the early 1980s saw ethnic minority actors play their own racial/national roles in LWT's *Mind Your Language*, a (by today's standards) pretty crass (white-scripted) series which nevertheless starred actors like Dino Shafeek, Albert Moses and Pik-Sen Lim, and did mock everyone, regardless of race, creed, colour, though the effective bottom line was still: foreigners are clowns with silly habits who cannot speak English. Hard to believe all that was only twenty-odd years ago.

But there was another side to the popular entertainment coin. In the mid-1980s, Paul Scott's Raj Quartet tetralogy was dramatized for television, and a little earlier his novel *Staying On* was memorably filmed with Trevor Howard and Celia Johnson. Asian actors played their own ethnic roles, and the characters they played were neither idealized nor monsterized. Art Malik's Hari Kumar is still remembered as a great performance by many.

These pieces showed a much more realistic view of the Raj than we had seen before, and revived interest in the work of the great British novelist E. M. Forster. *A Passage to India*, published sixty years earlier, was filmed in 1984 by David Lean on the back of the renewed interest in the British Raj. Other works quickly followed, but set in a contemporary context: 1985 saw the seminal Stephen Frears/Hanif Kureishi *My Beautiful Launderette*. Later came the softer *Bend It Like Beckham*. In pop music, people like Nihal and Rishi Rich have become prominent. In sport, we have had the privilege of watching

Nasser Hussain (the first England cricket captain of mixed ethnicity) and fellow cricketers Mudhsuden Singh – known as 'Monty' – Panesar (born in Luton in 1982 of Indian Sikh parents), and Sajid Mahmood (born in Bolton of Pakistani Janjua Rajput descent); and in boxing the electrifying Amir Khan (Mahmood's cousin, also from Bolton). There are, however, very few professional South Asian footballers yet.

The first generation of South Asians in this country italicized the work ethic – get your head down, get educated, and get into a profession. The more integrated second generation might take a more relaxed view, though Muslims in particular, who used to take an unassuming stance, are becoming more assertive. In short, a vibrant, talented, confident generation has emerged from decades of complex family history and travels, reflecting the many threads of personal and political history across the world, and of course the great deal of hard work it took to arrive home.

An estate agency in Bradford in 1967 with signs in Urdu for immigrating residents.

EPILOGUE

The world shifts constantly. We live in the evening of Western dominance, and the ghost of the Soviet Union, despite its oil and gas reserves, is a paper tiger. The new powers are China and India, and they are already making more than overtures to the last seriously exploitable, peopled continent, Africa.

Fragments of Empire still exists: Britain still holds some Caribbean islands. She also has Ascension Island, once classed as a ship and now leased to the United States. She still has St Helena, where she sent Napoleon to die. And she has the Falklands, which she fought for in the last official colonial war in 1982. Britain has Bermuda, the Tristan da Cunha group: Gough, Nightingale and Inaccessible as well as Tristan itself, named after its Portuguese discoverer (in 1506). She still holds on to Gibraltar and the British Indian Ocean Territory.

Hong Kong went in 1997, the same year as the death of Princess Diana, which latter event sparked a public reaction that killed much respect for the Royal Family, though it still commands a measure of sentimental sympathy, and the Queen is still Head of State in some former dominions.

Our positive heritage – and it is not great compared with what it might have been, though no empire is remembered for its benevolence – is our culture, our language, our tolerance (for all our faults), our legal system and our solid if bureaucratic administrative set-ups. There have been unpleasant operations, such as the notorious refugee camp Sangatte (now closed) and Lunar House, Croydon (which Kafka himself would have had difficulty in imagining), but they are not especially British or French nightmares, and they are probably unavoidable.

The British Empire, apart from a scattering of islands, is gone, and the Commonwealth is no more than an association of independent states which, nevertheless, if the call ever came, might pull together for the sake of the unity they once had, and the beliefs they hold together. Britain itself today is a small European state which has not quite shed the memory of its glory days, and indeed, when one considers how recently the Empire still existed, that should not be surprising. But even though the sun has set, and despite the many and often grievous faults and injustices we perpetrated, we can, I think, still hold up our heads when we look at the indelible way in which our once mighty governance has shaped the world.

RESOURCES

'See, that's what's important about history; that you can sort of be alive when you weren't really alive. That's why teachers should tell you about the people who were alive then, and not just the things that happened. Because then you can pretend that you were alive too, when they were alive, or you'll pretend that you will be alive when you know you won't be alive any more ... That way, learning about history is like making believe you could live three different lives instead of just one life: the life you have, the life people had before you were born, and the life people are going to have after you die.'

Doreen Grainger (assumed name),
London-born Jamaican, aged 11, 1970s.

This final section is designed simply to help people explore further. Most of the books mentioned are relatively inexpensive and easy to find, either in bookshops, via the web, or in your local library, if you are lucky enough still to have one. I've also made a note of a few interesting websites (which have links to others), and of museums and institutions.

Here, too, is a list of current member states of the Commonwealth, the loosely knit, almost informal collection of nations which retain links to Britain as the mother country, though today that is a very relative term, just as the Commonwealth is a very nebulous concept.

For those of you who'd like to link significant people with significant dates, there's a list of British monarchs from about 1750 to 1950 (giving regnal years and ending with the current incumbent, Elizabeth II), as well as one for prime ministers from about 1750 to 1980, when empire effectively ended, giving their times in office.

The British Empire left a very deep impression and I'd like to give you one final example of it. In the 1950s and early 1960s, the massive, 1.91m tall, figure of Queen Salote of Tonga (1900–65) was as well-known in Britain as the Queen Mother. Her father had been so taken by empire that he'd renamed himself George, after King George III, and he christened his daughter Salote – the nearest pronounceable Polynesian equivalent to Charlotte – the name of George III's wife.

Because of the complexity, I have marked with an asterisk the books which I personally consider the best to start with. The others are equally good, but are either more specialized or more complex. The asterisked books are the ones which are best adapted to giving the general reader a good overview of it all.

This is a select bibliography and I have only mentioned one work of fiction. Readers who wish to look at novels and so on related to or inspired by the Empire can find writers' names dotted around the book, notably in the Prologue. Some of **George Orwell**'s essays describe his own empire experiences; Victorian imperial novelists like **G. A. Henty** may be hard to track down. **Rudyard Kipling**'s *Kim* is still readily available, as is **Erskine Childers**'s *The Riddle of the Sands*. **David Lytton**'s *The Goddam White Man* originally published in 1962 is, I believe, a brilliant novel of apartheid South Africa.

BIBLIOGRAPHY

(alphabetically by author)

1: Empire

Alexander, Joan, *Voices and Echoes: Tales from Colonial Women*, Quartet, London, 1983

Allen, Charles, *Soldier Sahibs*, John Murray, London, 2000

Blake, Robert (Lord Blake), *The Decline of Power, 1915–1964*, Paladin, London, 1986

Butler, David, & Anton Gill, *Lord Mountbatten: The Last Viceroy*, Methuen, London, 1985

Cohn, Bernard S., *Colonialism and its Forms of Knowledge: The British in India*, Princeton UP, Princeton, 1996

*Douglas, Roy, *Liquidation of Empire*, Palgrave Macmillan, London, 2002

Ferguson, Niall, *Empire*, Allen Lane, London, 2003

Foster, R. F. (ed.), *The Oxford History of Ireland*, OUP, Oxford, 1989

Foster, R. F., *Modern Ireland*, Penguin, Harmondsworth, 1989

Gill, Anton, *Ruling Passions*, BBC Books, London, 1995

Hakluyt, Richard (ed. John Hampden), *The Tudor Venturers*, Folio Society, London, 1970

Hobsbawm, Eric, *The Age of Empire 1875–1914*, Weidenfeld & Nicolson, London, 1987

—— *The Age of Extremes 1914–1991*, Michael Joseph, London, 1994

Holmes, Richard, *Sahib: The British Soldier in India*, HarperCollins, London, 2005

Hopkirk, Peter, *The Great Game: On Secret Service in High Asia*, John Murray, London, 1990

Hughes, Robert, *The Fatal Shore*, Collins Harvill, London, 1987 (about Australia)

Hyam, Ronald, *Empire and Sexuality*, Manchester University Press, Manchester, 1990

Lawrence, James, *Raj*, Abacus, London, 1998

*Lawrence, James, *The Rise and Fall of the British Empire*, St Martin's Press, New York 1996

*Judd, Denis, *Empire*, HarperCollins, London, 1996

Lapping, Brian, *End of Empire*, St Martin's Press, New York, 1985

Livingstone, David (a portrait), *Dr Livingstone the Great Missionary*

Traveller, Compiled from Reliable Sources, Tyne, London, nd but *c*.1882

Louis, Wm Roger, *Ends of British Imperialism*, I. B.Tauris, New York, 2006

Meredith, Martin, *The State of Africa*, The Free Press, London, 2005

Moorehead, Alan, *The Fatal Impact*, Mead & Beckett, Sydney, 1997

Morris, James (now Jan), A three-volume history of the British Empire: *Heaven's Command*, *Pax Britannica* and *Farewell the Trumpets*, Penguin, Harmondsworth, 1979

Orwell, George, *Burmese Days*, Gollancz, London, 1935

Pakenham, Thomas, *The Scramble for Africa: 1876–1912*, Weidenfeld & Nicolson, London, 1991

Park, Mungo, *Travels in Africa* (modern edition), Everyman, London, 1969

Schama, Simon: *Rough Crossings*, BBC Books, London, 2006 (on the slave trade and the foundation of Sierra Leone)

Strachey, Lytton, *Queen Victoria*, Chatto & Windus, London, 1921

Stein, Burton, *A History of India*, Blackwell, Malden, MA, 1998

Urban, Mark, *Generals*, Faber, London, 2005

Williams, Eric, *From Colombus to Castro; the History of the Caribbean 1492–1969*, Deutsch, London, 1970

2: Immigration

Hansen, Randall, *Citizenship and Immigration in Post-War Britain*, OUP, Oxford, 2000

Leese, Peter, Beata Piatek & Izabela Curyllo-Klag (eds), *The British Migrant Experience, 1700–2000: An Anthology*, Palgrave Macmillan, London, 2002

Phillips, Mike & Trevor, *Windrush*, HarperCollins, 1999

Sirett, Paul & Paul Joseph, *The Big Life*, Oberon Modern Plays, London, 2004

Visram, Rozina, *Asians in Britain: 400 Years of History*, Pluto, London, 2002

*Winder, Robert, *Bloody Foreigners: The Story of Immigration to Britain*, Abacus, London, 2005

WEBSITES

The National Archives runs a very good website on immigration:
http://www.movinghere.org.uk/
The London Transport Museum has an online exhibition on its Caribbean
workers:
http://www.ltmuseum.co.uk
See also:
http://www.bbc.co.uk/history/british/modern/arrival
http://www.bbc.co.uk/history/british/modern/windrush
http://www.bbc.co.uk/radio4/history/empire
http://www.casbah.ac.uk/links .stm
http://www.commonwealth.org.uk

PLACES

The British Empire & Commonwealth Museum
Station Approach
Temple Meads
Bristol BS1 6QH
tel: 0117 925 4980
web: www.empiremuseum.co.uk

The Museum of Immigration
19 Princelet Street
London E1 6QH
tel: 020 7247 5352
web: www.mytowerhamlets.co.uk
& www.24hourmuseum.org.uk
(ring before you visit as this museum doesn't yet have regular opening times)

CURRENT MEMBER STATES OF THE COMMONWEALTH OF NATIONS—HEAD: Queen Elizabeth II of Great Britain

The Queen is Head of State of sixteen of the Member States.

The Commonwealth Games, held every four years, is second only to the Olympic Games.

The four largest economies in the Commonwealth are India (US$4,300 bn), Britain (2,000 bn), Canada (1,220 bn), Australia (700 bn).

Military outlay: Britain (US$48 bn), India (21 bn), Canada and Australia (10.5 bn).

Tuvalu (formerly The Ellice Islands) is the smallest member, with 11,000 inhabitants.

Membership is voluntary and non-binding. There used to be economic links, and some strong business interests remain, but otherwise those that remain, it has to be said, are largely sentimental; though pressure can theoretically be brought on members who violate the Commonwealth's moral/ethical code.

Members:

Antigua and Barbuda
Australia
The Bahamas
Bangladesh
Barbados
Belize
Botswana
Brunei
Cameroon
Canada
Cyprus
Dominica
Fiji
The Gambia
Ghana
Grenada
Guyana
India

Jamaica
Kenya
Kiribati
Lesotho
Malawi
Malaysia
Maldives
Malta
Mauritius
Mozambique
Namibia
Nauru
New Zealand
Nigeria
Pakistan
Papua New Guinea
St Kitts and Nevis
St Lucia

St Vincent and the Grenadines
Samoa
Seychelles
Sierra Leone
Singapore
Solomon Islands
South Africa
Sri Lanka
Swaziland
Tanzania
Tonga
Trinidad and Tobago
Tuvalu
Uganda
United Kingdom
Vanuatu
Zambia

BRITISH MONARCHS (REGNAL YEARS) FROM 1760:

George III: 1760–1820
George IV: 1820–1830
William IV: 1830–1837
Victoria: 1837–1901
Edward VII: 1901–1910
George V: 1910–1936
Edward VIII: 1936 [abdicated]
George VI: 1936–1952
Elizabeth II: 1952–present (2007)

BRITISH PRIME MINISTERS (YEARS IN OFFICE WITH POLITICAL AFFILIATION) FROM 1762:

Earl of Bute: 1762–1763 (Tory)
George Grenville: 1763–1765 (Whig)
Marquess of Rockingham: 1765–1766 (Whig)
Earl of Chatham (William Pitt the Elder): 1766–1768 (Whig)
Duke of Grafton: 1768–1770 (Whig)
Lord North: 1770–1782 (Tory)
Marquess of Rockingham – again: 1782 (Whig)
Earl of Shelburne: 1782–1783 (Whig)
Duke of Portland: 1783 (Whig)
William Pitt the Younger: 1783–1801 (Tory)
Henry Addington: 1801–1804 (Tory)
William Pitt the Younger – again: 1804–1806 (Tory)
Lord Grenville: 1806–1807 (Whig)
Duke of Portland – again: 1807–1809 (Tory)
Spencer Perceval: 1809–1812 (Tory) [the only British PM so far – 2007 – to have been assassinated]
Earl of Liverpool: 1812–1827 (Tory)
George Canning: 1827 (Tory)
Viscount Goderich: 1827–1828 (Tory)
Duke of Wellington: 1828–1830 (Tory)
Earl Grey: 1830–1834 (Whig)

Viscount Melbourne: 1834 (Whig)

Sir Robert Peel: 1834–1835 (Conservative [Con.])

Viscount Melbourne – again: 1835–1841 (Whig)

Sir Robert Peel – again: 1841–1846 (Con.)

Lord John Russell: 1846–1852 (Whig)

Earl of Derby: 1852 (Con.)

Earl of Aberdeen: 1852–1855 (Peelite)

Viscount Palmerston: 1855–1858 (Whig)

Earl of Derby – again: 1858–1859 (Con.)

Viscount Palmerston – again: 1859–1865 (Liberal [Lib.])

Earl Russell – again [previously Lord John Russell]: 1865–1866 (Lib.)

Earl of Derby – once again: 1866–1868 (Con.)

Benjamin Disraeli: 1886–1868 (Con.) [Only Jewish PM to date – 2007]

William Gladstone: 1868–1874 (Lib.)

Benjamin Disraeli (later Lord Beaconsfield) – again: 1874–1880 (Con.)

William Gladstone – again: 1880–1885 (Lib.)

Marquess of Salisbury: 1885–1886 (Con.)

William Gladstone – once again: 1886 (Lib.)

Marquess of Salisbury – again: 1886–1892 (Con.)

William Gladstone – fourth term: 1892–1894 (Lib.)

Earl of Rosebery: 1894–1895 (Lib.)

Marquess of Salisbury – once again: 1895–1902 (Con.)

Arthur Balfour: 1902–1905 (Con.)

Sir Henry Campbell-Bannerman: 1905–1908 (Lib.)

Herbert Henry Asquith: 1908–1916 (Lib.)

David Lloyd George: 1916–1922 (Lib.)

Andrew Bonar Law: 1922–1923 (Con.)

Stanley Baldwin: 1923–1924 (Con.)

Ramsay Macdonald: 1924 (Labour [Lab.])

Stanley Baldwin – again: 1924–1929 (Con.)

Ramsay Macdonald – again: 1929–1931 (Lab.)

– and again as National Labour (a kind of coalition), 1931–1935

Stanley Baldwin – once again: 1935–1937 (Con.)

Neville Chamberlain: 1937–1940 (Con.)

Winston Churchill: 1940–1945 (Con.)

Clement Attlee: 1945–1951 (Lab.)

Sir Winston Churchill – again: 1951–1955 (Con.)

Sir Anthony Eden: 1955–1957 (Con.)

Harold Macmillan: 1957–1963 (Con.)

Earl of Home [Sir Alec Douglas-Home]: 1963–1964 (Con.)

Harold Wilson: 1964–1970 (Lab.)

Edward Heath: 1970–1974 (Con.)

Harold Wilson – again: 1974–1976 (Lab.)

James Callaghan: 1976–1979 (Lab.)

Margaret Thatcher: 1979–1990 (Con.)

John Major: 1990–1997 (Con.)

Tony Blair: 1997–2007 (Lab.)

The next General Election is due in 2009 at the latest.

INDEX

PICTURE CREDITS

Key: t = top, c = centre, b = bottom, l = left, r = right.

Courtesy of the Advertising Archives: p167. p173. p248.

Bridgeman Art Library: p18; Biblioteca Universidad, Barcelona, Spain, Index. p27; Private Collection.

The British Cartoon Archive, University of Kent: p156: ©Associated Newspapers plc/Solo Syndication. p166; ©Associated Newspapers plc/Solo Syndication. p205; ©Associated Newspapers plc/Solo Syndication. p226; ©William Papas. p245; ©William Papas.

By Permission of the British Library, London: p20-21; (Maps.19.b.21). p37 br; (Add. 27254). p49; (Maps.1.Tab.7). p72; (Add.Or.2). p92; (Ac.6182).

©Camera Press, London: p268; NCNA. p269; NCNA.

Crestock.com: p38; ©Carsten Reisinger. p110; ©Carsten Reisinger.

Mary Evans Picture Library: p233; Maurice Ambler.

Getty Images: p26; Time Life Pictures/Mansell Collection. p35 t; Hulton Archive. b; Hulton Archive. p36; Time Life Pictures/Mansell Collection. p50; Kean Collection. p54; MPI/Stringer. p55; Stock Montage. p56; MPI/Stringer. p60; Veer/Jim Barber. p70; Hulton Archive. p76; Time Life Pictures/Stringer. p78; Hulton Archive/Stringer. p79; Hulton Archive/Stringer. p81; Hulton Archive/Stringer. p82; Hulton Archive/Stringer. p85; Felice Beato/Stringer. p87; Alice Schalek/Three Lions. p89; Hulton Archive. p90 tl; Topical Press Agency/Hulton Archive. p90 tr; Topical Press Agency. p91; Rischgitz. p95; General Photographic Agency/Hulton Archive. p96; Hulton Archive. p99; Time Life Pictures/Mansell Collection. p100; I Heyman. p102; Hulton Archive. p103; W & D Downey. p104; Three Lions. p106; Hulton Archive. p109; Ejor. p123; Central Press. p124; Hulton Archive. p125; Hulton Archive. p127; W & D Downey. p138; Veer/Jim Barber. p149; Topical Press Agency. p151. p160; Time Life Pictures/Mansell Collection. p164 tl; Margaret Bourke-White/Time Life Pictures. p164 tr; Wolf Suschitzky/Pix Inc/Time Life Pictures. p169; Simmons Aerofilms/Hulton Archive. p170; Peter Stackpole/Time Life Pictures. p174; Stockbyte. p186; Davis/Topical Press Agency.

p187; Keystone. p191; Felix Mann/Picture Post. p192; Fox Photos. p198; Keystone. p201; Keystone/Hulton Archive. p202; Charles Hewitt. p206; Veer/Jim Barber. p217; Topical Press Agency/Hulton Archive. p219; Keystone. p220; AFP. p225; Douglas Miller. p227; Keystone. p228; Fox Photos. p229; Chris Ware/Keystone Features. p230; Express Newspapers. p231; Haywood Magee/Picture Post. p232; Thurston Hopkins/Picture Post. p236; Haywood Magee. p238; Haywood Magee. p239; Bert Hardy/Picture Post. p241; Ron Case; Keystone. p242; Bert Hardy/Picture Post. p245; James Jackson/Evening Standard. p247; Frank Barratt. p250; Mark Kauffman/Time Life Pictures. p251; Charles Trotter/Keystone. p252; Keystone. p253; Keystone. p254; Central Press. p255; Bellamy. p256; Central Press. p257; Keystone. p258 tl; Ted Russell/Time Life Pictures. p258 br; Stroud Express. p259; George Rodger/Time Life Pictures. p260; Terrence Spencer/Time Life Pictures. p261; Mike Lawn/Fox Photos. p263; Mike McLaren/Central Press. p265; Thurston Hopkins/Picture Post. p265; Terrence Spencer/Time Life Pictures. p267; Terrence Spencer/Time Life Pictures.

Imperial War Museum, London: p159 (Q691); Ernest Brooks. p190 (CH13438). p193 (CH12263). p195 (D6210).

iStockphoto.com: p16; Chris Schmidt.

The Kobal Collection/Diamond Films: p98 tl; p98 tr.

The Library of Congress Prints & Photographs Division: p222; M H Zahner.

The National Archives: p30 ref. FO84/1310 Crown©. p32 ref CO 137/181 (114); Crown©.

The National Maritime Museum, London: p25; Thomas Cavendish, Sir Francis Drake, Sir John Hawkins. p29 t. p29 b. p34. p59. p71. p75.

National Portrait Gallery, London: p24. p31. p53.

The Royal Collection © 2007, Her Majesty Queen Elizabeth II: p94 tl. p94 tr.

Topfoto.co.uk: p86. p97; Edward Linley Sambourne.

Copyright © V&A Images, London: p37 bl.

BUY EMPIRE
HOME ANI

R.S.W.BD. ISSUED BY THE EMPIRE MARKETING BOARD.